"For zeal for your house has consumed me, and the insults of those who insult you have fallen on me."

PSALM 69:9

Zeal for Your House

By Bishop James E. Walsh
Edited by Robert E. Sheridan, M. M.

OUR SUNDAY VISITOR, Inc.
NOLL PLAZA, HUNTINGTON, IN 46750

ISBN: 0-87973-892-8
Library of Congress Catalog Card Number: 76-6211

Cover Design by James E. McIlrath

Published, printed and bound in the U.S.A. by
Our Sunday Visitor, Inc.
Noll Plaza,
Huntington, Indiana 46750

892

Contents

3
Sere and Yellow Years (1970-1975)

Introduction

Who is Bishop James E. Walsh of Maryknoll?

He is best known for his incarceration as witness to his vocation — the man imprisoned for twenty-two years (1948-1970): under house arrest for ten years, in the Detention Prison awaiting trial for two years, and ten years of his long sentence.

Reading this small volume may answer most questions asked. However, some minimal background may provide an outline of his life.

Bishop Walsh was born in Cumberland, Maryland, April 30, 1891. His grammar and secondary education were in his parish school, later he was graduated from Mount St. Mary's College in nearby Emmitsburg, and after working two years joined the newly founded Catholic Foreign Mission Society of America as one of the first group of six in 1912. Ordination to the priesthood was in the beginning of his fourth year of theology, December 7, 1915, an anniversary date Americans would remember for another reason many years later.

After teaching in the Maryknoll minor seminary, Father Walsh was assigned to China in 1918, and became superior of the small group of American missioners upon the death of the Maryknoll co-founder, Father Thomas Price, in 1919. Less than ten years after his arrival in the Middle Kingdom, he was named Bishop of Kongmoon, China, and continued there until elected to the highest office in his young missionary society, its

7

Superior General; that was for ten years, 1936 — 1946. In 1948 he was back in China — Shanghai — where he remained until 1970.

Today he is in comparatively good health, shares the life of the whole community, enjoys walking around the Maryknoll Seminary grounds for recreation, does some reading and has given a limited number of conferences, written copies of which have been located for this compilation.

This little book is not intended to be a biography or a memoir. The reason for presenting this particular selection of Bishop James E. Walsh's writings and remarks — his experiences in China, his own role as Superior General, his long imprisonment, the world-wide response to his release — is an attempt to share the Bishop's thoughts on a variety of occasions and situations.

It is more than half a decade since he last saw Shanghai, and only on rare occasions has he left his little corner of Maryknoll, New York. He belongs to the Church and in a special way to American Catholics.

The theme of this compilation is missionary, actually the *raison d'être* of Maryknoll which was established by the American archbishops as the Catholic Foreign Mission Society of America and of Bishop Walsh's own lifelong dedication.

Robert E. Sheridan, M.M.
December 7, 1975 — Sixtieth anniversary of Bishop Walsh's ordination to the priesthood.

Bishop Walsh with French bishops following his consecration,
Sancian Island, May 22, 1922

First four Maryknollers to leave for China, 1918. Bishop Walsh is seated left; Father Thomas Price, co-founder died a year later. Father Francis X. Ford, later bishop, died in a Chinese Communist jail. Father Bernard Meyer (standing) died 1975.

1

Early Years (1918-1945)

Most of the writings of the first young American missioners assigned to the Orient were published in the Ecclesiastical Review and a dozen other Catholic periodicals of that period, and also in two volumes of that era, Maryknoll Mission Letters. The present compilation attempts to concentrate on writings which have not been published.

The first spoken and written words of Bishop Walsh on the occasion of his consecration as a bishop on May 22, 1927, seem a fitting beginning for these selections. He chose Sancian Island, death place of St. Francis Xavier and a mission of Kóngmoon, as the site of his consecration. Latin was a lingua communis for early missioners, who often mingled with Europeans of different tongues and Chinese priests (very fluent in Latin from their seminary training). This address was communicated to such a segment and also to many pilgrims who came down from Hong Kong on a modern steamship, quite unlike the sailing boats that carried St. Francis Xavier to so many distant ports.

Of the half dozen whom Bishop Walsh thanked in his address, two French missioners are singled out as having some relevance to the 1975 generation. It was Bishop Fourquet of Canton, whose rectory was a haven for the earliest Maryknollers, and Father (later Bishop) Gauthier who lived with the American pioneers. Bishop Fourquet helped them to establish themselves and shared his vast missionary experience with the earliest arrivals in South China.

All Things in Him

St. Francis will thank everybody who honored his island with their presence on this little occasion and he will reward them, I am sure, with spiritual favors. The grace and inspiration that come from a visit to his tomb are indeed worth the trouble of a visit to the island hallowed by his death.

And indeed, that is one reason why I chose this holy spot for the consecration. I feel so deeply my own need of special grace. Never was a man more unworthy, never was a man more unfitting raised to the office of the episcopacy. Of course, I have consoled myself much with the promises of St. Paul in Phil. 4:13: *Omnia possum in Eo qui me confortat,* (I can do all things in him who strengtheneth me), and in 1 Cor. 1:27-30: *Elegit Deus ut confundat sapientes et infirma mundi elegit Deus ut confundat fortes. Et ignobilia mundi et contemptibilia elegit Deus et ea quae non sunt ut ea quae sunt destrueret. Ut non glorietur omnis caro in consepectu Ejus.* (But the foolish things of the world hath God chosen, that He may confound the wise; and the weak things of the world hath God chosen, that He may confound the strong. And the base things of the world, and the things that are contemptible, hath God chosen, and things that are not, that He might bring to naught things that are: That no flesh should glory in His sight).

Yet, in spite of all is it surprising that a man should

13

tremble when he thinks of his own weakness in the face of the great responsibilities of the office of a bishop? I confess freely that my only feeling at this time is one of diffidence. And I thus welcomed the opportunity to come to St. Francis' tomb and receive the oils of consecration on the spot sanctified by his holy death, with the prayer that he would bless from Heaven his successor so weak, so unfitted, so unpromising, so altogether unlike himself, and yet one, I hope, animated by the same motive: *Da mihi animas Sinensium.* (Give me the souls of the Chinese). And indeed if he will bless and you will pray, perhaps the burden will be borne and the work accomplished that God has, in His Providence, for our little mission. It is with confident trust in that help both from Him and from you that I will endeavor to trace in my small way the footsteps of the great servant of God who has gone before me.

I could never recite all the favors and helps extended by the missionaries of Canton to our little budding mission. But one thing that stands out with a prominence that calls for expression is the extreme goodness of its Vicar Apostolic, Bishop Fourquet, a father and a brother who have given both paternal advice and fraternal assistance, anything that was needed. We never went to Bishop Fourquet without being aided. "All things to all men," we found him and we owe him more than we can ever repay. He will disclaim all this — I doubt if he is even conscious of it — *quia nescit sinistra quid faciat dextera ejus*, Mt. 6:13, (Let not thy left hand know what thy right hand doth). But it is all true, he has helped us, steadied us, encouraged us, made possible our success, and may God bless him for it. It was to me then a personal pleasure to receive consecration at his hands — one of the few consolations I have in assuming this heavy burden. I pray that God will reward him with special help for his own far more weighty tasks of guid-

14

ing the destinies of the Church in that pivotal spot of South China, in the city of Rams.

If I have this great consolation, I also feel today an equally great privation that is the absence of one to whom our little mission owes an equally great debt, one who left his own work temporarily, to come over into Macedonia and help us, who helped us, taught us, trained us, who was guide, philosopher and priest and that when we most needed such help, during our first years as tyros in the mission fields. What a joy it would have been to have him here today. But, God willed otherwise and Bishop Gauthier is instead looking down upon us from Heaven. *In itineribus saepe*, 2 Cor. 11:26, (In journeyings often). How well he described his own apostolic life in the words of his motto. For truly he spent himself in those journeys over the hills of China searching for the lost sheep of the house of Israel and now he has taken his last journey — the last journey — and the best of all for it leads to the throne of God. The traveller is home, his journeys are over, and that apostolic heart that only beats for God's other sheep is now to reap the reward. He has fought the good fight, he has run the course. May he bless us from Heaven, may he help us to walk in his footsteps, may we profit by the precious example he has left behind. To his bereaved missionaries we extend our fullest sympathy: in the literal sense we suffer their loss with them, and their sorrow is our sorrow.

To our own missionaries I only want to say one word. I am the least among you. Look upon me as your servant. I am made a bishop chiefly to help you. It will be my chief concern. If my help sometimes takes the form of direction, I hope that you will realize it is intended to help just the same. But, I think we understand each other; we are a happy family; may God and St. Francis bless us with the same affectionate union.

15

In an address to the St. Paul Guild in New York City in 1937, Bishop Walsh gave what seemed a series of vignettes but which quickly sketched the religious beliefs of the Chinese people. Today these vignettes give us insights into pre-Communist China and lead one to ponder what the long-range effects of Maoism will be.

Religions of China

On the Blue Express leaving Peking some years ago I remarked an elderly gentleman, who was obviously a fellow-countryman loose from his moorings, bearing all the earmarks of a stranger in a strange land. A few words of conversation revealed the fact that he was seeing China for the first time, and the further fact that he was a lawyer from Boston, bearing the name of a former American president. "What impressed you in Peking?" I asked him, expecting the usual comment of the tourist about the strange food and the slow trains. To my surprise I received a very discerning answer that told me at once I had met an intelligent man. "Everything impressed me," he replied. "There is nothing in Peking that did not excite my admiration, from the Forbidden City to the ricksha coolies. But if you mean what impressed me the most, the answer is quite easy. It was the Temple of Heaven. And it was not merely the beauty of the place — although it is one of the finest pieces of architecture that I have ever seen — but it was chiefly the idea behind it that I found touching and inspiring. The marble altar in the open air — the emperor going in person to stand upon it, looking up to the sky — and offering there the aspirations of his four hundred million people to the powers above — such a religious ceremony is a surprising thing to find among pagans. It was a simple and gracious form of worship that proves to me that God does not abandon His other sheep."

17

Actually my friend had stumbled across what was probably the purest and simplest form of Chinese worship, as it was also the most primitive. It was indeed a striking conception for a pagan nation that their chief form of worship should have consisted in this act wherein the emperor, as the father of the people, went out on a simple marble platform, open to the four winds of the universe, and simply looked up to the blue sky, there to report the progress of his people for the past year, while invoking upon them the blessings of heaven for the coming year. This is an example of the worship of the power of Heaven — whether personal or impersonal is disputed. It is the Primitive Religion of China, and it is surely an indication that the people of China, in their instinctive plea for help from above, were searching for the unknown God, if haply they might find Him.

*   *   *

I made a practice in China of inviting the government officials of the district, all of whom were pagans, to attend the celebrations at the mission every Christmas and Easter. They would come for the solemn services in the church, at which they assisted with the utmost reverence, and would stay for tiffin, which was in the nature of a banquet.

Last Easter one of my best friends in this group, the treasurer of the local government, excused himself right after Mass, saying that he was obliged to go out and worship the mountain. Easter Day had coincided with the Feast of the Pure Brightness, an occasion on which the great majority of the four hundred million Chinese go out to the tombs of their ancestors on the hillside to sweep and decorate the graves, and to make a sacrificial offering of food and drink. With their strong practical sense, the Chinese do not leave the food and

18

drink on the grave, but having duly offered it to the ancestors, they then eat it themselves. This is Ancestor Worship, which is also a primitive form of Chinese religion, its origin being lost in the dim regions of pre-history. It is safe to say that every Chinese, who is not a Christian and has any religion at all, engages in some form of this cult, believing with the vast bulk of his people that the peace and prosperity of himself and his family will largely depend upon the honor paid to the spirits of his dead.

*   *   *

One day I was coming down the West River on a steamboat, when the cry went up of "A man overboard!" The captain stopped the ship and we all rushed to the rail to see an old Chinese farmer struggling in the water. Several small sampans were quite near the man, but nobody raised a hand to help him. The officers of the ship were incensed at this indifference and they shouted strenuously to the sampan people, urging them to pick up the drowning man. When this proved of no avail, the captain went in to his cabin and returned with a rifle, which he pointed at the sampan people. He had no intention of firing at all, but between the menace of the rifle and the repeated urging of everybody on board ship, one sampan was finally persuaded to assist the drowning man. The sampan people rowed over to him so that he could catch hold of the side of their boat. The man, struggling in the water, was by this time too weak to climb into the boat and he fell back into the water after repeated efforts to do so. Nobody in the boat would put out a hand to touch him or help him. This brought the rifle into play again, with much urging and shouting on the steamship, until finally one of the sampan men grudgingly put out his hand and assisted the drowning man to safety.

"Why did they not help him?" I asked a Chinese passenger on the ship. "The water devil wanted him," he replied laconically. "They feared that if they helped him out, the water devil would be angry and take it out on them." This is Animism, another form of Chinese religion, by which people believe that the mountains, rivers, stars, clouds, soil, trees, flowers, and almost everything in the whole universe, are dwelt in by spirits, or devils, that have power to harm people, and therefore need to be placated by all sorts of avoidances, abstentions, renunciations, and other performances.

*　　　　*　　　　*

A little boy was herding water buffaloes one day in a vacant field next to the mission, when one of the buffaloes got excited and gored the youngster with his horn. The injury was not fatal, but made a rather severe wound. The boy was taken off to a medical dispensary, where his wound was treated, and he then went home. Some hours later his mother appeared on the scene armed with joss-sticks and paper money. She went to the exact spot where the accident had occurred, placed the incense sticks in the ground and lit them, and then proceeded to burn the paper money, as a sacrifice to the spirits. Asked why she did this, she replied that the spirits of that particular spot were evidently inimical to her boy, and that she wished to placate them in order to prevent further harm coming to the child.

This may be said to be a form of Taoism, a religion indigenous to China — one that began its career as a philosophy that sought to explain the universe and everything in it by a lot of nebulous language containing little or no meaning. It soon evolved into a septum of magic. Today it is a great collection of divinations, sorceries, rites, ceremonies and observances that are invoked to ward off all the evils to which flesh is heir.

20

A friend of mine in China was Dr. Wong Chenk Naam, whose son was the local magistrate of the district in which I lived. Dr. Wong was the highest priced practitioner of Chinese medicine in the City of Canton, and also personal physician to the governor of the province. He and all of his family were Buddhists in the sense that they supported a Buddhist temple that had been established by their ancestors, believed certain Buddhist doctrines, and practiced them to an uncertain extent. I was present at the family dinner, when Dr. Wong announced that, having reached the age of sixty, he had "entered the way," and from then on would observe the strict Buddhist fast by abstaining from meat, fish, eggs, and anything that contained life, and would also take up the serious recitation of the Buddhist prayers. I spoke afterwards with his sons, asking them if they had done the same. "Oh, no," they said. "It is too soon for us to enter the way. It is only when you get old and become tired of the world that you enter the way and begin to fast and pray." "That seems to be a very convenient religion," I replied. "In other words, you give up the world after the world gives you up. Is that the idea?" They laughed. "That is about it," they agreed. "We Chinese are that way. We take our religion by degrees." Buddhism is, of course, an Indian religion imported to China, and the Chinese have warped it to their own uses, as they do with everything that comes their way.

*   *   *

When Confucius was consulted about the next world, he made this answer which has become famous: "I do not yet know men, so how can I know the spirits." Confucius was a great humanist in the sense that he assimilated the best human traditions that lay to his hand, and from them tried to construct a system that

21

would regulate the conduct of life. He had no messages from Heaven to give the people. He told them what to do here below, but he told them nothing about a hereafter up above. They were to pattern after the great models among their ancestors, and all would be well. By observing the customs and practicing the virtues of the ancients their individual lives would be peaceful and prosperous, and in the aggregate would insure a well ordered and well governed country.

To this he added some ethical teaching of a negative character. A good sample of it is his version of the precept of charity, which he cast in the negative form: "Do not do unto others what you would not like them to do unto you" — a striking contrast with the positive injunction of the Gospel that commands: "Do unto others as you would have them do unto you." Confucius has very little teaching of a positive character, and for this reason there was in his doctrine very little incentive or inspiration to make people to live up to it.

Confucianism is an ethical system, or a philosophy of life, rather than a religion, but it has been called a religion because the veneration for the great Sage ended in his being deified and having temples erected in his honor. Whether it is a religion or not, however, it has influenced the Chinese more than all their other religions put together, and has in fact determined their attitude towards those religions. That attitude is one of concern for this life, and a tendency to view the religious problem as a question of how best to regulate human life by human means. It is thus practical and eclectic, instead of being idealistic and transcendental: "this-worldliness" it has been called, in contrast to the other-worldliness that must characterize any real religion.

*   *   *

We may now ask: "Are the Chinese people religious?" Very. They have not only one religion, but six, and the average Chinese is a mixture of all these six. With the practical instinct they bring to every problem, the Chinese chose from all these religions whatever seemed to their purpose, and that purpose was the eminently practical one of carving out a good life in this world. They reverence Heaven with their ancient Emperors, keep up their immemorial Ancestor Worship, erect their buildings on animistic ideas of the relation of the site to wind and water, and call in Taoist monks to exorcise devils at their funerals, while their wives all flock to the Buddhist Goddess of Mercy to implore her aid in childbirth. In fact, they have taken practices from one or another religion to apply almost all the problems of existence, and with such amazing ramifications indeed as to extend to almost every detail of their lives. Every stalk of rice or mulberry planted, every silk cocoon reared, every tree cut down, every journey undertaken, every shop opened, every matriculation of a child at school, every birth, marriage, sickness, death, and so on, are all surrounded with religious observances of one kind or another. For a parallel to it one can only think of St. Augustine's City of God, wherein he describes the great profusion of vain observances that existed among the pagans of Greece and Rome.

This practical instinct of the Chinese to try to obtain every advantage that is available from any source sometimes leads to amusing complications and one fairly common one today is the desire on the part of some parents to put one child in the Catholic Church, and another in the Protestant, while they themselves remain free to keep up their own pagan practices, thus securing to the family, as they fancy, whatever good there may be in all the religions. It has been remarked also that when they attend the horse races in Hong Kong and Shanghai, they play the horse across the board.

23

In the sixteenth century the Jesuits launched an effort to convert these people that promised in a very short time to give God the whole Orient. Francis Xavier, Matteo Ricci, Adam Schall and Ferdinand Verbiest were the spearheads of this thrilling attempt. Xavier was the pioneer who died in the first rude assault after making the breach and pointing out the way. Matteo Ricci was the extraordinary character who wormed his way into one end of the forbidden country under the barest toleration and so impressed the people by his combined knowledge of European science and their own Chinese culture, that within twenty years he had landed in Peking as a friend of the emperor. Father Schall and Father Verbiest built on this. Due to their proficiency in astronomy and mechanics, they successively occupied the position of Director of the Astronomical Board and this gave them the familiar friendship of the emperors of their time, over whom they had great influence. They used it to obtain concessions for the Church and soon China was filling up with missionaries of their own and other orders who were making converts everywhere. Hopes ran high. But they staked all on the favor of the court, and with the disfavor of the court they lost all. A question arose about whether certain Chinese rites connected with the honors paid to ancestors were suitable for Christians. The emperor said "Yes." The pope said "No." It was a moment that made history. The emperor was so incensed that he withdrew his favor. He retained some friendship for the missioners and let their work go on in a limited way. But the handwriting was on the wall. The officials and literati all over the empire, jealous of the new religion, were waiting like wolves for their chance to spring, and it came with the next emperor, the son of the man who had been the missioners' great friend. A general persecution ensued which practically wiped out the budding Christianity through exile and the sword. A great effort had failed — though it was an effort so bold, so daring, so apostolic, so well conceived and so well executed, and so nearly successful, that it was magnificent even in its failure, and it remains an eternal credit to the zeal of the men who attempted it.

Today in China we still attempt to convert the leaders, but we do not put all our eggs in that basket. We seek above all to make leaders out of the converts, which is a slower but surer policy from the human point of view. For it is found more generally feasible to add leadership to China's unspoiled farmers, who are our converts, than it is to add conversion to China's spoiled gentry, who are our leaders. And moreover, the present leadership is not likely to lead very long, converted or otherwise. In China, as in most countries, it is the young blood from the farm that presses forward in each generation to take the reins of power from the palsied hands of the urban population. The educated farmer is our man. He is only our convert of today. But he will be our leader of tomorrow.

We find our harvests of converts mainly in the farming villages rather than in the towns, and the reason is that same practical instinct of the Chinese that is exemplified in their native religions. The approach to these people is not speculative, but practical. That does not necessarily mean the mere material, but it does mean a spiritual help or principle that has tangible application to the present life. "By their fruits you shall know them," is for the Chinese the great criterion — and they want to see those fruits here and now.

In the villages we find that there is usually a poor provision for some or all of the four basic and elementary needs of human life and we try to supply the lack. Where we do it successfully, we convert whole villages at a time.

25

These needs are: livelihood, protection, education, health.

In the city these needs are met, as the larger community can both demand and finance them. We make individual converts in the city. They are always possible anywhere. But as there are no corporate needs to relieve, we can find no principle of cohesion in the city by which to convert people in groups. We fish with a line in the city, whereas in the village we fish with a net.

It is not the mere fact of relieving a need in the village that converts it. You can help their livelihood problem by getting their taxes reduced, solve their protection problem by organizing a home guard of policemen, open fifty schools or as many medical dispensaries — and never make a convert.

You bring home to them in meeting their need two basic things: (1) That only the Church, out of a wish to save their souls, is interested enough in them to come into their village and make its progress her own problem; and (2) That only membership in the Church can unite them and strengthen them in such a way as to render their progress and well-being any way permanent.

This is what the elders of the village have been waiting for four thousands years to hear. Their consuming life interest is in that village. They want to see it peaceful and prosperous, its children disciplined and educated, its sick cared for — and they are always scanning the horizon for the means to bring it about. They find that means in the missioner — and the conversion of the village is the result.

We cannot say that our three million Catholic converts of China are all well educated, but the aim is to make them so. Our school system is strong at the top and the bottom, but lags somewhat in the middle. We have three Catholic universities for our grown young

26

men, and we have innumerable elementary prayer schools for our baby children. We are a bit weak on the intermediate grade and high schools, but we have many excellent ones, and every mission is straining hard to add to the number. On the whole we feel that our educational effort is not too bad. Our seminaries incidentally are numerous and of the very highest standard. We are thus fairly well equipped to turn out an excellently trained clergy and an educated laity. We think that all we need to insure good progress is to keep on keeping on.

And yet there is a problem remaining if we are to give the Orient to Christ — for it must be confessed that we have not yet fired the popular mind. The Orient has only dimly glimpsed the strength and beauty of our divine religion, and has not even vaguely suspected the tremendous currents of life and grace that are there — and until it does, it will remain groping about amid the partial philosophies that it already knows. There is probably some good in every one of them — or at least some elements that God in His Providence has used in preparing the people for His full revelation. Our task is to make a synthesis for them, showing them the good elements in their own human civilization, while adapting and incorporating them into our divine dispensation, much as St. Paul grafted the Gentile branches of the wild olive tree on the true stock of Christ. We must show them that back of their instinctive worship of the blue vault of heaven lies the true Lord of Heaven. We must show them that their ancestor worship is a gracious sentiment that finds its true expression in the doctrine of the Communion of Saints, and that instead of looking down to worship the graves of their fathers at their feet, they must look up to reverence the Father of all above the stars. We must show them that there are no devils in the water, but rather that God is wonderful in the surges of the sea, and that the sun and stars and

27

rivers and hills and all creation are but vestiges of His beauty; for beauty is the hem of His garment, and He has scattered it all over His universe as one means of leading us to Him. We must show them that the contemplative spirit they learned in the picturesque courts and wooded vales of their beautiful temple enclosures, was a preparation to contemplate divine beauty in the courts of the Lord. We must demonstrate to their practical minds trained to this-worldliness in the school of Confucius, that the most practical thing in the world is to learn other-worldliness in the school of Christ. And we must take every detail of their lives, the hard and the easy, the fortunate and the unfortunate, the smiling valleys and the bountiful crops, the stalking famines and the devastating floods, and all the joys and miseries that go into the warp and woof of their lives; and we must make them see the beautiful pattern that is being worked out for them through it all by a Weaver Divine. In short, we must show them the splendor of order by fusing all the worthwhile elements of the Orient with the religion of the Occident in a compound that will give them our unity in their own variety. That is the definition of beauty. So our problem is to make a synthesis of beauty — that will seize the soul and effect the conversion of the Orient — in order to present it as a fit offering to Infinite Beauty — Who is Christ.

Formal portrait of the young bishop

In 1929, when this address was delivered at the annual Maryknoll Departure Ceremony, Bishop Walsh had a great advantage over many others invited to deliver this sermon: he had, himself, been a member of the departing group in 1918 and he understood, from personal experience, many of the observations that make up part of this selection.

In that era, missioners were leaving for ten years, across the country by rail and over the ocean by trans-Pacific shipping. Nobody dreamed in those days that millions of Americans would be sent to the Orient for radically different purposes within short years.

Times to Remember

When St. Francis Xavier went to the Far East, his friends looked upon him as a fool. They looked upon the glorious career that lay before him and which he was giving up, according to their view, to receive nothing in return. To his friends he was a fool, but a fool for Christ. He was ready to give up glorious prospects of a successful career in the world to take up the one thing worthwhile, and this was to preach Christ, and Him crucified. That was four hundred years ago.

Who is a fool now, St. Francis Xavier or his friends? As for his friends, who objected to this step, we do not even know their names. They are swallowed up in the multitude which was so taken up with the interests of their day, and we have never heard of them since. We remember them now only because they were his friends. There is no reason why we should remember them particularly. They were too wise to see beyond their own little sphere. Consequently, they were swallowed up in the past. St. Francis Xavier was a fool, but eternally wise. Yet it is not because we remember him that he is great. St. Francis Xavier is not great because he was famous. The judgments of man availeth nothing. The vision of man is a hollow thing. Xavier's greatness lies in the splendid task which he set before himself, and the extraordinary devotion with which he pursued that task, and that task was — the extension of God's Kingdom in the hearts of men. It is the only task worthwhile. It is, after all, the reason for which the world was created. That is why the flowers grow, the birds sing, to give praise to the Creator. "O, Lord, my God, how admirable is Thy Name in the whole earth!" That is the reason for the sufferings of Jesus, and for the sorrow of His Immaculate Mother — that the sons of men might have life, and have it more abundantly. It is not only worthwhile, but it is the only thing that is worthwhile. "This is eternal life, that they may know Thee, the one True God, and Jesus Christ, Whom Thou has sent."

We are not like St. Francis Xavier. He was a saint — we are far from that type. Yet, we take up the same task and we can try to imitate him. Strangely enough, the one point in which we can imitate him most easily is the one which was easiest for him. It is the characteristic that stands out throughout his life, his unbounded, childlike confidence in God. He set out for lands where the people were more or less savage. In fact, they had a habit of poisoning all strangers. He was urged to take some sort of antidote, but he refused. His only fear was that he should fail to have confidence in his loving Father in Heaven. His thought was, "He holds me in the hollow of His Hand." Confiding in the loving protection of Divine Providence, he would make no provision whatsoever. We can imitate him in this. "Our Father, Who art in Heaven."

We know that these young men go forth tonight to the other end of the earth, but they do not go alone. We know they are in God's hands, and that a loving Father cares for them every moment, in every circumstance, wherever they may be. He has more care for them than any earthly father could ever give. We know that the Holy Trinity, Father, Son and Holy Spirit, dwells in the souls of these young men, wherever they go; we know that God's Mother will always be near them. Why, then, should we not have confidence? Let us realize the assurance which our holy Faith gives us.

Three young men of the Passionist Order were recently done to death in the missions of China. We think first only of the heartrending external details and yet we realize that it was a sublime privilege on the part of a loving Father to give these young men such a glorious opportunity. We know that God was always with them, and He was never closer to them than at the moment when they yielded up their souls to Him when surrounded by bandits. Let us have confidence in the Providence of God, and not think that these young men are going forth, abandoned and cast off at the other end of the earth. It is true they will be separated from their friends, but we have the very best of Friends always with us. "Though I should walk in the midst of the shadow of death, I shall fear no evil, for Thou art with me." God is with us — we go with Him.

As they go forth tonight, I would wish for them the gift of remembrance. It is not listed among the virtues, so far as I know; perhaps it is a compound of many virtues. Remembrance will lighten your burdens, brighten your sorrows; it will go far to seeing you through.

Remember, first of all, your devoted parents. Yours is the privilege — theirs the sacrifice. They are giving you up to God. Remember always the sacrifice they are making. They could have looked forward to the day when you would be near them, to strengthen their declining days, yet they have given you to God. They make the sacrifice. Remember to soften that sacrifice as much as possible. Pray often for them, that God may shower His blessings upon them. Keep in touch with them. They are glad to make the sacrifice, but we must remember to soften it as much as possible.

Remember Maryknoll. In remembering Maryknoll, always think first of him who has been its father. It is

33

no extravagance to remember him and to pursue him always with your messages of affection and gratitude. Remember your great model, St. Francis Xavier. We should see God in our superiors.

Remember the seminary — the lessons you learned here. Above all, remember the ideals you found here for your apostolic life, and if disillusionment comes in later years, remember that it is due to yourself. These ideals will still be true — they are the eternal truth.

Remember Maryknollers. Remember the ideals and guiding lights given to you. Finally, let us remember the great privilege we have of cooperating with our Divine Lord in the Redemption of souls. Let us try to remember when trials come — and they will and must come — let us remember how we stood so often in the chapel at Maryknoll and, looking at the crucifix, promised that we would give all to Him.

When sorrow and trials come, if we could only remember this there would be nothing but joy in our sorrow. We should see things in the eternal light.

If we do this, it will bring to us a life of complete happiness. A life of pleasure? No, but it will be a life of happiness. It is guaranteed; and our love and gratitude will bring a smile from our Lord and His Immaculate Mother at the end of the road.

Bishop Walsh had no idea of the storms ahead when this picture was snapped in Hong Kong Harbor.

August is a sweltering month in South China. Further, burial follows almost immediately after death in such a warm and damp climate, and Bishop Walsh in 1931 was much too far away to be present for the obsequies of one of his distinguished missioners, what with lack of roads and other difficult transportation.

This account is more the record of a man who thanked God for his apostolic vocation by staying on the job, working hard at his allotted task; it is the story of a busy and fruitful life more than reflections on death.

Appreciation of Father Taggart

Father Philip A. Taggart, who died at Yeungkong, August 4, 1931, was one of Maryknoll's early students. He was born in Brooklyn, N.Y., in 1893. He entered Maryknoll Seminary in 1914, the third year of the Seminary's existence. He was ordained to the Holy Priesthood on May 21, 1921. That same year he was appointed to the missions, and in September of that year he sailed as a member of the fourth annual departure group destined for the only Maryknoll mission that then existed: the present Vicariate of Kongmoon in Western Kwangtung, South China. This departure group, besides Father Taggart, consisted of Fathers Paschang, Murray, Meehan, Joseph Sweeney and Brother Albert. Also sailing at that time was the first group of Maryknoll Sisters ever to seek the missions, numbering Sisters Paul, Lawrence, Rose Monica, Barbara and Imelda. Finally accompanying the party were Father General bound for his first mission visitation, together with his travelling companion, the Rev. James F. Kelly of Boston. The entire party arrived at Hong Kong in October 1921. Almost immediately Father Taggart proceeded to Yeungkong to commence his life as a missioner. He was to labor just a decade in Cathay.

Father Taggart began his mission career as curate to Monsignor Ford, the then pastor of Yeungkong. There was a large community at Yeungkong in those days.

Buildings in the Vicariate were so few that there was little place to put the young priests coming out. The Yeungkong rectory was never good but it was better than no rectory at all, and for some years, as a consequence, Monsignor Ford accommodated perforce a number of young curates with some kind of makeshift quarters while they made their first steps in the language. A year later the Yeungkong Convent was occupied by the Maryknoll Sisters, and from that time forward the Yeungkong community usually numbered five or six Sisters in addition to its three or four priests.

Father Taggart was not a man to mind rough living conditions. Tall, strong, rugged and vigorous, he was the sort to breast physical hardship as a matter of course. On the other hand, his forthright and decided temperament tended to fix him early in life in definite grooves of habit, and he accordingly found the great and inevitable adjustments of the first years in China, physically supportable indeed, but morally trying. In this he was like nine out of ten men who come here. A man of quick impulse and great nervous energy, he had to struggle against the angularities of disposition inherent in his type and now enhanced by the great demands of his new life in China. But he possessed solid spiritual qualities that were to carry him through this difficult preliminary adjustment and over later and sterner hurdles as well. A strong spirit of faith, extreme generosity, and a very active zeal were the qualities that marked everything he did — even his mistakes. His was the story of the big-hearted and impulsive man whose excellent intentions and eternal trying offset gloriously the little false starts that are in their real essence but signs of life, and therefore of hopeful promise in young missioners. Typically American in his piety (of which he had plenty and said nothing) his way did not take him into any of the bypaths of the spiritual life, but seemed to lie along the highroad of fidelity to prayer and the essential practices of the priesthood.

Father Taggart spent two formative years at Yeungkong under Monsignor Ford. Here he learned enough of the language to perform the essential work of the missionary priest. While a bright and clever man, he had no gift of tongues and he never became a thoroughly proficient speaker of Chinese; yet he continued his studies throughout his missionary life, and this perseverance eventually enabled him to understand readily and to be understood, as also to preach an effective sermon.

At the beginning of his third year in China (Fall of 1923) he was given his first mission, being appointed pastor of Tungchen. Eight hundred rather fervent farmer people make this one of the best and most consoling missions of the Vicariate, and Father Taggart liked his people and his place from the start. This mission, however, entails a great lot of work, as the Christians are scattered in seventy different villages and must be continually visited. Full of activity and diligence, Father Taggart was equal to the constant visiting and generally exacting demands of this far-flung mission, and here he spent three busy and happy years. In addition to taking care of his people, Father Taggart began here to display the practical talents that made him so highly successful in the physical organization of the mission stations that came under his stewardship. Without being an architect he had all the practical artistry that goes to make one; he was also a finished gardener with an extraordinary knack for landscaping. Everything he touched grew, and growing coalesced into a picture. At adopting, finishing, or furnishing a house or a chapel he was equally happy: he could not be in a place long without turning it into an object lesson in both practicality and beauty. Tungchen Mission with its big expanse in its rural location already possessed in the rough all the elements of a medical mission compound: under Father Taggart's hand these quickly evolved into a harmonious and picturesque whole.

In March 1927 Father Taggart returned to America to spend a year in doing propaganda for the Vicariate which was sorely in need of funds. In this quest he proved equally untiring and successful. He received permission to collect in his own native diocese of Brooklyn where he raised a substantial sum of money through a continuous round of Sunday preaching in parish churches. He returned to China by way of Europe, regaining the missions towards the end of 1928. He was immediately appointed to Yeungkong, thus coming back as pastor to the mission where he had begun his career as a young missioner on his original arrival from America.

The Yeungkong Mission had passed through many vicissitudes. Ever since the departure of Monsignor Ford for Kaying, it had been without any permanent pastor of long tenure, owing to sickness and other unavoidable circumstances that made constant changes imperative. The Sisters had been obliged to leave against their will during the great unrest of 1925 and had not yet been able to return. The Christians of this mission, never very fervent nor well instructed, had naturally become even less so. The place was in a discouraging state in general. However, all it needed to regain its former status of a fairly promising mission was a careful, zealous and permanent head to direct it. This it now found in Father Taggart. Times had greatly improved: the anti-Christian agitation had simmered down, while the resources of the Vicariate both as to men and means had been somewhat bettered. The Sisters were ready and anxious to return. They did so. Father Taggart was thereby made very happy. In addition he was given the assistance of a curate. Yeungkong was to know again its former halcyon days of big mission staff and corresponding mission activity.

Yeungkong had been and is a hard mission. Its people if likable, are tricky and exigent. They make good friends, difficult converts, and careless Christians. Generations of devotion and sacrifice will probably be needed to bring any considerable number of them to the full stature of Christ. Father Taggart, however, was an optimist and a man of plans. He took up his work with vim. His first attention settled on the physical improvement of the compound, a task for which he was specially fitted. The gradual and patient acquisition of various little adjoining huts and plots by his predecessors had finally accumulated to give the once small mission a good area. Father Taggart was thus able to proceed to carry out literally the injunction of the Prophet: "I have set thee to destroy and to plant and to build." He razed huts and raised walls; he patched and adapted and added; he sowed and planted and hedged; in general he improved and adorned. This was his metier; soon the rambling old labyrinth of a mission straightened out and blossomed forth into the attractive compound it is today. The garden particularly was a success; from a vacant lot fit for stray cats and old tin cans it became over night a bower. The Sisters' Convent was given the necessary repairs; the mission chapel was brightened up; St. Anne's Home for old women and blind girls was repaired and augmented. Yeungkong is not even yet a model mission compound by any means, but only a special talent coupled with untiring devotion could have rounded out its slight possibilities so expertly as did Father Taggart. The plant today is an object lesson in the mission principle of making the best use of what little you happen to have.

Yeungkong, while it has an enormous area, possesses few Christian villages. There are only twenty stations to visit, and thus the travel required of the pastor is much less than at Tungchen. With less travel to do, Father Taggart found extra time which he spent in repairing his out chapels. He rebuilt the Maan Shui chapel with such extensive repairs that it necessitated a housewarming — much to the delight of the Christians. He repaired several other stations. He made plans, bought land, and scraped money to repair more. A builder to his fingertips was Father Taggart.

In his ordinary daily round he was genial and lively, fond of company, a forceful and interesting talker; in a word, something of a mixer. There is no better quality for a missioner in a country where everything is based on friendship. Father Taggart was a maker of friends. Everywhere he went he knew many people, had many visitors. His generosity helped to cement them. No missioner in China can meet every demand for aid, but Father Taggart naturally of a generosity approaching the lavish, found a way to meet many of the most pressing appeals. He was particularly interested in students, many of whom he assisted to get an education in the hope that they would later repay the investment by reflecting credit on the Church.

During one year he taught English in the Government Middle School, at a great sacrifice of his own time in order to cultivate relations with the student element of the city in general. This was only one of many ways in which his active zeal found an outlet. To the Sisters he was kindness itself, leaving nothing undone that he thought could aid their work or consult their well being. He spent his days as a solicitous pastor and a zealous missioner.

That those days were not to be many nobody had any inkling. In his ten years in China he had never been sick a day. He was strong and rugged; the apparent picture of health. Coming from a swimming party with some Chinese students (he was from a boy a magnificent swimmer and very fond of the sport) he complained of feeling a bit unwell. It was the last week of July 1931. For a day or two he fought off the feeling of sickness, thinking it to be some temporary indisposition. However, Father Connors, his assistant, became alarmed and called the doctor. At that time the American doctor attached to the Presbyterian Hospital was absent. The only available doctor, however, was Doctor Lee, a young Catholic Chinese doctor doing general practice in Yeungkong. Dr. Lee, as it happens, is an extremely able physician; he was professor of medicine for some years at Canton's best Western medical school and he recently was employed at Nanking by the Central Government to revise the official Chinese pharmacopia after it had been drawn up by a group of international experts. Dr. Lee at once found that Father Taggart was suffering from acute uremia and said immediately that there was little if any hope to save his life. He tried every possible known means, but Father Taggart did not respond. Meanwhile, Father Connors removed Father Taggart to the Presbyterian Mission Hospital at the invitation of Miss Rauch, a registered nurse who was then in charge. Miss Rauch gave Father Taggart the best quarters the mission afforded and herself left her ordinary work to do the nursing. Mr. and Mrs. Lewis, the only other foreigners spending the summer at the Presbyterian Mission, also helped with unsparing devotion to care for the sick missioner. Father Connors and the Sisters spent almost all their time at his bedside. Dr. Lee was very assiduous. But it was God's summons. The uremic condition could not be relieved. Father Taggart got steadily worse, steadily weaker. On August 4, at 2:30 p.m., just one week after the attack had declared itself, with Father Connors and the Sisters reciting prayers at his bedside, he quietly died. Father Connors had that morning

43

given him the last sacraments and fully prepared him for the sleep that is an awakening. Father Taggart ended his mission career where he began, at Maryknoll's pioneer mission of Yeungkong after just ten years of journeying for Christ. The next morning after Father Connors had offered the Holy Sacrifice of the Mass for the repose of his soul, he was buried in the little Catholic cemetery at Yeungkong by the side of Sister Gertrude Moore. Father Connors gave the absolution while the Sisters and Christians stood by adding many prayers. Another Maryknoller had given his life for the other sheep; the pagan soil of Yeungkong guards the precious remains of another young modern apostle who left all things and followed where the Master called. "And every one that hath left house, or brethren, or sisters, or father, or mother, or wife, or children or land for My Name's sake, shall receive an hundredfold, and shall possess life everlasting" (Matt. 19:29).

Bishop Walsh in Chinese dress

Bishop Henry A. Pinger, O.F.M., was alive, thirty eight years after this homily was delivered, still active in a limited sense in his retirement in Indianapolis, Indiana. He has kept in touch with Bishop Walsh since the latter's return to the States.

On the occasion of the Chicago consecration, September 21, 1937, the late Cardinal Mundelein spoke to the preacher of the day, after the Mass, and reminded him that much of what he had been given credit for — the saving of the missions in Shantung after World War I — was actually due to the wife of the late William Randolph Hearst who took special interest in the very delicate plight of the missionaries at that critical time.

This homily is a swift survey of chapters in the evangelization of China over the past centuries.

Franciscan Footprints

"Ye men of Athens, I perceive that in all things you are too superstitious. For passing by, and seeing your idols, I found an altar also, on which was written: *To the unknown God.* What therefore you worship, without knowing it, that I preach to you" (Acts 17:22-23).

In the city of Peking, the old capital of China, there is a striking parallel to the situation that St. Paul found in Athens. There, many centuries ago, man erected a religious monument called the Temple of Heaven. It is a thing of beauty, consisting in an elaborate altar constructed of the purest white marble, and set out in the middle of a beautiful park, where it is exposed to the four winds of heaven. It is a temple that has no walls except the green trees that line the park, and the cupola of the temple is the blue sky above. To that unique place of worship, the emperor of China went every year to perform the official religious ceremony of the empire. There he offered the aspirations of his people and invoked upon them the blessings of Heaven, looking up to that sky and imploring the Power that lay behind the veil but that had not yet fully revealed Itself to his people. This was the expression of the most primitive religion of China, the belief and trust in the Creator Who dwelt in Heaven and had power to regulate the affairs of earth. He was called the Upper Ruler, and was worshipped as a personal God. He was dimly perceived, but

47

He was sought after. It was a touching attempt on the part of China and its people to put themselves in communication with the unknown God, if haply they might find Him.

The man who bore the role of St. Paul in this Oriental setting, who first appeared on this scene and confronted this situation so reminiscent of Athens, was the spiritual ancestor of the bishop who is being consecrated today. He was John of Montecorvino, a Franciscan priest, who became the first Catholic missioner to take up his residence in China. He went to China in the Middle Ages. He was welcomed immediately by the Chinese people, whom he found to be very religious. He was received with favor by the emperor himself, and was aided in his ministrations by the imperial court. Within five years time he had baptized six thousand people, eager to worship the unknown God he had come to announce to them. He was appointed Archbishop of Peking by the Holy See. He made great progress, establishing Catholic churches in various parts of the imperial city and also in the outlying districts. He labored for thirty years during which time the Faith continued to spread widely. Then he died and was mourned by the entire city, since many had learned to recognize in him the ambassador of the God Whom they sought. It was a good beginning, but unfortunately nobody came forward to build on the foundations so well and truly laid. Events conspired against the continuation of the work. The Black Death ravaged Europe at that time, rendering it impossible to recruit missionaries among the depleted clergy and religious orders. On the other hand, the Mongols swept down from their desert plains to ravage China, and in the chaos that ensued the churches were disrupted and the native flocks were scattered. These untoward circumstances caused the cessation of the work that had begun so promisingly.

All this happened in the year 1300. There is something amazing in this circumstance. The Franciscan order was founded in 1200. Ninety years later, we find it sending missionaries to a country that was then regarded as lost in an impenetrable labyrinth of difficult travel routes at the end of the earth. We recall that the very first thing St. Francis himself wanted to do was to leave his own country and to go to convert the Saracens. Perhaps there is a spiritual lesson lurking here, for this same desire seems to have been an element in the formation of all the great congregations in the Church. When St. Ignatius had only six men in his order, he sent one of them to pioneer in the missions of the Far East, and we know him as Francis Xavier. St. Vincent de Paul was inspired to found his congregation by his experiences among the pirates of the African Coast, which was the most obvious foreign mission of that period. Similar influences are traceable in the foundation of many of the great religious families. Even the contemplative orders, whose actual life is far removed from the missions, seem to partake of the same spirit, so that we find St. Teresa beginning her career by actually running off to be martyred by the Moors. And another St. Therese expresses herself from her cloister in modern times as wishing to travel in all lands and preach the Gospel to all creatures, and to do it to the end of time. There is a spiritual law discernible here, and it is that those who are really filled with the spirit and the life of Christ are filled to overflowing, so that they can never rest content while Christ remains the unknown God, saying with the Psalmist: "I will be satisfied when Thy glory shall appear" (Ps. 16:17). They are restless and would launch out and communicate that spirit and that life to other souls, until there is no country and no people that remains outside the circle of redemption with which Christ intended to girdle the earth.

The work of John of Montecorvino was not lost. It was treasured in the memory of the Church and it was treasured above all in the traditions of the Franciscan Order, and in this way the prosecution of the work was not abandoned but merely delayed. When the time became ripe and conditions feasible, modern Franciscans resumed the continuation of the work that Montecorvino had begun, flocking into China and setting about to erect a new edifice on the old foundations. They found success. For they also found a people who were still looking for the unknown God, and they found it was easy to make Him loved where they were able to make Him known.

The search of the Chinese people for God is a very interesting thing. From the dawn of their history, they have always had a strong religious sense which has expressed itself in many different forms. Far from being irreligious, the Chinese rather have too many religions. There are at least six distinct religions that have been practiced in China for thousands of years. Today they are merged in one big eclectic pantheon, and the four hundred million Chinese are accustomed to shop around among these various religions, taking one ceremony from this and another custom from that, as they chance to feel the need in their continual groping for the Divine. In this way the ordinary Chinese pagan is practicing religion in some form or other all day long, his life being a succession of acts which have a religious significance. We call these acts superstitions, just as St. Paul spoke of the Athenians as being superstitious — and for the same reason, namely, that they are not directed in the proper manner to the known and true God. However, the salient fact is that a superstition, wrong though it be, indicates recognition of the need for help from a higher power, and this can only be a search for God. The fact is that all men are naturally religious and no race of pagan people was ever discovered who did not cherish and practice a big assortment of religious beliefs. The only people to be found in the world who are non-religious are the spoiled Christians of America and Europe, who have turned their backs on the light of the Faith, and ended up with nothing. Incidentally, the only Chinese pagans who are non-religious are those few who have been educated in American and European universities and have learned from Christians that religion is useless. The rank and file of the Chinese people, on the other hand, are very religious, and are engaged in a constant search for Divine help outside themselves, and this makes a great mission opportunity. For while they do not recognize Christianity as the religion they seek, yet the need is there for anybody who can meet it.

The missions of the Franciscan Fathers in China have forged ahead rapidly in the modern period. They have had their problems and their hardships, and they have had their martyrs, but they have gone ahead, working in the face of all difficulties, and they have won through to success. The Franciscan missions in China are many, but the territory of Shantung Province, where Bishop Pinger is assigned to labor, is a particularly successful field. The missions of this province are conducted by the Franciscans and by the Divine Word Fathers, and for many years they have been regarded as models of mission organization for the whole country. Thus Bishop Pinger has found his lines cast in goodly places — at least from a mission point of view. He has had the privilege to be a neighbor of Bishop Henninghaus, the Divine Word Bishop of Yenchowfu, who is looked upon as one of the grand old men of the Chinese hierarchy. The Vicariate of Yenchowfu, under his direction, developed into a model mission, and when missionaries from other sections of China wish to discover the best methods and the most efficient means for the evangelization of the Chinese, it has long been the custom to look to Yenchowfu. These missions, incidentally, were some years ago in grave danger of a great catastrophe, and were only saved from it by a peculiar intervention that traces back right to where we stand, here in Chicago. The missions of Shantung, both Franciscan and Divine Word, were largely manned by priests of German nationality, and during the World War (World War I: Ed.) that saw so many people affected with unfair prejudice against the German race, there was a movement on foot to remove the missionaries from this promising field which they had built up at great sacrifice and labor. This would have been a death blow to missions that rank among the most successful in the whole of China. It was prevented by the wisdom of the Holy See, and to some extent through the instrumentality and urgent insistence of the present Archbishop of Chicago, who is a member of the board of the Sacred College of Propaganda that presides over all the missions of the entire Church. The influence that was used to preserve these missions intact was a service that insured the future of Shantung. The occasion is therefore historic, even unique, that finds His Eminence consecrating an American Franciscan to preside as bishop over the same mission territory that he formerly helped to preserve.

Bishop Pinger is an American working in this promising field. He is, by the nature of the circumstances, a man appointed by God to carry on three great traditions. He is placed over a territory in a most promising part of China which already has a record of great development, and is thus expected to continue the fine tradition of Shantung. He is carrying on the tradition of his own Franciscan Order, which has the honor of having inaugurated mission work in China, through his great predecessor Montecorvino. Finally, he is the continuator and the representative of a third glorious tradition, namely, that which involves the contribution of America to mission work in the Orient, and the contribution of American Franciscans in particular. For just as Montecorvino began the work of the Church in the Orient, so the American Franciscans began the participation of America in this same work. The first American priests ever to work as missionaries in China were Franciscans, and Bishop Pinger is the successor of that band of pioneers from his own Order, who already constitute a long and distinguished line. May he live long and labor zealously to add glorious new chapters to all these splendid records.

The Bishop is being consecrated, and is going to return to his mission at a time when the field of his labors is reverberating with shot and shell. Some will question his wisdom in doing so. However, there is a sufficient answer to such hesitancy, and here it is. The need of the people is more important than the safety of the missionary. The need of the people is the opportunity of the missionary. And the need of the people is the reason why God sends the missionary. The physician does not desert the patient on the operating table, and neither does the missionary desert his flock when they are in their greatest need. The search for the unknown God is still on in China. And more so than ever in these periods of stress and trial — and somebody must be there to show the Chinese people where to find Him. St. Francis would be there — and he is there in the person of his sons. John of Montecorvino would be there — and he is there in the presence of his successors. Bishop Pinger will be there both as son and successor — directing his missionaries, feeding his flock, spending and being spent, living the life of a successor of the Apostles, doing the work of a bishop of the Church of Christ, helping His people to find the unknown God.

Father Gerard Donovan was one of three brothers ordained and sent overseas as Maryknollers. His violent death in 1938 — when bandits forcibly entered the sanctuary of the chapel where he was kneeling for Benediction of the Blessed Sacrament, held him for ransom and left him to die on a lonely mountainside in Manchuria — continues to our present generation as a strong reminder of the price that an apostolic vocation has demanded in the past and might well be an indication of what the future, too, holds. This sermon was preached at the Funeral Mass after Father Donovan's mangled body was returned to the United States.

A Martyr Priest

"Brethren, I do not count myself to have apprehended. But one thing I do: forgetting the things that are behind and stretching forth myself to those that are before, I press towards the mark, to the prize of the supernal vocation of God in Christ Jesus" Phil. 3:13-14.

When it seemed good to Almighty God to demonstrate the coming of age of the American Church, He first chose two American priests whom He had carefully molded to fill the role of leaders in a movement that would signalize this point of departure. In His providential plan these two men were taken from two different sections of our country as if to indicate that the movement launched by their instrumentality and under their guidance was to be a truly American movement, representing every section of this favored land and reaching into every nook and corner of it. The movement was the foreign missions in particular, but in its broader aspect it was to emphasize the apostolic character of the American priesthood in general. It meant that the American priest was called to be a true apostle in the exercise of Christ's Ministry whether at home or abroad.

This movement was new only as applied to a stage of development in America; in itself it was as old as the Catholic Church. The founders of Maryknoll knew that they were making no discovery, inventing nothing, establishing nothing new. They recognized that they were merely drawing on the existing reservoir of the Church and applying one of its most sublime exigencies to present conditions. They drew their inspiration from many sources. They themselves were products of the American Church and they represented the best traditions of the pioneering priests of their own country. They knew America could be missionary because they remembered that it had always been missionary. They thought of the great figures of the past who had climbed the mountains and scoured the plains in our own pioneer missions to lay down a missionary tradition at the very outset of the Church's work in America. They themselves, in some measure, had personally labored in work of this same character. One had been a pioneer in the ideology of the apostolate, laboring to instill the mission spirit in the hearts of the people by his devoted activity as director of the Propagation of the Faith Society. The other had been prepared through the actual performance of mission work in his own person, in all its trying details and under the most difficult circumstances to be found perhaps anywhere in America. These things, however, were only items in the formation of their background. As in the case of all providential men chosen for a special work, they were close to God and they were enamored of His Church. Their hearts beat in unison with the Church; they knew its history, palpitated with its life; and they tried to share in all the inspiration that its divine economy has had to offer to its children for two thousand years. They ascended to the pure font of inspiration revealed at the very establishment of the Church in the divine definition of what its work was to be, their hearts vibrating at the sound of Christ's direct command to go and teach all nations — very much as if they had stood with His apostles on that solemn day and heard those words from His divine lips themselves. They shared the campaigns of the apostles and the apostolic journeys of St. Paul and they were entirely conscious of the struggles of the martyrs in the Colosseum and the arena, wherein were written in blood the secret of the progress of this divine Entrant into the lives of men. They followed the course of the apostolic Church through its history, reviewing the apostolic labors of all the great missioners of the Church down through the ages, and perceiving quite clearly from that living history the difficulties and demands that were inevitably entailed in the prosecution of the work they were chosen to launch.

They were penetrated with a solemn conviction as to the stern character of mission work; they were perfectly cognizant of its difficulties and dangers and pitfalls; they were acutely conscious of its needs; and they were also on fire with its glory and so when they felt the inspiration of God sounding the call to action, they did not hesitate.

In their survey of the problem, all factors pointed to success with the possible exception of one. The only question in the equation was the American priest. Could he measure up to the demands of this apostolic vocation? It was necessary to face the fact that those demands might eventually include the very extremes. The work was Christ's work, the essential objective for which He had come on earth, the cause for which He lived and died, and the motive for which He established His Church. There was no question about the necessity of the work being done; then the question was the ability of the American priest to do it. The founders were obliged to ask themselves if American Catholic youth were capable of rising to the heights of sacrifice and selflessness needed to pioneer for Christ. Could they give up home and country and family and friends? Could they stand the isolation of exile, the discouragement of slow plodding and occasional failure, the rigors of climate, the thousand and one demands of life on the frontiers of the world? In short, could they live dangerously and die cheerfully? For the question was could they do it, not for a short period, but for a lifetime of long and arduous years, working against odds and hoping against hope, keeping their hearts pure in the midst of pagan surroundings, preserving their loyalty and love and zeal when everything around them tended to tarnish and compromise it, persevering to the end? And finally, could they actually lay down their lives in the performance of their work, meeting death itself for Christ, and regarding it in their willing generosity as the sublime privilege that it is? For this also was a distinct possibility. The founders of Maryknoll did not know the answer to this question, but they believed that the answer would be given in the affirmative by the Catholic youth of America. They staked all on the caliber of the American priest — assisted of course by the grace of God. They were not to be disappointed.

Father Gerard Donovan has answered this question. He was selected by God to answer it once and for all in his own person. It is a sublime role and a historic one. The career of this young priest is a double glory to the American clergy, harking back to the pioneer days of the American missionary tradition that produced him, and pointing gloriously to the future of the American priesthood that will be emboldened to follow him. In selecting Father Donovan to embody in his own person the divine stamp and seal of approval and success for the growth of America towards the full stature of the priesthood of Christ, Almighty God has brought us to a new point of departure. The Catholic priest is not only a minister of Christ, but he is also a follower of Christ and indeed another Christ, willing to go the whole way with his Divine Master, living as He lived, dying, if need be, as He died. This crystallizes the true conception of the priesthood. For the true ideal of the priesthood can only be that which exists in the mind of Christ, Who established that priesthood, and it is that His priests be like Himself, the Eternal Priest, Who not only preached to His people, but also offered Himself for them.

Father Gerard Donovan embodied in his person and in his career much more than the simple ability to face death with a smile. He faced life also with a smile — which is harder to do — and consequently when he made the supreme sacrifice he was only dying as he had lived, according to a Providential law which often allows the final touch of a man's life to be in keeping with his preliminary career. And it is for the reason that Father Donovan faced life so well that he was chosen by God to face death so triumphantly. The background of this sacrifice is nine years of selfless devotion, untiring zeal, and smiling courage. This involved the daily decisions of nine long years under the hardest missionary conditions, and these daily decisions were always to forget the things that are behind and keep pressing on to what lay before, the supernal prize of the vocation in Christ Jesus (Phil. 3:13). What were the activities of this constantly active priest? Only one, but that was the most important activity in the world, and in fact, the only activity in the world that is important at all — helping other people. Christ made men important by dying for them, by that act revealed the purpose of the universe as a simple problem of helping and saving men. Whatever activity is helpful to the souls of men is thereby worth doing in the world, and whatever fails to contribute to that end is futile, and what retards it is harmful. This is a true touchstone, and one by which we can confidently assess the worth to the world of any instrument of God.

The mission of Manchoukuo is not an easy one. It is a field which presents all the usual difficulties of a foreign mission territory together with some unusual hardships peculiar to itself. There is perhaps no mission where it is easier to be daunted by the prospects, compromised by the dangers and doubts, inhibited by the oppositions and barriers, worried and preoccupied by the troubles and anxieties — no mission where it is easier to have the native hue of resolution sickled over with the pale cast of thought — and to forget to smile.

Yet a man who forgets himself will not forget to smile, because in thinking of others he smiles for them. Father Donovan was close to his people. He understood their hard conditions, sympathized with their little problems, shared their rugged lives, admired and loved their simple humanity. He gave them his heart and in doing so he entered into their hearts. He lived for the people. He would climb the highest mountain in Manchoukuo to save a single soul. He actually spent his nine years in Manchoukuo in climbing many mountains to save many souls. And into the mountain forests where he penetrated and into the lowly villages where he was welcomed he brought his smile. He was gracious and deferential towards the old people; he had active sympathy and help, comfort and consolation for the ablebodied folk; he had his own cheery inspiration and a smile and a blessing for the young people and the babies; and he had the doctrine of Christ for all. Living for the people, he also died for the people, as far as we can piece out and reconstruct the circumstances of his final sacrifice. He was taken in a strange manner from the very sanctuary, with his people all about him. He was a young man of great spirit and courage and of keen intelligence. The possibility of resistance was certainly the first thing that flashed across his mind. This flash must have been immediately followed by a second thought for his flock and the possible consequences to them of any resistance on his part. In another flash he made his choice, and apparently it was the choice that Christ had made before him, of offering himself as a sacrifice in order that no harm should come to the people. So there was no outcry, there was no resistance, there was only the simple acceptance of the sublime role for which his life had prepared him — to forget self and help others in death as he had done in life — to follow in the footsteps of Christ to the very end.

Thus the keynote of his life was emphasized and crystallized in his death, and we have before us a type and model of the sort of apostle that America was destined to produce. It is the type of a simple, cheerful, smiling, courageous, and totally unassuming young man, who concentrated on the one thing necessary, namely, to love the people for whom Christ died and to imitate Christ Himself in giving his own life to save them.

This day is overshadowed with divinity. This day brings God very near. We go now to a little plot of ground that has been selected by Almighty God to enshrine and memorialize a great providential plan that may well play a major role in the history of His Church. Here close together will lie the precious remains of three men who in their careers and in their own persons have proved the apostolic character of the American priesthood. Here lie the three protagonists of the movement that has given a new impetus to the speedy realization of the purpose for which Christ came on earth. Here are the two founders who showed us the way to realize the fullness of Christ's priesthood, and here with them will lie their first young martyr who actually walked that way. It is fitting that they should lie here together, for they are the providential instruments associated in the building and completion of a common work. Maryknoll is complete and America is apostolic. They are here for a grace and a blessing and an inspiration, an ever-living reminder of the sublime principle which they sealed both in life and in death, these three men who were chosen by God to embody the supreme ideal of the apostolic priesthood. They have opened the skies, and they lie here to point the way to the stars.

Maryknoll feels the spiritual glory of this triumph. And Maryknoll is proud of the sublimity of this moment when it is privileged to offer to God the pure sacrifice of this ardent young priest who walked so courageously by the side of his Divine Master. But Maryknoll also feels very sharply the grief of separation, for if Maryknoll has gained a glorious model, yet Maryknoll has lost a son and a brother. Every heart at Maryknoll shared the anxiety of his captivity, shared the pain of his loss, hopes to share the triumph of his victory. And in addition to our own personal grief, Maryknoll likewise shares in a particular way the heavy sorrow that is involved in this sacrifice for his father and mother and his devoted family. No words of ours could fully assuage their sorrow, and for a full understanding of this mystery we can only commend them to the divine consolation of Christ Himself, in Whose footsteps their manly son so courageously walked, and to the maternal comfort of Christ's Immaculate Mother who stood near their son in his trial just as she stood near her own Son at the foot of the cross. Time will soften their sorrow as it reveals to them the spiritual glory of the sublime role for which their own son has been selected. Now they are paying the price of greatness, the human pang that comes in yielding the loved one to a great spiritual role that involves sacrifice, the vocation to live on that elevated plane by which God establishes an example and an inspiration for the general good of mankind. The role of Father Gerard Donovan ever will be history at Maryknoll, and generations of young apostles yet unborn will pray for the grace to share his spirit, catch his generosity, to inherit his smile. He lives in Heaven with God. And he will live on our hilltop forever.

May the angels receive him. May they present him at the throne of God — Maryknoll's pure offering, our son and our brother, the most beautiful flower in this garden of God's planting, our joyous apostle, our martyr priest.

The founders of Maryknoll have been vindicated in their judgment regarding the apostolic character of the American priesthood. They have been justified in their estimate of American youth. They made no mistake.

There are two Bishops Walsh — James Anthony Walsh and James E. Walsh. The former is the Co-founder of Maryknoll, consecrated in 1933, three years before his death in 1936. The younger bishop, James E. Walsh was consecrated earlier, in 1927, and — thank God — is still very much alive at eighty four.

Father James Anthony Walsh, the Priest

To the very early students of Maryknoll, and no doubt to later ones as well, the spirituality of Father James Anthony Walsh always seemed to be a very priestly type of spirituality. A constant exemplification of the basic virtues and disciplines of the priesthood in his daily life, a strong emphasis on the ideals of the priesthood in all his principles and attitudes, and an evident love of the priesthood in his heart, were among the characteristics that caused this universal impression. Maryknoll students had many occasions to see, and to admire, many sides of their gifted Superior, but they always looked upon him first and foremost as the pious, fatherly, highminded, priestly priest.

All this was the more surprising perhaps, or at least the less to be expected, in view of the Co-founder's unique role at Maryknoll, which was that of the busy executive from the very first. True, he was Superior of the Seminary from the very first also and for many years after. No doubt he was very conscious of the responsibility of this important office, and this may account in part for the pronounced priestliness he always exhibited in regime and habit, in speech and demeanor, in action and reaction. However, it could hardly account for the whole deep-dyed make-up of the man altogether. It probably had something to do with the meticulous care he lavished on the little regulations, customs and appurtenances of the seminary, with his manifest concern for the liturgy and the studies, with his personal interest in every seminarian, and with the marvelous fidelity he brought to all the seminary exercises in the midst of his other engrossing, time-consuming occupations. But it could not have been the sole explanation for the constant, notable, indelible priestliness of his character as displayed in the council room as well as at the altar, when chained to his desk, in his moments of relaxation, in every detail of his life. This was not something he could put off and on according to the exigencies of a particular office; it was his personal possession.

A many-sided man, if there ever was one, Father James Anthony Walsh impressed even the least observant as primarily the deeply spiritual priest to whom other things had been added, not as the divided personality who tries to sandwich in the essentials of the priesthood amid other interests, distractions and duties. The episcopal motto he later chose was more than an accident. "Seek ye first the kingdom of God" (Mt. 6:33) was not only a lifelong favorite text of his but was also, if all unconsciously on his part, a perfect summation of his own life and its entire spiritual orientation. God and His justice were the deep, primary interests in his philosophy. The other things were added to him, some as rewards according to the scriptural promise perhaps, some by his own acquisition, but all as outgrowth, results, incidentals, accretions. It seemed eminently fitting when he finally received the fullness of the priesthood, for he had always been fully a priest.

When one considers the multiplicity of the "other things" that made up his life, this marked priestliness of the Co-Founder is all the more revealed as a basic, permanent part of him. It had to be. Busy executive is a mild word to describe his assignment. He was the initiator, promoter, organizer and administrator, both on the practical and the spiritual plane, of a work which was at once brand new, wholly unknown, capable of great development by its nature, and very anxious to grow and to grow quickly by its inner urge; and he was all these things at a time when help was scarce, helpers few. Meanwhile he was also Superior of the Seminary and of the whole Society. Thus he had to be a business man, a literary man, and executive officer, a household manager, a family father, a spiritual shaper and leader, and something of a peerer into the future, all at the same time. Many a priest finds himself combining some or all of these activities in some moderate measure — or trying to — on occasion. But there was at least a threefold marvel in the way in which he combined them, in the dexterity with which he met their varied, constant demands. In his case: (1) each separate function was carried out in what might be called extravagant measure, in full and absorbing degree, (2) each function was carried out with notable success, and (3) he remained the eminently priestly priest through it all.

No doubt there are various shades of spirituality, a difference of emphasis, of development, of personal bent to some extent, of divine leading perhaps at times, even among priests. No doubt also the peculiar variety in each case, the particular development is often affected by occupation. However this may be, the Co-Founder of Maryknoll must have had a certain basic spirituality of his own that was not unduly affected by anything. He may have been developed in character and ability by his demanding occupations — probably was; but his priestly spirit was only intensified by them, not obscured, diluted or changed. He came to his work as a priest, performed it as a priest, and ended it as a priest. In doing so he built on true foundations, put first things first. His own spiritual edifice was solid, and as a result the building he erected was sound.

If one seeks the reason for this, a very strong and providential one occurs at once to the mind. We do not know what originally made Bishop James Anthony Walsh, the man, such a priestly priest. It may have been his good youth, his excellent formation in a Sulpician seminary, his later development as an active diocesan priest, his own personal cooperation with the grace of God; or, as is more likely, a combination of all these influences together. In any case his earliest students do not know this particular about their spiritual father, as we were not his contemporaries but his children of a later generation. What we do know is why the Co-Founder of Maryknoll was such a priestly priest. It was because God evidently planned it that way. Thus we do not know where or how he got his priestliness, but we know where and why God got him. It was because Maryknoll needed such a type of father and leader, produced by and taken from the American priesthood, to give it a healthy and propitious start, and to further its ultimate success.

A new work like Maryknoll faced a double danger, one external, the other internal; and this very quality of eminent priestliness on the part of Bishop James Anthony Walsh went a long way to provide against both. These dangers were inanition at home and superficiality abroad. It was easy to launch a new movement by dint of pen and promotion, but only the confidence inspired by a thoroughly priestly leader could insure the domestic encouragement and support that was so crucially needed, especially at first. It was easy to gather a lot of young men together and send them out to foreign countries, but only the strongest emphasis on priestly ideals and fundamentals, reinforced by the living example of their leader and model, could insure their development into serious, self-sacrificing, apostolic missioners. Maryknoll's future was bound up in the type, the character, the spiritual stature, of its creators and leaders, its two Co-Founders, to a considerable extent. That is the ultimate reason, it would seem, why God provided men for this role who were so advanced and confirmed in priestly virtues, Bishop Walsh and his collaborator, Father Price.

The present writer first met Father James Anthony (as he was then called, not by us, but by his intimates in the priesthood) at Hawthorne in the autumn of 1912. I had had the temerity to present myself as a new student for the newly projected, still non-existent, foreign mission seminary. I did so with a feeling of trepidation which lasted about two minutes, the length of time it took to receive the greeting of my new Superior. Father James Anthony was a reassuring figure to begin with, a man of settled composure with a dash of kindly, interested animation. I forget his first words, but I recall my pleased impression that he did not regard me as a stranger, greeted me rather as a person already known, made me a member of the family without the slightest preliminaries.

I recall his second and his third words. The second was that the water supply was low, and that I could help Francis Ford to manipulate the hand pump in the front yard, if I cared to. The third was: "Are you a singer?" It was about time for Benediction of the Blessed Sacrament, and he was preparing for it. As it happened, the question was a poser. Nobody could ask me a more embarrassing one, either at that moment or at any other. My heart sank in my boots, perhaps my face fell also. Nothing to do but come out with it, I thought in consternation. "My best friend would never accuse me of that," I replied, and waited for the sentence.

It never came. In place of it there was a chuckle that I was to come to know well before much ivy had grown over Maryknoll. "Well, don't worry about it," he hastened to interject. "In that case we'll call you a Wheeler and Wilson."

Father James Anthony was not above a pun, indulged in them frequently, distinctly liked them. It was an item in the ever-ready humor of a man who combined a perfect sense of proportion, a good degree of wit, and the elevated, understanding view of a fatherly priest towards the foibles of humanity. From that time on (my first day) I felt at home at Maryknoll.

After the incipient seminary moved to Maryknoll on the Hudson, one of my early assignments was the care of the Co-Founder's room. I made the bed, emptied the waste basket, and dusted the pictures. The place of honor was held by the well-known picture of St. Francis of Assisi with one arm of Christ reaching down from the Cross to embrace him. I recall entering the room on one occasion to find Father James Anthony gazing at it with fixed attention. It was my impression that the picture meant much to him. I also recall an occasion when I brought to him, seated at his desk, the relic of the True Cross which was kept in the Seminary chapel. I do not remember the reason why the relic was brought to him at that time, but I remember distinctly the avidity with which he took it from my hand, the fervid kiss he quickly pressed upon it — reactions of a kind not often seen in a man so composed, restrained and undemonstrative.

Those who knew him well will not doubt that the Cross and the Passion of Christ held a very high place, if not the highest and most central place of all, in his devotional life, in the underpinning of his spirituality. It is the true fountain of living water, after all, for the priest who would drink deeply of the spirit of Christ, be more than His pious follower at a safe distance, identify his own life and death, fortunes and desires, with those of his Master. No man of half measures, Bishop James Anthony Walsh was that kind of a priest.

The Spiritual Reading talks given by the Co-Founder in my day were eagerly looked forward to. Almost invariably they took the form of little homilies based on incidents in the life of Christ as described in Holy Scripture. Disarming at first in their quiet simplicity, these informal talks were soon found to be gems of apt expression, graceful and cogent, sometimes even beautiful. He had a talent for description, and he used it frequently to recreate scenes from the life of Christ which were very effective. Christ in the Temple, Christ at the well, Christ with Martha and Mary, Christ with Mary Magdalene, Christ in the Upper Room, Christ in many scenes with the Apostles, became pictures that students carried away with them and remembered. These talks were not polished discourses, gave no impression of having been meticulously prepared. To us they seemed more like the natural and spontaneous expression of a mind and heart long nourished by, steeped in, the spirit of the Gospel.

Shortly after I was ordained a priest, the Superior of Maryknoll gave me a pleasant surprise by announcing that he would accompany me to my home parish on the occasion known as the First Mass. I was surprised because the journey from New York to the place where my family lived (Cumberland, Maryland) was a long and inconvenient one. We spent a night on the train together, and he preached at my First Mass on the following morning. I fear I may have been too preoccupied with my own new experiences to pay very close attention to the sermon. I merely noted at the time that it was an effective and pleasing one. However, it impressed one of the parishioners so much that he spoke of it to me some ten years afterwards. This was a Mr. James Gaffney, a very pious and good man and, as it happened, my godfather. "I remember," said Mr. Gaffney, "how beautifully he spoke of the Blessed Sacrament. And about the priest being like the Blessed Mother. It has always remained in my mind."

This remark caused me later to look up the record. This is a part of what the Co-Founder said on that occasion: "This young man, who went forth from here a few years ago as a lay worshipper in this his parish church, returns now to intercede for you at the altar of his youth. He comes back another Mary. His fiat will also bring down Jesus Christ from Heaven; his consecrated hands, like hers, will hold the Babe of Bethlehem; his eyes will rest upon God laid in the snow white manger of this new Bethlehem, this house of Bread. And he comes back another Christ. The words that his lips will shortly utter — words which break through the clouds and reach Heaven — the mighty words of consecration — will not be, 'This is the Body of Christ,' but 'This is My Body.' Christ will use his lips, his tongue, to perpetuate the unbloody Sacrifice that goes on from the rising of the sun to its going down. He is a priest; the power of Christ will operate through him."

Such incidents illustrate a priestly characteristic of the Co-Founder that was very typical of him. It was his great deference towards other priests, consideration for them, even for the youngest among them. This was often remarked at Maryknoll and elsewhere. Seminarians accustomed to being seen and not heard were surprised to find themselves suddenly treated like kings the day after their ordination. Young curates at big functions liked the way in which he sought them out for attention, took as much interest in them as in anybody else present. He had all the graceful traits, the tastes, the interests of the man who has become the priest in every fibre, all over. The priesthood flowered in him, shaping, dominating his whole character.

These little reminiscences, trifling in themselves, bear on a point that is not a trifle. The Co-Founder and first Superior General of Maryknoll had to be a very priestly man, if he was to serve as a model for his spiritual sons of the early or the later days or of the great future. If priests were to be apostles, they had to be true, whole souled, single-minded, priestly priests at bottom to begin with. Otherwise they were building on sand, would lack the whole foundation and the essential powerhouse of the apostolate. It was part of Bishop James Anthony Walsh's role to provide this model in his own person. He did it well, as he did so many other things, spiritual and material, that were required for the strong, healthy development of Maryknoll.

The consecration of Bishop Raymond A. Lane in Lawrence, Mass., June 11, 1940, would be the first of three sons of that strongly Catholic city to become bishops within the Maryknoll Family. Assisting Bishop Walsh in the ceremony were Bishop Joseph E. McCarthy of Portland, Maine and the Auxiliary Bishop of Boston, later to become its Cardinal, Richard J. Cushing.

Interesting, too, the new Bishop would, six years later, return from a PW camp in Manchuria to succeed his consecrator as Superior General of Maryknoll, the latter to return to China for his many years of imprisonment.

Bishop Lane's Consecration

There is a presence here, that while unseen, has dominated this ceremony from the first step to the last. That figure is truly present in every episcopal consecration, which by its nature can take place only through the direction and specific command of this personality. The consecration of a bishop is the act of the Holy Father, and it is to him as the chief actor of the scene that our hearts go on such an occasion. What we actually saw in the church this morning was but a young missionary priest consecrated bishop through the instrumentality of several brother bishops and accompanied by the prayers and support of many zealous members of the clergy and the laity. What we did not see, but what actually took place, was a drama behind the scenes in which the Vicar of Christ on earth, the Holy Father, who alone appoints the bishops of the Church, reach out from his august throne and select a man to represent him in sharing his responsibility of the world-wide apostolate for his precious flock. Again behind the reality lies another deeper reality, equally unperceived except by the eyes of faith but no less true. It is the picture of Christ Himself present in our midst to add another member to His band of apostles just as truly as He once called His first apostles by the shores of Galilee.

The present occasion provides a good example of the Holy Father's action in directing his world family. The consecration of a missionary bishop is a constructive act, a measure of progress, a step forward, a provision for the development and rehabilitation of the people. This is a great contrast. While men are tearing down, the Holy Father is building up. While men are led astray by false ideas of fancied progress that they seek to attain through strife and conflict and highly questionable means, the Holy Father keeps on indicating in every act, the paths to true progress by peaceful and lasting means.

It might seem to men that the provision of a missionary bishop for a far-flung corner of the pagan world is a small item to cast into the seething cauldron of world conflict that exists today, but actually it provides a good example of the theory that lies back of the whole policy of the Church. The Church possesses the solution to all the needs of every people, and the head of the Church, the Holy Father, is prepared to provide those specific solutions as they become practical and necessary. However, he does not seek to impose his solutions upon a world that is not prepared to receive them, nor has he any undue optimism about the acceptance of his concrete proposals by populations who remain gravely at variance in the first principles that underlie the proposed measures. The kingdom of God is within you, and the Holy Father knows that the people of the world must be converted and prepared in heart before they will accept and act upon his practical prescriptions. He counts upon us to do the spade work, to propagate the Catholic faith that will rectify the hearts of men, to give the Catholic Sacraments that will strengthen the souls of men, to prepare the people of the world to accept generously and spontaneously the prescriptions of the Vicar of Christ that will insure the happiness and peace of men. Therefore he sends his missionaries to do this work. He says in effect: The Church has the answers to all the needs of the world, and I myself will give those answers to the world at the proper time. Do you go and prepare the people of the world to accept them and to act upon them when they receive them.

This commission is well expressed in the motto of Bishop Lane: *Facere et Docere* — "To do and to teach." This is in effect what the Pope tells us to do, to go to this people, to the scattered members of his whole family and there among them to do and to teach what Christ Our Lord first did and taught. This is the way to prepare a world that will be willing to accept God and to be guided by the counsels and commands of His Vicar on earth, and this is accordingly the basic and permanent way in which to secure the happy acceptance of God's world program for the peace and happiness of His people.

Finally, whether by accident or design, there is a circumstance in the present consecration that would seem to augur well for the significance of this event in the plan of preparing the pagan world to accept the message of Christ. Bishop Lane has been given the episcopal title that was bequeathed by Bishop Henninghaus of Shantung. To be the successor of this man in any sense at all is a privilege and a responsibility. Bishop Henninghaus, recently deceased, was in his time the grand old man of the Chinese missions, the perfect bishop, the great organizer, the wise father, the apostolic leader. Scarcely more than five feet tall, his mind and his heart were as big and broad as his body was small, and he was not only loved by his own priests and people but he was revered by every missionary in the Far East, as the perfect type of missionary leader. His vicariate was so noted for its splendid organization and apostolic drive that it was widely regarded as the model mission of the entire Far East. Bishop Lane is honored to receive the title relinquished by those hands, and we can surmise that the Holy Father when he was bestowing it may have had a kindly thought and a fatherly hope that the new bishop would carry on his work in the same spirit and with the same success. That work and spirit were characterized by a complete devotion to the people, a tireless and energetic apostolic zeal, a total immersion in Oriental culture and a deep regard and appreciation for every aspiration and good quality manifested among the people, in short, an identification with his people that made him their true father and will keep his name in benediction among them for generations.

Maryknoll is grateful to the Holy Father for this expression of confidence by which one of its young missioners is entrusted with the grave responsibility of bringing Christ to six million people. In this moment, our hearts go to the Father of the family and we pray Almighty God to support and bless him in the tremendous burdens that he is shouldering today. We know, however, that in spite of the grave anxiety he must feel, and the deep sorrow of his paternal heart over the troubles of his children, that he retains the Catholic outlook and deep confidence that are rooted in the divine assurances to the Church. "We have rejoiced for the days in which we have seen evils" is the motto inscribed on the Fisherman's ring, and the successor of St. Peter will remain rooted in that Catholic confidence that is founded on the rock of faith amid all the storms and evils that afflict the passing scene. May God bless and protect our Holy Father, the one hope of a distracted world, the one source of the divine guidance and direction that the world needs, just as it needs Christ Himself Whose place he takes, and may his new missionary bishop fulfill the confidence that the Holy Father reposes in him today, by walking in the footsteps of the apostles, by giving himself to his people, by preparing their hearts to accept all the directions that the Vicar of Christ may give for the happiness and peace of the world.

Back at Maryknoll as Superior General, 1937 found him talking in the Seminary entrance to a Maryknoll Sister.

Sister Mary Clare entered the Maryknoll Sisters on February 1, 1920. Her name was Gertrude Miltenberger and she had been born, like Bishop James E. Walsh, in Cumberland, Md. Their pastor, Father Wunder, was a friend of Father Price, later co-founder of Maryknoll, but then a missioner in North Carolina and editor of the magazine Truth, *founded by him in 1897. In 1900 (December issue) and in many later issues of* Truth, *Miss Miltenberger is listed as a solicitor. Later, in the spring of 1918, Father Price was doing promotion work for Maryknoll in Pittsburgh — his most successful work as a promoter — and Gertrude Miltenberger was living there and had already founded the* Maria Mission Circles. *This eulogy was given at her funeral in 1946.*

Eulogy for Sister Mary Clare

God has been here, and He has taken from us the earthly presence of Sister Clare, calling her soul, that came from His own hand, back to Himself. We both grieve and rejoice while we wholly accept His divine will — that is equally adorable to us in all the circumstances, hard or easy, of life and of death. We know grief because we feel the separation that death brings — the deprivation of a gracious presence and the loss of a helpful worker in the community. We experience joy because we also know the victory that death brings — in setting the seal on a faithful life and translating it to the vision of God. "As it is written: That eye hath not seen, nor ear heard, neither hath it entered into the heart of man, what things God hath prepared for them that love Him. But to us God hath revealed them by His Spirit; for the Spirit searcheth all things, even the deep things of God" (1 Cor. 2:9-10). We live here in the religious life. We live with God, in a life consecrated to the extension of His Kingdom on earth, in a round of duties designed to lead others to heaven, in the practice of virtues that directly prepare ourselves for heaven. For this vocation we are highly privileged. We have known the things that God has prepared for them that love Him — at least in their great essentials — for God has revealed them to us by His Spirit. He has done this to strengthen and enlighten us beyond the common lot of men. He has opened to us His treasures and made us the almoners of His charity, and the dispensers of His mysteries. He has confided in us, trained us, revealed and explained things to us, walked closely with us, made us His trusted and intimate friends; and so we have loved the beauty of His house and we have known the place where His glory dwelleth. We have consecrated our lives and all our energies to carry His grace and truth, His hope and His glorious promises, out over the mission fields of the world and share them with other men. We grieve for Sister Clare, but a thousand times more do we rejoice, for we know what things God hath prepared for them that love Him; we have preached them to others, and we would not halt the favored soul among ourselves that now leaves us to fly to this reward.

Sister Clare joined the Maryknoll Sisters twenty-six years ago, and was to celebrate the Silver Jubilee of her first profession this year. She had been a teacher in the world and she was a teacher for a good many years as a Maryknoll Sister. She taught for a long time in our school for Orientals in Los Angeles, and subsequently for seven years she taught in the Hawaiian Islands, first being Superior of the Maryknoll Convent in Heeia, and later teaching in the school in Wailuku on Maui.

There is reason to believe that she was a very competent teacher; certainly she was a person of cultivated mind, good balance and sure taste. It was not my fortune to be associated closely with Sister Clare in any Maryknoll work, and I did not know her intimately, although she lived in the same town that was my own original home. I knew her family better — and a better Catholic family I am sure I never knew. But I had occasion only recently to review a production of hers that I take to be indicative of her spiritual development and her character. I was given a long series of meditations to read that she had prepared for children. They were based on devotion to the Blessed Virgin. I began to read with perfunctory interest that soon changed into absorption, and ended with amazement. I can think of no other word to describe the piece of work except the one word: beautiful. The penetrating understanding of the child mind, the solid and sensible spirituality, the judicious selection and emphasis, the tasteful, chiseled English, and the restrained but ardent love for the Blessed Mother that breathed from every page, made the book a sort of spiritual treasury for children, and must have revealed something of the writer. I do not know if the work will ever see the light of day, but I believe that the Sister who produced it was very much in tune with the light of heaven — whither we trust God's mercy will soon conduct her.

When a good religious dies, there is no sadness that is not immediately swallowed up in joy. Sister Clare was an unselfish worker, a faithful religious, a gracious spirit, an exemplar of charity, an asset to her community. Charity is the ticket to heaven because charity is God's life, and without charity nobody enters there to live with God. Let us pray for her that her soul may be adorned with charity and immersed in it, so that all the little stains of earthly imperfection may be speedily swept away and she may find peace and rest and joy in the arms of God.

Years ago, priests around the United States were wont to remark on a particular spirit of the new Maryknoll society. Difficult to define, it was simply called the Maryknoll Spirit. After Bishop Walsh sent this 1942 Christmas letter to Maryknoll priests, Brothers and seminarians, many felt that it was the best description put on paper that captured that elusive spirit.

The Maryknoll Spirit

Christmas will unite us all in spirit, or rather it will find us so united, separated and distant though we may be in the body, as we scatter up and down two continents in the pursuit of our vocation. And indeed, there is much to unite us, whereas I hope and trust there is nothing more serious than material space to divide us. We are members of the Mystical Body of Christ, sharing in common the participation in His own divine life that the Head diffuses to the members, bound to God and to each other by all those sacred ties that make up our birthright in the household of the Faith. We have a common vocation, and a sublime one, that centers our lives on the pursuit of one great and identical aim, and likewise provides us all with the same set of inspiring ideals as a spur to its attainment. We differ naturally in many little accidentals as individuals; we have different dispositions, different perceptions, different gifts, different opinions. But we do not differ in our aim or in our ideals, and I know that what I seek you seek, and that what you cherish I cherish, and that what we all seek and cherish together is the reign of Christ in the hearts of the people, along with the grace to embrace every labor and sacrifice necessary to bring it about.

At Maryknoll and among Maryknoll men there has been a traditional spirit, early evident and long persistent, by virtue of which the members of our Society have become noted for their whole-souled acceptance of each other. In the atmosphere created by bringing men together for the common pursuit of a soul-stirring aim, close ties of mutual respect and thoughtful charity became the rule, and we found ourselves going through the spiritually healthy process of making friends, not merely because we chose them for natural reasons, but because God gave them to us for a supernatural purpose. It is my belief that this spirit of brotherly interest and family forbearance not only remains strong among us but is becoming stronger as we grow and learn and develop, although its external manifestations do not always remain the same, some changing, some abating, some increasing, with our later history and providential growth. You cannot know five hundred men as intimately as the handful of pioneers could know each other, but you can esteem and prize five hundred men by virtue of the Maryknoll bond that creates your relationship with them, and this I trust you do. The spirit of our organization does not necessarily depend upon the little intimacies of daily contact for its nourishment and continuance, for God Who gave us the spirit knew that such means would not be available to men living oceans apart. The criterion of the spirit is not how well you know a Maryknoll man, but how quickly you accept him and how sincerely you esteem him.

So in all essentials the Maryknoll spirit ought only to increase as time goes on, for each passing year brings joys and trials, labors and successes, that we share together, engendering fellow feelings that should make us wondrous kind. We now have experience enough to realize and appreciate the price of our success; the labor and anxiety that goes into the classrooms, missions and promotional activities at home, the zeal and sacrifice that underlie all our progress in the mission field abroad. We now know and understand the difficulties and dangers that confront our men in every department of the work — yes, and the failures and the weaknesses and the lack of success, for these, too, are part of the history by which we learn to help and sympathize with each other. In short, our successes and failures alike should bring us together, keep us together, deepen the meaning of the Maryknoll bond. And if at times some events are not clear, if puzzles arise, if actions are not fully fathomed, if individuals are not fully understood, it will be wise to classify all these things as part of the experience God judges it necessary for us to have. Let us not say too quickly that the spirit of Maryknoll has changed, but rather that we are changing, growing, and above all, that we are *learning*. Most of us are still comparatively young men, whereas it is the work of years to understand all the principles of action and all the facets of character of even good men. Do not make the mistake of oversimplification; of judging everything under the sun by the few primitive criteria of childhood; of misunderstanding every character that does not happen to fit into some little preconceived category of your own. The Maryknoll spirit has not changed, but we are living and learning and growing big, and we need that spirit more than ever so as to enlarge our horizons both within and without.

The spirit of any religious group is a special cachet that God imparts to the particular organization as one means of fostering its success. Usually it will emphasize or reflect in some way the special aim of the institution, and always it will embody characteristics of a nature to support and weld together its members in the pursuit of their aim. It is no small help. However, the Maryknoll spirit alone is not a complete recipe for the total spiritual success either of ourselves or our work, for it is only a partial and special application of a larger and deeper spirit that is, and must be, common to all successful religious activity. We speak of what is called the spirit of the Gospel. There is a spirit brought into the world by the smiling Infant we worship today, and instilled and exemplified in every act and word of His life from the Crib to the Cross, and recorded and explained and emphasized by His Church, both in its written traditions and its unfolded history, that was intended to preside over and animate every single item of progress and success that was to be secured in His Name. And it follows that no real success will ever be obtained without it. This means that supernatural work will always demand supernatural motives and viewpoints, supernatural inspirations and helps, in the same sense that those who propose to do a work for God must do it in loyal and unselfish subservience to God. Strangely enough, this seeming restriction does not narrow down the field of our practical activities but actually enlarges it, for it opens the way to any and every legitimate human effort in any way calculated to cooperate with the designs of God. "Love and do what you will," says St. Augustine; it is the spirit that counts, and therefore the saints did well even in their smallest actions because they performed them with the pure and devoted intention of accomplishing something for God. And, on the other hand, we have seen big efforts to convert nations end in almost nothing, because men forgot the larger spirit of consulting only God's interests, and got lost in party punctilios of their little organizations and their own.

The spirit of the Gospel breathes in every word of the New Testament, but the pictorial illustrations of it are found in the histories of the saints who lived it. Can we look at the principles of St. Paul, and fail to understand the ideals we are supposed to espouse in the pursuit of our similar vocation? Can we witness his ardent championship of the cause of Christ, his complete possession by it, his single-minded zeal in advancing it, and doubt the measure of our own consecration? Can we see his love for souls, the labors and woes he underwent to reach them, the love and sympathy he expended to retain them, and question what our own attitude towards our people should be? Can we observe his boldness and perseverance in following out every logical step of a vocation that linked a whole hostile world against him, running the full gamut of opposition and persecution with death at the end, and still debate the terms that should define and limit our own perseverance? And what about the zeal of St. Francis Xavier, the enormous travel, the unremitting labor, the constant danger, the single-handed lifetime battle on a vast front with almost no help and every possible obstacle, and the sublime confidence in God through it all? There is the sharp adherence to the perfect principle so evident in the life of St. Vincent de Paul, the enormous goodness and total self-forgetfulness of St. Alphonsus Liguori, the exquisite charity of St. Francis de Sales, the boundless sacrifice for souls of the Curé of Ars, the calm commitment to go the whole way on the part of Theophane Venard; and so on through the whole litany of those models given to us by God to illustrate what the spirit of the Gospel means.

If we cannot have the virtues of the saints, we can have their principles. If we cannot run the way with their giant footsteps, we can at least direct our own humble steps along the same correct path. The spirit can be right, even if the performance is limited.

What is the result of this spirit in the life of a man? In a general way, I think it is the transference of his interest from himself and his petty prerogatives and pretensions to God and his neighbor. Its first fruit is the open mind, its full growth the big broad mind, and its final flower the thoughtful and loving mind. It issues in magnanimity — that classic mark of the great man, and it is found in all the saints, for all of them were great men. It merges into charity, for it bears all things, suffers all things, hopes all things, and tries to understand all things. It directs all the aspirations and energies away from self to concentrate them on something loved more than self, and thus it comes to live in a world of shining ideals where life is primarily an opportunity to love God, hold truth, and help souls. It rules out many things, and first and foremost among them are all preconceived prejudices and pet notions in regard to men and events, methods and results, recognitions and rewards, injuries and affronts, circumstances and situations. It knows no jealousy of others' gifts, it entertains no envy of others' fortune, it holds no grudges, it maintains no defenses, it has no reserves. It sorrows with all and it rejoices with all, and it never rejoices more than when it can witness or assist or bring about the success of another, because it finds its happiness in gratuitous giving and it cares little to receive.

It does not say that a proposal cannot be good because I was not the one to propose it, that a method cannot succeed because I did not think of it first, that a result cannot be efficacious and permanent because it differs from my way of obtaining results, that an event or measure or decision cannot be helpful because it did not accord with my opinion, that a man cannot have good motives because his actions seem strange to me, that an appointment cannot be God's Will because it is not my own will, that a recognition cannot be merited because it did not come to me, that an injury must be unremerited because it did come to me, that a situation that came about in God's regular providence is unbearable because it is unpalatable to me.

The man of big soul, open mind, and thoughtful charity is the fit instrument to embody and manifest God's love for His people in the apostolate of souls.

Filled with the spirit of the Gospel such men will seek success where it truly lies, in any and every feasible human effort that is animated by the supernatural principle of utilizing and subordinating everything to the Kingdom of God and the welfare of souls, and they will dominate and subdue the countless little unregenerate human foibles and susceptibilities that seek constantly to clog and devitalize their divine program. And animated with the Maryknoll spirit, they will love the brotherhood, cherishing each other with fraternal affection, bearing one another's burdens and forbearing with one another's weaknesses, slow to pain and criticize, and quick to console and help, as they set about the work God gave them to do, intending that they should accomplish it not dividedly but together.

*   *   *

A year ago I sat alone in a hotel in Kamakura and wrote this message, intending to greet you with it last Christmas, and hoping against hope that it would find you and your people entering upon a new era of constructive development and blessed peace. It was not to be. World forces had been set in motion that were enormously difficult to harmonize and control, and all efforts to avert the cataclysm failed. So the Christmas that came brought you conflict instead of peace, increased anxiety instead of alleviation, new difficulties added to the old. The year proved to be one of stern trial, and that not only for our missioners and ourselves, but for all the people of the world everywhere. The tide of disaster was only mounting to the flood.

I send the little message again, believing that we cleave to the same principles in stormy days as in calm, reflecting that our vocation is above and beyond earthly turmoil, hoping that the bond which unites us to God and each other will strengthen us in war as it has consoled us in peace. May our Divine Visitor from the skies increase in all our hearts the spirit He wants His Mary-knoll men to bring to His work. May it inspire them with large-minded affection for each other, flaming championship of His people, close and loyal fidelity to Him.

Maryknoll's Superior General in a relaxed moment.

Cumberland, Maryland, had been a center for Irish immigrants of whom the grandfather of the Bishop was one, later to become a representative in the U.S. Congress. His mother, from Houma, Louisiana, was a Concannon — enough identification for the Friendly Sons!

In May 1943, Bishop Walsh gave an address to the Friendly Sons of St. Patrick of New York.

Friendly Sons
of St. Patrick

I appreciate the privilege that is mine tonight. These are days when words and ideas are flying through the air as thick and fast as bombs and bullets, and some of them are almost equally explosive, equally productive of good or harm. We have both a war and a peace to win. A block buster that lands in the right place will surely aid in winning the war, and a small word that lands in the right place may help in its own way to win the peace. My little message concerns peace, and I think it is going to land in the right place when I address such a representative group as the Friendly Sons of St. Patrick of New York.

St. Patrick, by the way, is one of the special patrons of Maryknoll, the Catholic Foreign Mission Society of which I am the Superior. He was designated as such by the Founders of Maryknoll, not because he was a great Irishman, but because he made the Irish people great. He did it as their saint and apostle by bringing them the Faith that develops nobility of character in men, and we believe that the same Faith will make any race or nation great. So we have gathered up young men from the sidewalks of New York and the farms of the Middle West — or to be more exact, God has gathered them up from almost every State in the Union — and we are sending them out to distant lands to repeat St. Patrick's performance. We also believe that St. Patrick made the

95

Irish people peaceful — though not too peaceful when a good fight is going on — but in the sense that those who fight for the right are the true peacemakers in the end. And we believe that the Catholic Faith will make all the nations peaceful, if they will accept it, or if they will only live up to a few of its essential principles even without accepting it. The pity is that many nations do not do even this much, and we think this is why peace remains so elusive; but we continue in our hope that the spread and influence of the Faith will bring it closer.

China is the country I personally know most about, as I lived there for eighteen years. I learned to regard the Chinese as the most gifted people in the world in all the natural endowments of intellect and character, but I never knew them to enjoy any real peace. I never saw a people who deserved so much or who were content with so little, and I never knew a people who loved peace more or had less of it. They asked of life only a little rice to eat and a roof over their heads, but their hard, simple lives were constantly visited by every sort of trouble, from bandit raids and Communist uprisings to large-scale civil war, and this condition was finally followed by the present major external war. I used to invite the officials of my district to Mass every Christmas and Easter. None of them were Catholics but all were good friends of mine, and the head man of the group was a young prefectural governor whom I count to this day as one of the truest and best friends I ever had. One Easter I took "Peace" as the subject of my sermon, and this man, who was an excellent official deeply interested in the welfare of his people, came to me afterwards with this remark: "If your religion can bring peace to China, it will be welcomed by every Chinese. Peace is what we all want the most and it is the one thing we have never had."

I had many consolations and a few hardships in my

eighteen years among the lovable people of China. However, I did have one little venture in which I spent a week in a bandit camp a good many years ago. The bandit chief who took the town — with me in it — told me he had come to establish peace in the place. He did not succeed very well, and when the Government soldiers came and laid a siege to retake the town, he asked me to go out and talk peace with them. "My aim in life is peace," he said, "and we must compose this matter on a basis of reason." I agreed to take his message. "Go away slowly and come back quickly," he said in the polite Chinese phrase as I was leaving. I fear I was less polite than he was, for I took good care to reverse his suggestion. I went away quickly and did not come back at all. My poor Robin Hood friend later made his peace with the hangman when the soldiers had rounded up the whole band. But I always retained the impression that it must be a very peaceful nation where even the bandits are men of peace.

The following sermon was written but not delivered because of a last minute cancelation of the testimonial dinner during those war days in 1943, when it was originally planned to have Bishop Walsh speak.

In years past, many of the best retreats given to and for Maryknollers were by English Capuchins who were establishing their community in the States. Today, a good proportion of the students in our seminary, as also members of the theological faculty, are Capuchins from nearby Garrison, New York.

A Capuchin Bishop
Is Consecrated

Invited to be consecrator for Bishop Niedhammer, I was a little surprised because I felt it was a case of the mountain coming to Mohammed, the young vigor of Nicaragua to an old bench warmer long exiled from China, New York to the rustic reaches of Westchester, the experienced and tried and true mission army of St. Francis to the comparatively young beginnings of Maryknoll. And I was honored and delighted for precisely the same reasons, seeing in them a gracious compliment to Maryknoll — that is no less welcome because it may not have been fully deserved.

In a prominent place in the main corridor of the Seminary of Maryknoll is a large picture of a Capuchin, put there to inspire the young men of Maryknoll with mission spirit. It is the picture of Cardinal William Massaia, Apostle of Ethiopia, one of the great figures in the modern mission period of the Church, and the Order that produced him must be right in the main stream of Catholic mission tradition. Of course we have pictures of St. Francis also, who is one of our special patrons and who may be regarded as an even greater missioner, great in himself and great in his sons, who have carried out his vision of building the Church by covering the world with missions and missioners.

It was through his sons that St. Francis began the evangelization of China with John of Montecorvino, and

99

it was largely through his sons that the entire continent of Central and South America was given to the Church. We do not doubt that the same St. Francis will put the finishing touches in Nicaragua through another of his apostolic sons, our new bishop who has just been consecrated for the task.

So Maryknoll takes inspiration from St. Francis and his Capuchins, while they in turn are humble enough to believe that they can derive some benefit from the spirit of Maryknoll, which means, I hope, that we are both something more than Capuchins and Maryknollers — that we are both members of a much greater organization — that we are brothers in a still more wonderful family — that we are, all of us together, Catholic sons of the Catholic Church.

If we need any more saints to enlist for this occasion, we have the two greatest of all the apostles, Saints Peter and Paul, and I invoke the fullness of their spirit and their blessing for their newest successor, Bishop Niedhammer. I once attended the consecration of a Franciscan bishop in Chicago, and I heard this comment from the Father Provincial who took occasion to welcome the guests. "If there is anything lacking, please put it down to our inexperience," he said. "We often produce saints in the Order but seldom bishops. We are not much accustomed to these consecrations. A canonization would be more in our line." Apparently there was some opposition between a saint and a bishop in the good Father's mind, and he might be right, although I believe there are some members of the clergy who do not share his view, if I may judge by their pious belief that their own bishops have richly earned their reward, and deserve to be translated to heaven, or at least to Halifax, right away. At any rate, we do not want to see Bishop Niedhammer translated to heaven for awhile, but rather to see him translate heaven to Nicaragua by bringing his lovable people the fullness of the Catholic faith. And if he can do that successfully with the grace of God, perhaps he may solve this little problem of the divergence between a saint and a bishop by combining the two vocations in his own person.

The Bishop of Bluefields has a romantic name for his Vicariate, though I fancy the romantic part does not impress him particularly as he rides horses around its jungles, swelters in its tropic heat, and counts up his bills payable in the wake of its hurricanes, earthquakes and volcanos. Yet there is plenty of romance, beautiful romance in Bluefields, and it is contained in the example of himself and his priests, who are willing to do all this in their quest for souls, willing to do it for men who are their brothers, willing to do it for Christ and the Church. May there be blue skies over Bluefields, and may they symbolize the blue mantle of Mary, Mother of God and Queen of the Missions, as she extends it in loving protection and blessing over the bishop and his missioners in their labors for the people of Nicaragua. To Bishop Niedhammer and to the Capuchin Fathers — ad multos atque aureos annos (many and golden years).

Mission education has been a necessary element in keeping alive apostolic interest around the country. The annual Mission Sunday celebrations in most dioceses are indicative of this spirit and these thoughts are still relevant to the mission cause in 1976. This address was made in Rochester, N.Y., in 1945.

Mission Sunday

"He looked for a city that hath foundations; whose builder and maker is God" (Heb. 11:10).

Mission Sunday in the year 1945 can well be regarded as a key date in the modern world. It comes at a time when mankind is at the crossroads. The human race is emerging from the worst tragedy in its whole history. The shooting is over, but the sorrow remains, and the eternal puzzle of elusive progress. Where is it and what is it? We, all of us — blood brothers in the same human family, have recently been obliged to devote all our efforts to killing each other, and the efforts were very successful. All over the world we have dead men, full hospitals, blighted lives, disrupted families, broken homes, devastated cities and saddened people. Our own country suffered severely, although it suffered less perhaps than any other. But all suffered enough and even much too much. This is the price of that crucifixion of humanity called war. And now we survey the ruins and count the cost. And we tell ourselves wistfully, longingly — too hesitant to hope, yet too concerned and anxious to despair — that we must keep this peace so dearly bought and that such tragedy shall not happen again. The world is sobered rather than happy. The world is relieved but worried. It is a turning point in human history.

The mental attitudes and preconceived notions of human beings are the hardest things in the whole universe to change. We can tear down a mountain and alter the course of a river, but it is difficult to change the minds of men. However, God can change them and He can bring good out of evil by letting men see their own mistakes as revealed in the tragic consequences of war. The late Pope Pius XI once stated to me that nothing short of the Communist revolution would have sufficed to dislodge the Russian people from the inveterate prejudice caused by a thousand years of stagnation under the Czars and the Orthodox Church. Then he went on to predict that another similar upheaval would still be necessary before the minds of the Russian people were fully opened to the consideration of the claims of Catholic truth. We think that the minds of all people everywhere today have been forced open by the awful tragedy visited upon them in global war, and that they are now open in the sense that they are dissatisfied and disillusioned, anxious and alarmed, groping and seeking. Nobody wants to go through the misery of world war again if there is any escape from it. And since nobody knows where or how to find the escape, everybody is looking for it. Men find themselves in a wilderness of confused thought and discarded plans. The world has been literally knocked down, and those who are left in it are now faced with the problem of building it up again. This is humanity's chance to build it better, to look for the city that has foundations, whose builder and maker is God.

Mission Sunday reminds us that the missions of the Church are actively engaged in promoting the ideal world of Christ. The true peace of the world that God envisions for His children all over the earth is the one that will be established when the missioners have preached the Gospel to every nation and when the fullness of Catholic truth has been accepted by the generality of men. If we consider the vast numbers yet to be converted, this devout consummation may appear as a dream to be realized only in the dim and distant future, if at all. Yet, there is no reasonable doubt that this great objective has been brought measurably closer by prayer, and other hands will save the souls of the future. Old Bishop Jarlin of Peking used to say that he was responsible only for the present. When taxed with lack of foresight in devoting all the mission resources to evangelizing and conversions instead of diverting it into big institutions and other works of more advanced development, he would reply: "God asks us to do the work that is possible and open to us now; He will provide other hands and other means for the needs of the future. Every generation has its missioners. We are the missioners of this generation."

For 1900 years the Catholic world has thought it a great and vital thing to have the vocation of an apostle. We have it and we think so, too. Let us ask for the grace to fulfill it faithfully and well.

Two diocesan priests, James Anthony Walsh of Boston (he was the Propagation of the Faith Director) and Thomas Frederick Price (the first North Carolinian ordained to the diocesan priesthood) submitted their proposal for an American mission society to the American archbishops in 1911, who gave their approval to the project; Propaganda and Pius X were agreeable when the plan was presented and, on June 29, 1911, the Holy Father gave his official approval. It is customary on this anniversary for the head of the community to give something of a State of the Union conference. The following is typical of this tradition.

Foundation Day 1945

Thirty-four years is a long time in the life of a man — a short time in the life of a religious society. Maryknoll is young, but some of us are getting old. Our little cemetery, that chosen corner close to us and to God, is beginning to fill up a little. Our two Founders have been there these past few years, and some of the best men God ever gave to Maryknoll now lie beside them. Others of our members lie where they fell — some in the mission compounds where their brothers of Maryknoll are continuing the work they well began; some in isolated outposts in the mission fields here and there; some, we fear, in unknown graves, that is, unknown except to the eyes of God. Some of those members of our Society met death peacefully and some violently; some in fairly consoling circumstances and some in human abandonment and distress; some after long lives filled with zealous labors, and some in the first promise of their youthful years. But all of them met it courageously, we believe; all of them met it in the faithful pursuit of their vocation; and all now rest in the loving arms of God.

There will be more of this thinning out in the ranks of our Society as time passes, but there will be much more filling up of the ranks from the youth of America whom God will call to this work. We are witnessing this phase at this very moment when the mounting list of vocations to Maryknoll can only be described as "heaped up, pressed down, and running over." Maryknoll is young and Maryknoll is growing, and growing fast. We ought to take account both of our youth and our growth, our modest record of the past and our solid hopes for the future, because this is our Foundation Day, and it means something special to each and everyone of us in the plan of God.

Our foundation gave us two great apostolic leaders and a great apostolic vision of which they were possessed in common. The vision and the plan merited the approbation of the Vicar of Christ, and it also enlisted the prayers and support of the friends of Christ, some of them known to us and many of them unknown to us, chiefly in our own country, but also all over the world. Our files, our records, our whole history are filled with testimonials and evidences of this fact; we have not lacked the confidence of the Church and the enthusiastic support of the people. Whatever this vision and plan may mean to us who live so close to it, it thrilled this country of ours from one end to the other, particularly among the thoughtful clergy and the more zealous laity, who saw in it the crowning gift of America's charity, and the logical response of a faith that was now full blown. They saw, and they hoped and they prayed — and seeing the plan they wondered what the building would be.

It was given to our Founders to build well in their own lifetime and it has been given to us, their successors, to see their building spread and rise and develop and expand. There are some beautiful stones in that building that are seen by all eyes, and there are some deep foundations seen by few but God. We all think naturally of the successful external activities on the record of our Founders, but we might also think of the faith and the charity and the prayers and the courage that were always in their hearts. We think with pride of the

108

chosen ones who were privileged to give their lives openly and violently for God, but we must think also of those who daily and silently have given and are giving their lives for God. I think of the missioners who have died in China, and of the missioners who are living in China today sharing the wartime sacrifices and privations of their people. I think of our missioners who are still interned, and of all who have been interned, counting the litany of their hardships patiently endured as a precious offering from Maryknoll to God. I think of our missioners of the Philippines and the generous spirit that they brought to the recent severe ordeal they had to go through — priests and Sisters alike. I think of our missioners in Latin America who are going through the first difficult pioneering steps in very primitive living conditions and in an environment that is often unresponsive and discouraging. I think of the unseen sacrifices of our missioners in the Hawaiian Islands where there are also plenty of conditions that try men's souls. And finally, I think of our members in the homeland, of the zealous feats of some, of the habitual virtues of many, of the honest efforts of all — and I think, too, of the prayers that incessantly go up from all our hearts and of the blessings that continually come down.

These are some of the assets of Maryknoll on its Foundation Day. I could list the liabilities just as easily. I could speak of the weakness, the dangerous tendencies, the pettiness and immaturity, the mistakes, even the serious defections — of which we have had our share. Maryknoll is young; Maryknoll is still on trial. We still have many shortcomings to correct, many lessons to learn, many virtues to acquire. But today we can leave them to the mercy of God perhaps, by which He has delivered us from so many dangers, by which we hope He will yet also deliver us. It is only necessary for us to be humble and not proud, to be eager for the zealous work

109

of the future and not to rest in the little record of the past to understand that God has been very good to us and that we have very far to go in gratitude if we are to make a fitting return to Him.

Meanwhile, the mission tide is rising, the mission needs are increasing, the mission countries are calling, and we have the immense privilege of representing the mission work of the Church at this crucial period in the history of the world. Maryknoll wants to represent that cause well, but Maryknoll can only do it through you, its members. May our Foundation Day confirm us in our mission vocation. May the critical nature of the times and the miseries of the people inspire us to give our best for God. His people need us. "Remember thy congregation, which thou hast possessed from the beginning" (Ps. 73:2) and make us apostolic men of charity and courage, worthy of our trust in these critical days, worthy of the bright promise of Maryknoll.

Bishop Walsh dedicating new novitiate for Brothers in 1945

An address to the graduates of Power Memorial Academy in New York City was an opportunity to express gratitude to the Irish Christian Brothers for making their schools open to appeals for vocations and it also provided a platform to spread the message of the missions and, possibly, obliquely invite some young men to give their lives to the work of modern apostolate.

Thoughts for Youth

This is one of those occasions that brings a lot of happiness to a lot of people — and perhaps a little uneasiness to a few people. The uneasiness comes to those who are to make the speeches, and sometimes to those who have to listen to them when they are not tempered with brevity and mercy — but that only includes the audience and the speakers, and we are just the scenery for a graduation, so we are relatively unimportant. The important people at this affair are made very happy, and they are the graduates, their parents, and their teachers. For them the graduation marks the completion of a lot of work, the culmination of a lot of hopes and, we may add, since the outcome has been successful, the cooperation with a lot of grace contributed to the enterprise by God. So they are all made happy by this fine step forward, this milestone of successful effort, and the rest of us forget our uneasy minor role and find ourselves sharing their joy. We are happy because they are happy.

The first pat on the back, it seems to me, goes to the parents of the students who had the discernment and the good fortune, to send their sons to Power Memorial School. They picked out the school with as good an endowment as could be found anywhere in the world — an endowment better than most and equal to any. I have not seen the balance sheet of the school, I do not know its financial status problems and headaches, but I speak of a much more important endowment than money. The real endowment of a school consists in its aim, its spirit and its traditions. The aim here is Catholic education. The spirit is Catholic loyalty. And the traditions are those of the Irish Christian Brothers. These three combine to make the ideal Catholic school. This is a precious endowment — worth more than all the grandiose buildings, empty names and sham prestige of all the schools in the land that have lower standards and lesser ideals. The parents have selected the right kind of education in sending their boys to Power Memorial — they could not have chosen better. They receive the first installment of their reward today in the happy completion of their children's education. They will receive bigger installments — greater rewards — as the future unfolds before these chosen graduates and their Catholic education contributes to make their lives purposeful and useful. These young men will be an element of strength to the Church, an asset to their country, and a credit to their families. The Church, state and family will owe much of this to their teachers, the Brothers who imparted to them their Catholic education.

This is not the first time I have visited a school conducted by the Irish Christian Brothers. Over three months ago I was in one of their schools that is famous all over India — the Brothers' School is in Bow Bazaar, in Calcutta, where I had tea with Brother McLoughlin and the community. A little later I visited their school in New Delhi, the capital of India. Two months ago I was in their house in Rome with Brother Clark where I said a prayer with the community for the canonization of their founder, Brother Edmond Rice — one confirmed of deep Catholic faith, warm Irish courtesy, and keen educational emphasis. So I feel very much at home among the Brothers today and I reserve for them my second pat on the back, warm congratulations for work well done, a school well developed, and well conducted, and a graduating class well prepared. Much water must flow under the bridge before we can reach a day like this — and the Brothers are the energizing agents that keep it flowing, that keep things moving.

I have an added reason to feel at home here, to feel a special tie that binds me to the school. The Power Memorial School has contributed an extraordinary number of vocations to Maryknoll. At present there are eleven young men from Power Memorial studying in Maryknoll houses for the foreign mission priesthood — this is a gift for which Maryknoll is grateful. It puts the school in the front rank of Maryknoll benefactors, for no greater gift can be given than these young lives and total dedication. And incidentally, the circumstances make a good commentary on the character of the school itself. There is nothing wrong with the ideals and influence of the Power Memorial School when it can pour such a contribution into the life stream of the Church in America. My dear Brothers, for eleven young apostles in the making, Maryknoll thanks and salutes you. May their lives to be spent for God and His needy people bring credit on us both.

It is not customary to reserve the last pat on the back for the graduates themselves, but they will not mind if I suggest that they are finishing a minor job compared to the one they are beginning — they finish school but they enter life and life is the real story to which school writes only the first introductory chapter. What will the story be like? I do not know, but I think I know what will be the determining factor in it. It will be the magic word *development* and the equivalent word that has no magic in it at all, the plain everyday, unattractive word, *work*.

The graduate who will make the best success of his

life is not he who makes the best mark in school but he who makes the best development after he leaves school. And he will develop the best who does the most and the hardest work. Work is 99% of the success of any endeavor, but when I say that I really mean work, not perfunctory punching of a time-clock, but hard, unremitting, brow-wrinkling, nerve-exhausting, time-consuming labor. It is this sort of severe and responsible effort, spiritual, mental and physical that exercises the faculties of men giving them solid strength of soul and great powers of mind, rounding them out into keen, active and well-balanced men who touch life at many points and ornament all they touch. This is development; talents are to be used not laid up in a napkin, as our Lord reminds us. Success comes through development, and development comes through work.

There has been a good investment here. Work from the teachers, solicitude from the parents, and at least a mild form of assimilation on the part of the students. We should be grateful for this investment, treasure it, and make it all count for God, for country, and for our own souls and the souls of all around us. Heartiest congratulations to all concerned and may God bless, preserve and perpetuate the work of Power Memorial School.

2

China Again
(1948-1970)

In 1948, the Bishop was back in China for a second long assignment. The Catholic Central Bureau was established by Archbishop Riberi, the Inter-Nuncio to China. Bishop Walsh was named the Executive Secretary and with him were Chinese and foreign priests, the latter representing nine European and American countries. All members brought their extensive experience to the new organization, pooled their vast knowledge of the Middle Kingdom, vigorously approached their newfound freedom, after the Japanese surrender. The common language of Bureau headquarters was Latin and the common fate of almost all members was imprisonment, expulsion and in the case of two courageous priests, death.

It was 1950, two years after his arrival, that the Communists took over Shanghai. The next year they closed the Bureau. While under house arrest, the Bishop was permitted to visit the French Jesuits and, as explained in his Hong Kong interview, he became engaged in research and writing. Before the noose completely tightened an extensive list of manuscripts had been smuggled to Hong Kong, one of the articles even reaching the office of The Voice, publication of St. Mary's Seminary in Baltimore.

In 1958, arrest, trial, sentence and twelve years were served. His older brother was permitted on two occasions to visit him but otherwise it was silence until in 1970, the Bishop walked across the border between Communist China and Hong Kong. Within a week he felt sufficiently strong for a large press conference and relatively little has been added to that account which is included in this series.

Last picture of Bishop Walsh before his arrest by the Communists. It was taken at the Catholic Center in Shanghai.

The following contribution was dated December 3, 1950, written in Shanghai shortly after the arrival of the Communist troops in that city. Years earlier Bishop Walsh had written: "I knew Father Price personally for seven years (1912-1919); I knew him by reputation all my life as he was a friend of my pastor, Monsignor Edward Wunder, and also an acquaintance of my father." Father Thomas Frederick Price, a veteran missioner in North Carolina, joined Father James Anthony Walsh in founding the new mission society in 1911.

Memories of Father Price

Simplest, humblest, most unpretentious, honest and open of men, Father Price was not a puzzle, although he puzzled a good many people. Among those who met him only casually, knew him only superficially, there was a wide range of opinion concerning his character, just as there was only one common, definite, strongly held opinion of it among those who lived close to him, knew him well. To a man, the early Maryknollers, priests, Brothers and students, regarded Father Price with a curious mixture of smiling toleration, strong affection and downright veneration. Others, knowing him less well, shared the smiles without going on to the better understanding and the resultant esteem. Some may have added sneers on occasion; so at least it was reported, and so indeed it was easy enough to believe. Such reactions, however, must have been of a rather mild variety where they existed at all; for even those who failed to like him could scarcely be brought to dislike him. Yet it is a fact that he was not always and everywhere equally understood and appreciated. What holy man is? His character was seen and assessed with different eyes according to the viewpoint, the proximity, of the beholder; and in some degree, no doubt, according to the character of the beholder himself.

There is a reason that would appear to explain the peculiarity of these estimates in both cases. Father

Price, if not a puzzle, was something of an anachronism. He was a priest of the horse and buggy days, of a generation that was passing, that had indeed already passed as far as the great urban strongholds of the Faith, the experience and recollection of most of the faithful, were concerned. He came to Maryknoll from a lifetime of rural mission work in primitive, pioneering conditions, and he came as that manner of life had made him and left him. He represented the village crossroads, barnstorming, half-gypsy type of old American tradition, and the stamp of it was on him.

Everything about his external appearance, from the square-toed Congress gaiters to the baggy trousers and the greenish black coat, not only spoke of another world by manifesting a complete contempt for this one, but spoke also of another generation. His manners, delightfully simple, unassuming and cordial, though not without a touch of old-fashioned courtliness on occasion, also seemed reminiscent of the past to the hustling and bustling mentality of his contemporaries, especially the younger ones among them. His shoulders were stooped somewhat, as if accustomed to bearing burdens more real than that of mere age; his eyes were downcast for the most part, his gait rather shuffling and ungainly, his smile frequent, benign, lovely. Add to all that a gift of prayer that carried him to all sorts of unique extremes, rendered him completely indifferent to his surroundings, and vented itself in a variety of pious customs and practices which appeared, at first sight at least, as bordering on the eccentric and the bizarre.

Such were some of the first impressions that Father Price was bound to make on anybody. The composite picture he presented as a man, a priest and a personality was of such unusual, story book outlines that one could only believe he was either the relic of a bygone age or else the wonder of this one.

Speaking for the early Maryknoll seminarians, we thought he was both. The world of our own day was too much with us, early and late, however, to give us an entirely correct light on his total unworldliness. No boy is inclined to like oddities, real or apparent (except his own); or has enough experience to understand the reasons for them, good or bad. And we were little more than boys; for what is a seminarian after all but a boy plus a purpose? So most of us joined patronizing smiles to our genuine admiration, mixed amusement with our sincere and growing affection, perhaps even added a little mild disdain at times from our own confident stories of superior, up to the minute modernity. May we be forgiven for it.

> I know it is a sin
> For me to sit and grin
> At him here.
> But the old three-cornered hat
> And the breeches and all that
> Are so queer.

He was the last leaf on our tree, and we took our little fun as a part of the general gaiety spread all around us — supplied by Divine Providence for our special benefit, we never doubted — during our novice years.

It would be a mistake to think, however, that we were not all very fond of him from the very first. To us the true, unselfish, unworldly priest was always much more evident and dominant in Father Price than the old-fashioned man. One was the essence; the other, the trimming. Indeed we soon began to like the trimming also, or at least most of it. As more discernment came, a more unqualified esteem went hand in hand with it, growing apace. One thing that made understanding relatively easy was the circumstance that most of his unusual practices and attitudes seemed to stem from his great attachment to the Blessed Mother. That gave us pause, as it well might; for we also thought, much like himself, that no virtue or devotion could be very extravagant, could fail to please heaven, that had her for its object. The smiles eventually gave way to increased respect, sympathy, even a little wistful envy perhaps. Thus all the early Maryknollers quickly learned to love and venerate Father Price; it was hardly possible to do otherwise. And even those who may have continued to smile at some of his more extreme forms of devotion, rigorist views of life, and general nonconformity with the world about him, loved and venerated him, it may be supposed, no less than the rest.

With those who only had chance contact with Father Price in the big world outside of Maryknoll, the case was naturally different; and the difference again, was of a twofold variety. Many outsiders esteemed Father Price even more than we did. This was true, as a rule, of the more mature among the priests who knew him well; it was true likewise in the diocesan seminaries and in the many convents of nuns he periodically visited, at least for the most part. It was universally true, beyond any doubt whatever, of every lay man or woman who ever saw, saw even momentarily, the personification of prayer, poverty and piety his long, hard, faithful years had made him.

Lay people seldom mistake the character of a true priest, never that of a holy one. On the other hand, it was only to be expected that good numbers of priests, and perhaps some Sisters as well — both sufficiently critical races of beings at best — who did not know him personally and intimately, or perchance did not know him at all except by hearsay, should have dwelt more upon his striking oddities than his unobtrusive goodness, and should have drawn some uncomplimentary conclusions in his regard. Visionary, extremist, impractical, harmless, ineffectual, pious simpleton, eccentric devotee, were some of the mental images formed about him in these well meaning but well informed circles; and there were even some occasions, no doubt, when judgments of the sort were expressed in downright words. Father Price himself must have been well aware of this, but the knowledge cost him nothing, one may be sure, except perhaps an occasional act of thanksgiving for the privileged pain, remarkably common to all holy people, of being misunderstood.

"An American version of the Curé of Ars" was the description of Father Price once given to the present writer by an elderly layman who had known him well. It is an apt description, it would seem; and if so, it is surely sufficient in itself to explain whatever puzzle, anachronism, departure from the herd, or what not, was to be remarked and wondered at in his character. The stern contempt of the world, incessant immersion in prayer, complete living for God, so prominent and characteristic in the lives of St. John Vianney and himself, could not be an ordinary, everyday phenomenon, more's the pity, in any place or any age. Such a life is too holy to be common. The other term of the comparison is perhaps no less apt. He was too American as well, in a sense, too incapable of posing, too insensible of human respect and opinion, too much of the old style, realistic, rough and ready, matter of fact, take me as I am, frontier type of American to change one jot or tittle of his makeup in real or fancied conformity to his changing environment, or to be readily understood by those who had already changed. The men of his cast iron cut were disappearing from the American scene, although it can surely be hoped, let us say in passing, that the rugged, homespun honesty they personified may never disappear from the American character. Other times, other manners. But honesty, simple, humble, truthful, four-square, is always the self same; and it was deep in the warp and woof of Father Price. If then, for his complete inability to pose he was sometimes rewarded by being taken for a poser, it was because he would not, probably could not, make over his apparent singularity to merge with a new age like the rest of men.

Father Price was Maryknoll's first promoter. Indeed, if memory serves correctly, this work was his chief, and almost constant, occupation from the very foundation of Maryknoll until the day he left for China. This did not prevent him from giving his famous spiritual readings over long periods at times when his promotion field lay close to Maryknoll, being spiritual director for many members of the little pioneer family, and filling the chapel and corridors, the walks, woods and fields, with long, heaped-up unceasing prayers. But promotion was his work; and apart from the blessing of his holy soul, sturdy character, stirring example and wise advice, it was perhaps the great work, the most helpful contribution, among the things he did for Maryknoll.

Promotion is never easy at any time, and certainly it could not be hoped that it would prove so at the particular time when Father Price pioneered in it. Some of the disadvantages he labored under are surely obvious. He represented a work so new that scarcely anybody had even heard of it. Being new, it had nothing tangible to recommend it, no results to show, no record to stand on. Being foreign missions, it was not only a new development in the ordinary sense but bore the imprint, disturbing to some minds, of a radical, surprising, undreamed of, novelty. It had to be taken on faith, if it was to be accepted and encouraged at all; and that faith had to be based on the supposed practicality and opportuneness of a rather startling idea, plus a certain measure of confidence in the men who sponsored the idea. Such faith is a lot to ask or expect from the generality of men in or out of the Church, and particularly from a conservative body like the clergy with their combined experience and responsibility as leaders of the Church. To create the beginnings of confidence, to enlist support for a novel enterprise that had not progressed beyond the idea stage, was the special problem to which Father Price addressed himself.

The solution of this problem depended almost entirely on what attitude the clergy would take towards the new work, and both Father Price and Bishop Walsh knew that. Maryknoll had the good fortune to be founded by two men who embodied the best traditions of the American priesthood in their own persons, were themselves representative of the American clergy in the fullest sense. This circumstance had its own importance. It meant that they fully comprehended the hierarchical status of the diocesan clergy to which they had themselves belonged, even their prepossessions and susceptibilities. Knowing all this, cooperation with the clergy became their watchword. Thus they insisted from the very first on the cardinal principle that has always been the keystone of the arch in all Maryknoll promotion — and no doubt a primary cause of its success: the inviolable rule of basing every approach, conditioning every method, resting every undertaking, on the sanction and good will of the duly appointed pastors of the people. This conception is, of course, an essential feature running all through the whole administration of the Church herself; and the two Co-Founders, good administrators as they were in their own right, knew and adopted it instinctively.

This brings us to certain advantages that Father Price may have had as a promoter, despite the untried, uphill nature of the task he undertook. One was this very knowledge of the clergy, the long experience he had had with them, his well developed sense of what they

127

required in the way of cultivation. He was one of them and knew what to expect and not to expect. Their interest could be aroused, but only by gentle stimulation and correct procedure. Pastors, good and holy men, had their natural reserves, as was inevitable. Bàsically interested in everything vital to the progress of the Church, they were also heavily burdened administrators with troubles and needs of every description of their own. Meanwhile they were notorious targets for the troubles of others as well. All sorts of projects, activities, movements, sought their support, financial or otherwise. Appeals fell on their desks; appealers knocked on their front doors, maybe their back doors also. Salesmen lay in wait for them. In these circumstances they naturally tended to look upon every promoter, even one whose cause was worthy and commendable, as more or less of a wolf in sheep's clothing. This was no fault of theirs; it was merely one of the facts of life, human nature — and pastoral experience of it — being what they are.

Of this fact Father Price was well aware. This foreknowledge armed him with the proper caution needed in his delicate task, moved him to stress the long range aim of making lifetime friends for the work, taught him to forego any questionable short cuts, undignified methods, that promised to bring in money only at the cost of good will.

How much money Father Price raised by his promotion activities the present writer has no means of knowing. No doubt the facts are in the records. Whatever sums he obtained, whether great or small, must have been very welcome, even vital, in those days of struggle, for there was no time in the whole history of Maryknoll when the cupboard was more bare, the needs more urgent and universal. Our Co-Founders literally started with nothing. It fell to the lot of Bishop Walsh to plan carefully the whole campaign of underpinning the new work with a good system of enlisting popular support, and it fell to Father Price to take the field and give a good demonstration of the major approach, to make it work, chart its moves, dodge its pitfalls, iron it out in practice. Father Price did his part with great zeal and perseverance, certainly; it has always been believed, with considerable success.

There was finally, a whole set of advantages possessed by Father Price of which he himself was no doubt quite unconscious. This was the strong panoply of assets represented by his obvious holiness, his entirely unselfish character, and his widely known reputation as a man of God, to which may be added such accidents as his simple, engaging manners, his humble attitude, manifest poverty, venerable appearance. Along with all that he also threw into the scale a constant stream of prayer and a trustful, childlike, total dependence on the Mother of God whose newest little family stood in need of everything. These were helps indeed.

Brother Henry Corcoran, dear old Maryknoll fixture, once told me that he and Father Price between them had hit upon, more or less invented, the envelope and pencil system for parish church pews that added a measure of permanence to the interest momentarily aroused, while occasioning little fuss or bother to pastors and their helpers. Whether this report is strictly factual or not I cannot say; but the procedure was surely an efficient, helpful, fairly painless one, to all concerned, whoever may have invented it. In any case, it was adopted and employed by Father Price and his aides with good success, and Maryknoll had to look no further for a workable method of getting her message before the people. I believe the same system is still in use today. If so, time, also evidently on its side, must have found little fault with it.

If I had the memory I brought to China thirty-two years ago, I would doubtless be able to recall some interesting sidelights on Father Price's promotion work. Brother Thomas McCann, long since dead, was a frequent companion of Father Price in this work, and he was also a very close and intimate friend of mine. This young Brother was very devoted to Father Price. He was also a first-class promoter in his own right, besides being a man of parts in general. Among his other accomplishments he had the best tenor voice I ever heard at Maryknoll then or since. He used to get ten or twenty dollars at a time for singing a solo called "Face to Face" at funerals in Brooklyn, as he related to me, until Father Price told him to stop. Brother Thomas frequently regaled me with stories both edifying and diverting of Father Price's promotion experiences and his own; and as he was also something of a mimic, his stories lost nothing in the telling.

Unfortunately the memory of these particulars has long faded into the dim and irrevocable past, along with most of my hair, teeth, sunny disposition and other vanishing appendages of youth. However, the time comes back to me in vague outlines when Father Price and Brother Thomas stood at the rectory door of a well known pastor in Scranton (who shall be unnamed) to be greeted by a loud voice from the inner fastness bidding them to move on. Brother Thomas said that he was on the point of beating a strategic retreat when he turned to Father Price and found him immovable, smiling, holding up his rosary in one hand while he continued to thump vigorously on the door with the other. The door then presently opened to the tune of some splutterings, mumblings, whereupon a very tall, stern looking, gray haired old priest suddenly confronted the questing pair. Father Price said nothing, only smiled. The splutterings stopped. The old priest looked them over, saying not a word. Then he abruptly turned to Father Price. "Come in, Father," he said, "and tell me what you want." There was no clue to explain the unexpected change. Maybe he saw the rosary, or saw a priest of his own stamp and generation, or saw both. Father Price winked at Brother Thomas. They went in at the invitation — and stayed in.

"Hello, Fred, do you still chew tobacco?" was another greeting that met Father Price at a rectory door on one occasion, although at the time he was not calling to do promotion work. This was at the parish of a certain Father O'Neill in San Francisco who, it seems, had been a schoolmate or fellow seminarian of his. Father Price was then on his way to China, and this curious salutation was no doubt one of the last echoes of his country he took away with him to foreign shores. He met this onslaught also with a smile, tempered in this instance by a deprecatory remark to the young priests accompanying him. They, on their part, were delighted to see their revered Superior accosted on such a human, semi-affectionate basis, and to hear him return the compliment with some similar facetiousness of his own. The incident only serves as a tiny item in the pattern of his dealings with other priests, but it is perhaps of a piece with the general tenor of this relationship. Priests liked him, particularly the older priests, many of them simply on sight. Just what it was about him that they liked is, of course, anybody's guess. Was it his easy, approachable manner; his simple friendliness; his humble, modest attitude; his plain, poor, not to say poverty stricken exterior, his smile, his rosary, or what? Possibly all of them together; we do not know. If one may venture a guess, however, it would single out the obvious unworldliness, the simplicity and poverty, of his external appearance as a large factor in the equation. Nobody could look upon him without saying, "There goes a man of God." An external, visible disregard for the things of this world is not the only indication of a man of the other world, but it is an unmistakable one where it exists. And it existed in full measure in Father Price.

I used to see him cramming crusts of bread and hunks of cheese or meat into his pockets in the priests' refectory at the seminary on frequent occasions, when he was hustling through his breakfast preparatory to catching a train for promotion work in New York. It was my impression that he was providing for midday lunch in this fashion, preferring to munch sandwiches somewhere rather than to dine in restaurants. Where could he have munched them? The Radio City Music Hall did not exist at the time, and he would scarcely have been among its patrons if it had existed. Perhaps he ate on the street, in the subway, on some railway station bench. Deponent saith not because he does not know. What he knows is that Father Price lived like a poor man, had many of the practices of a poor man, loved poverty. This did not do him a bit of harm as a Maryknoll promoter.

Strangely enough, I do not remember, if indeed I ever knew, just what type of preaching Father Price used or favored in his promotion sermons. I have the impression that he could tear a passion to tatters when he wanted to, because I heard him give off a fiery, rousing, old style burst of oratory on two occasions. On neither occasion was he doing promotion, however; and this delivery contrasted so oddly with the ultra quiet, composed, simple manner of presentation he usually employed at the Seminary as to surprise me greatly at the time. I do not know if he used such old fashioned fireworks to any extent when doing promotion, but I rather think not. He may have thrown in some little flash of it on occasion. He knew how to thunder from the pulpit, express strong emotion, no doubt about it. However, one surmises that this manner of speaking was probably a relic from North Carolina mission sermons of his younger days, and that it was later largely discarded. At all events, I believe he used it sparingly, more often not at all, in his promotion work and during all his Maryknoll years.

His brief year in China has often been described, I believe; and in any case Bishop Francis Ford, who lived with him uninterruptedly during that period is the only person entirely qualified to describe it. What I chiefly recall is the excellent, even extraordinary, impression he seemed to make on all the people he encountered in that new and strange land, including missioners of all nationalities, travellers of all descriptions, and the good Chinese people themselves, as it happened, most of all. It is not without interest to note that this impression, particularly as regards the plain people — God bless them — was very much the same as the impression he had always created among those who had the privilege of knowing him well in his own homeland. This is no doubt a tribute to the superb powers of acute observation possessed by the Chinese people; and it may also be said that it is more of a tribute to Father Price himself than appears at first sight.

When a Chinese calls a man a Saint, one may rest assured that he must be a seraph and a cherub all rolled into one. Hard to be a hero to one's valet? We believe it, but it is a mild performance compared to passing inspection in the all seeing Orient. You cannot fool all the people all the time in any country, but you cannot fool any Chinese people at any time in a matter of this kind. Nobody can be a holy man in their eyes except a real one.

Father Price has been much admired for his humility, of which he surely had a plentiful store. The present writer is not among the number of those who marvelled at him on this account, as it happens, because he could never quite bring himself to marvel at anybody for such a reason. The possession of this particular virtue, rooted in the most elementary recognition of basic facts as it is, could never surprise me in the case of any semi-intelligent human being, let alone a holy one. All my wonder is, therefore, reserved for the blind, deluded, completely unrealistic individual who is so sublimely stupid as not to be humble.

There are degrees of humility, of course. It is well known that Father Price himself described dozens and dozens of them — the precise number I forget — in the memorable, frequent spiritual readings he devoted to this subject. It may be that he possessed all these degrees in his own person. I do not doubt in the least, nor fail to honor him for it up to a point. It was undoubtedly a favorite virtue with him, if not with me. But as for what seemed to me really noteworthy in his composition, what to my mind and recollection set him apart from most men, even from most priests, in a shining glory of his own, was a twofold possession which he evidently clasped and held and appropriated with every strong tentacle of his holy soul: his absorbed, complete devotion to the Blessed Mother of God and his deep, unfailing, exquisite charity.

We read about our Savior that He emptied Himself and humbled Himself (Phil. 2:7-8) and in very truth He did. We read that He was meek and humble of heart (Mt. 11:29); and He was indeed. We read about His Blessed Mother that God regarded the humility of His handmaid (Lk. 1:48); and indeed it was so. These are the only examples of humility that ever impressed me very much. But even this humility, sublime as it is when contemplated in such subjects, was yet, if I mistake not, but the prelude, introduction, first step, to something else, and to something far more intrinsically divine. It was but the primary motion of charity, the emptying of self that had been called forth by charity in the first place;

and that then served to initiate, in turn, the boundless pouring out of self in more charity, in the complete charity that He wrought on the Cross, that she accomplished under the Cross. Humility is only a beginning, equally a preparation and a manifestation, as it would seem, of something greater than itself. Humility lies at the root of charity, makes way for charity, calls to charity, as deep calls to deep. This is where it borrows its chief glory, as the matter appears to me. It is a great and basic virtue in itself, no doubt. But the real prize, the real prize, the true and intimate sharing of the spirit of God, the eternal principle that all goodness begins and ends in, the one pearl of great price that a man may give all he owns to possess, throwing in his life besides without a care of a question — is charity. I once had the privilege of selecting a device from Holy Scripture to be carved on the tombstone of Father Price at Maryknoll. I chose the sentence, "In caritate non ficta" (in love without pretense), thinking it befit him well. Father Price, simple, humble, honest, most unselfish, most unworldly of men, had charity. We think we know where he got it. Mary, God's Mother, was the star upon his banner, his teacher, his guide.

Bishop Walsh's exposition of his decision to remain with his flock during the chaotic days of the Communist takeover in South China, was recorded in the March 1951 issue of The China Missionary, *official organ of the Catholic Central Bureau in Hong Kong. In this same issue of* The China Missionary, *there follows an interview of the Prefect Apostolic with the Holy Father (exhaustive in its implications) that gives an understanding of the background, and further substantiates the Bishop's decision.*

Why the Missionaries Remain

Is it better for missionaries to leave China voluntarily so as to avoid being interned indefinitely in the place, or to remain and undergo internment, imprisonment, with its enforced inactivity? Neither alternative is very palatable, is it? However, the question is a practical, maybe an imminent one for us, I believe. I will give my own opinion about the matter since you ask it. There are certain considerations that make the duty of missionaries clear enough in this case — at least to my mind.

At a time when the Catholic Religion is being traduced and persecuted with the design of eliminating it from China, I think it is the plain duty of all Catholic missionaries, priests, Brothers and Sisters, regardless of age, occupation or condition to remain where they are until prevented from doing so by physical force. If internment should intervene in the case of some, or even death, I think it should simply be regarded as a normal risk that is inherent in our state of life, as a necessity concomitant to our responsibilities, and as a small price to pay for carrying out our duty, much as in the case of firemen and policemen who are sometimes required to give their lives in fires and robberies. In our particular case, moreover, I think that such an eventuality would be a privilege, too, because it would associate us a little more intimately in the Cross of Christ.

Some of the considerations that prompt me to feel this way are the following:

1. *The Wishes of the Church*

   Nobody can doubt that the Church wants all her priests to remain at their appointed posts whenever troubles of this sort arise. Why has she spent two thousand years praising and holding up as examples those who did so? Fidelity to the post is the settled tradition, of course. As for missionaries, there is a specific response from the S. Congregation of Propaganda Fide (still in force) which governs their case; the question was asked: In times of persecution by heretics and pagans is it necessary for missionaries to remain at their posts at the risk of life? The answer was affirmative, because during persecution the presence of the pastor is all the more necessary to the flock.

2. *The Desire of the Pope*

   The present Holy Father has expressed his desire to have priests and missionaries remain at their posts in spite of all dangers, unless I am mistaken. I have no citation or texts at hand in this case, but I recall both reading and hearing about some expressions of his to this effect. It is well known that his predecessor, Pope Pius XI, maintained this attitude very strongly. He pronounced on it apropos of troubles in China, Mexico and elsewhere on occasion. It would surprise me greatly if there was ever any pope who thought or spoke otherwise.

3. *The Canonical Responsibility*

   Regardless of what possibilities, troubles, dangers, etc., may arise, I cannot understand how any groups of priests engaged in the ordinary ministry

138

can leave their accredited posts, unless their bishop first obtains from the Holy See a specific release from the canonical responsibility which the mission society has assumed. This responsibility is certainly a contract with the Church, even if tacit, by virtue of which the Society involved and the specific bishop appointed, with the assistance of priests to be chosen, agree to (a) care for the existing flock, and (b) to promote evangelization. The departure of an occasional individual does not affect this responsibility, of course. But the departure of any large groups at this time (impossible for replacements to enter China) or of the bishop himself, would certainly be incompatible with the discharge of the responsibility. And I do not think it would be permissible in conscience unless the Holy See's specific release from it was first asked and obtained.

4. *The People*

That the faithful need the presence of the priest more than ever at this time, I think, is obvious. How can they, lay people with many fears and cares and mostly new in the Faith, be expected to keep up their Catholic practice, be true to it and not deny it, suffer for it (as most likely will be demanded of them) unless their priests give them an example of the same thing? Can that example be given in prison? Most assuredly — no place better to give it, nor any more forcible way to give it, to my mind. A priest in prison is an immense moral encouragement to our Catholic Chinese, while a priest on a ship leaving China in this emergency is an immense discouragement.

5. *China in General*

I think it is a providential period for the Church in

China. In normal times we are a handful of missionaries meeting a few people preaching a few sermons, doing a little good in some little corner. Our efforts are very limited, cannot reach far in this immense multitude of pagans. Today we are placed in the limelight, given the free, nationwide advertising we always desired. In these circumstances practically all of China's friends fall away, and we stand alone to preach a unique sermon to the masses that only the Catholic Church is capable of, namely the picture of patience, charity, sacrifice, living our lives for our brothers and so on. It is too good an opportunity to be missed, in my opinion. And that some great good for the Church in China is certain to result from it, I do not doubt.

6. *Vocation*

Our vocation is not simply our occupational work. The teaching, preaching, village visiting we usually do, it is something much deeper, permanent, indelible. It does not change if our work is impeded, if we are in prison, or for any other reason. One of the necessary conditions to carry it out properly, I think, is to accept in advance every trouble and contingency in connection with it that Divine Providence puts in our way. If we start to pick and choose for ourselves, it is very hard to tell if we are carrying out our vocation or running away from it. I suppose that St. Paul had his mission vocation while in prison, and that he carried it out there — also that such was God's plan in his regard. The only safe rule for a man with a mission vocation is, I think, to adhere to the clear indication of God's will (his appointed place where he finds himself) and to make no changes of his own volition. If he leaves China to escape imprisonment how does he know it was not a

140

part of God's plan to let him be imprisoned for the good it might do?

7. *Activity*

"Enforced inactivity" is a term that needs some distinguishing. Activity does not depend on the place; it depends on the man. Suffering patiently borne is activity, so is prayer, so is any kind of mental work — things which can be done, one would think, in prison as well as anywhere. What is really meant is a change of activity. This is something of a hardship to many men, I confess it — especially to those who are lacking in the faculty of imagination. However, we can all learn something new, or at least we can try to do so. If an example of prison life will help the Church in China, as I believe any suffering undergone for God will do, then, we are just being given another sort of activity for a time. There is no question of complete inactivity, I believe. That would be demoralizing and is hard for many. Again, if ministerial inactivity is meant, that is inability to care for the Christians, visit the villages and so on, then we can only say that a priest and a father does as much for his flock by suffering for them — and maybe he does even more. Another thing which, to my mind, ought to be left in the hands of God.

The Voice, *publication of St. Mary's Seminary, Baltimore, Md., secured the following which appeared in the June, 1953, issue. It was one of the last manuscripts out of Shanghai. The bishop mentioned here is Bishop Patrick A. Byrne, an early Maryknoller, who was to die under the Communists in Korea.*

The First Seminary in America

St. Mary's has always been a sort of spiritual home to me for various reasons. I do not know that I could analyze these reasons or even catalogue them; and I feel sure anyhow, that they would seem slight and inconsequential to many people. Still, they are substantial enough to me. So much so indeed that they make up a good keepsake in the aggregate, form one of the little lifetime treasures picked up along my wandering way.

I never was a student at St. Mary's. A few short visits — a day or a half day snatched occasionally in passing through Baltimore and repeated perhaps a dozen times in my whole life — represent the only direct participation I ever had in the life and the doings of the seminary of my own original diocese. This limited, random contact could not of itself forge much of a tie, create any great intimacy, between my humble self and the famous institution. Yet we have been friends, even close friends, I believe, rather than mere acquaintances. Somehow I have always felt a kinship with St. Mary's — indeed an affection for it — out of all proportion to my own proper knowledge of the place.

No priest can be associated ever so casually with any seminary, I suppose, without forming some little attachment to it. It is at least a living, memory-stirring reminder of his own vocational development, if nothing further. And if it should be particularly permeated with

143

all the best traditions of the priesthood, as is very likely to be the case in a Sulpician seminary, the effect will perhaps be heightened all the more.

My direct contacts with St. Mary's, though few and fleeting, span a long period. They began in 1915 with my first visit. And my indirect contacts, that is, my passing impressions concerning the seminary and its work, go back much farther than that.

The first awareness I ever had of the existence of the seminary came through Father Tanquerey, strangely enough, but not from his manuals of theology. All the efforts he poured into his books never made a theologian out of me, although I studied them at Maryknoll to the best of my ability. Years before that, however, their author had taught me a little lesson in another category. And the lesson was a useful one for a missionary, as I later found. It was not to be afraid of the water. A trifling service, as it might seem, but it stood me in good stead.

When I was five or six years old I spent part of a summer at Ocean City with my parents and my brother William. My brother was one year older than I was. I can remember still how ticklish our first little woolly bathing suits felt when we put them on. Not that we minded that very much. We ran up and down the beach, collected sea shells, played in the sand, had a good time altogether. We also admired the big ocean, but with certain reservations. We put our toes in the water, sometimes, but only to scamper back very promptly, as I distinctly recollect, from the boisterous, booming breakers.

We were in the middle of this performance one morning when a short, stout, oldish looking man, clad in a bathing suit, came down from the hotel veranda in our direction. He was a stranger to us. Without much ado he picked us up from the sand, put one of us on each broad shoulder, and waded into the ocean up to his waist. He stood there in the water for some time, letting the waves curl around us and spray over us, much to our enjoyment. Then he carried us back, deposited us on the beach where he had found us, and returned to the ocean for his swim.

Afterwards my father asked my brother and me if we knew who the man was who took us for the dip in the ocean. We shook our heads. "That is Father Tanquerey," my father said. "He is a priest who teaches in the seminary in Baltimore."

I do believe that I never feared the water in any shape or form after that. I never saw Father Tanquerey again to my knowledge, but the reassuring impression of that sturdy shoulder perhaps remained with me somehow. A few years later I had to be pulled out of the Potomac River in mid-winter by a benevolent colored man, as I had not then learned to swim. Many years later in South China I was often as close to drowning as was comfortable, particularly when I had occasion to make little mission trips along the coast in small, rickety fishing boats in semi-typhoon weather. But I never could regard the watery element in any mood as other than a playful friend. Once I plunged my horse off a culvert into a river and almost drowned before I could extricate myself from the confused tangle of reins, clothes, stirrups, and floundering, indignant animal. But the only thing that worried me at the time, as I recall, was how to apologize for my awkwardness and inadvertence, explain matters, to the poor old horse.

No student from my parish went to St. Mary's during the years when I was growing up in Cumberland. There was little to remind my rustic little circle of the seminary. I do not suppose we heard it mentioned once a year. However, the altar boys at St. Patrick's Church — among whom I had the good fortune to be counted — knew that Father Edward Wunder, the pastor, made occasional visits to St. Mary's Seminary and St. Charles College both, because he sometimes spoke about it. Also Father Eugene Connelly, who was curate in our parish for a time, used to play with us on the recreation ground behind the church; and I think that served to bring the existence of the seminary to our consciousness in some vague manner. What first made the seminary and its work something definite and real to me, however, was the time when one of the altar boys, Ambrose Ryland, finally left us to go to St. Charles College. I think I was away at college myself by that time perhaps; but in any case I was much impressed by the happening because this young man was my best friend.

Ambrose Ryland did not become a priest in the event; and that is a minor mystery in itself as he had every natural quality to make the perfect priest — generous disposition and good intelligence along with a lot of sunny, lively animation all his own. Maybe reasons of health intervened or something similar. He died since and went to heaven, taking the mystery with him. But, anyhow, he spent some years at St. Charles — where he became one of Father Tabb's intimate friends, as it happened; and he, being a very gregarious and a very articulate youth, used to regale me with stories and echoes of St. Charles and St. Mary's both.

My own vocation matured slowly, as it appears when I look back at it. I do not know what caused this particularly. Just my congenital cussedness perhaps. I scarcely think it could have been any fancied attraction in my own little world where I never saw much on the horizon, even in my young years, except work and more work, bill collectors and boredom. My family was poor; and so I believe I played with the notion of trying to be of assistance in that particular struggle for a time. But from Ambrose Ryland, and perhaps some others, I had heard a good smattering of gossip about St. Mary's Seminary before very long, and had frequently thought of the place, wondered about it. I also heard more about it at Mt. St. Mary's College where I went to school. And then, just as I was beginning to think of it more seriously, Father Price came along and said I would do for Maryknoll.

I made a little, passing visit to the old Paca Street place in 1915; and that was the first time I ever saw the seminary, if I recall rightly. I was a deacon at Maryknoll at the time. The seminarian's natural desire to escape a hotel bill was probably the reason for my call, or perhaps mere curiosity. At any rate, I landed among friends and was made to feel quite at home. And I have felt at home whenever I found myself within the walls of the seminary, whether at Paca Street or Roland Park, from that day on.

Father Dyer was the superior when I first visited Paca Street. He was very kind and attentive to me, causing me to wonder how such a busy man could spare so much time for a mere seminarian. I remember that he spoke to me about Father Patrick Byrne of Washington who had been ordained that summer at St. Mary's and had then hied off straightway to Maryknoll. Father Dyer evidently had been strongly impressed by the make-up of the young Washington priest — as one may suppose he had good reason to be, judging the matter in the light of the aftermath. Maryknoll has had no braver spirit, no more generous, self-forgetting soul, among its sons than Bishop Byrne — no more acute mind, either; and these were qualities which helped to fit him for his final role perhaps, forged him into a champion of Christ, in the turmoil of these latter years.

Father Dyer told me in effect that no student in his memory had enlivened the theology classes with such searching, difficult questions as Patrick Byrne; and he added that the young priest's teachers were proud —

and also somewhat relieved — when he finally completed the course and was ordained.

This sidelight from Father Dyer stayed in my mind; and it surprised me less and less as I came to know the subject of it better. At the time, I only knew that our two Founders, Father Walsh and Father Price, were very pleased with the accession of Father Byrne to our tiny ranks; and that, in addition, they regarded him as a man of excellent gifts. But it did not take very long for the rest of us to realize that they were entirely correct in their estimate and that the gifts were not only excellent but quite unusual. Notable among them, as soon became evident, was the quick, penetrating razor-like mind which Father Dyer had had occasion to remark. Bishop Byrne was a man who saw into most problems in a flash, at a glance; and he often saw right down to the bottom of a problem, too, when many others perchance did not see at all. Add the liveliest sort of a sense of humor, eternal and irrespressible, natural concomitant perhaps of the sharp insight which was so marked in him. Then add — and perhaps most of all — a very hearty contempt of the world. The flimsy, cheap, worldly world of human foible, that is; not the poor, plodding human beings in it whom he smiled on indulgently enough and, of course, sincerely loved.

I never knew a more completely honest and realistic man — fiercely honest is really the word; nor one who despised sham and pretense and vanity in every form more whole-heartedly. It may be that his early upbringing helped to form his pronounced outlook in this particular. I should imagine, at any rate, that Washington is as good a place as any to see and understand the tawdriness of the passing show along with the "littleness of reputed bigness"; and perhaps it is better than most. Empty honors and emptier titles, stuffed shirts and stuffy socialites and all solemn owls of every sort, were sure to provoke his ridicule, sometimes masked in his usual easy courtesy, but sometimes perhaps not altogether so. Neither did he have much more use for feathers and frippery in the Church than out of it. It was a jubilant joke to him when he managed to wiggle out of the purple twice (prefect apostolic in two different missions). The joke was on him in the end, of course, when it settled on his shoulders the third time for keeps; but by this time he was reasonably resigned, took it simply as a part of his purgatory in life.

On the other hand, no man could stress the simple realities of the Faith more than he. His conferences, retreats and so on were searching, logical, demanding, uncompromising. He had the most overweening love for the priesthood. He surprised me, I remember, on the day of my ordination by suddenly appearing with a present which he pressed on me. It was December and his present was an expensive pair of fur-lined gloves. I think I had never seen a pair of these luxurious looking things before and certainly I had never owned them. I thanked him but demurred, as I recall, asking him if it would not be better to give the gloves to some older person who deserved them more.

He fixed me with his sharp eye. "Listen," he said, "Yesterday you were nobody. But today nothing is too good for you because you are a priest."

That was a little inflation and deflation combined for me; and I suppose neither element did me much harm. The deflation part in my case was further completed the same day, as it chanced, by my own father. I had given him my ordination card and I thought he would be pleased with the motto I had carefully selected to emphasize the missions. "Satiabor cum apparuerit gloria tua" (Ps. 16:17) it read. He looked at it without any enthusiasm. "It's apropos in a way perhaps," he said somewhat grudgingly. "Had I been in your place, though, I would have taken the text, 'De stercore erigens pauperem' " (Ps. 112:7). (Lifting up the poor out of the dunghill).

Our superior at Maryknoll, Bishop James Anthony Walsh, was very much attached to Father Byrne all through the long years of their close association; and I feel sure that this attachment began very early. One day during those first years I was standing on our little seminary porch with Father Superior (as we then called him) when Father Byrne came out of the front door to take a waiting taxicab to the railway station. It was summer. Father Byrne paused a moment to make some joking remark. Then he flitted off with a parting wave to us, his straw hat perched a trifle jauntily on his head and his sharp, aquiline features softened in a flashing smile.

Father Superior seldom commented on one member of the little family to another. He was an ultra kind father, all his geese being swans pretty much, so this was perhaps just as well. However, he turned to me on this occasion as Father Byrne left us. "What an attractive figure he makes," he murmured in some sudden impulse of confidence. "And he is totally unconscious of it."

Yes, he was an attractive figure then and always, I truly believe; and not only externally but in his inmost character particularly and, indeed, in his whole singularly engaging personality altogether, as anybody who ever knew him would surely allow. Father Dyer's original opinion of him needs no revision, only addition. I cannot make the addition, fill up the picture, limn in the mission work and the missioner. All that would make a long story. I only signalize the obvious truth that St. Mary's Seminary sent a great and providential gift to Maryknoll in the person of Bishop Byrne.

While all my little visits to St. Mary's in bygone years were pleasant and rewarding, it may be that the visits made by its various professors to Maryknoll did even more to give me — and all Maryknoll with me — a strong taste of the spirit of St. Mary's. Yes, this must have been the case; it is certain from the character of the visitors, and the nature of the visits. A good number of these visits were for the purpose of preaching our annual retreat, kept the visitor with us for a whole week, made deep impressions. I missed any number of the retreats during the twenty-two years I spent in China and my other rovings but I attended a fair number of them also in my day. Father Bruneau, Father Vieban, Father Levatois are among the retreat preachers I distinctly remember. And then there was Father Reilly, the faithful visitor on frequent occasions, whom nobody is likely to forget.

I belong to the older generation. The priest I knew best — and who knew me best — is already dead something like seventeen years. This was Father Joseph Bruneau. Why he took an interest in me, showed me kindness, I do not know — simply because I was one of Father Price's boys perhaps; but, anyhow, I found in him a man who could always answer any of my difficulties with a word or two — and that from my seminarian days on. I did not see him often. I did not correspond with him except on the rarest of occasions — two or three times perhaps in my life. I visited him perhaps as many times at Paca Street when I was a young priest. I never sat in his class a single day, of course. I never saw the severe side of him for which he was famous. I never knew him well at all. But I always felt somehow that he knew me quite well and could give me a good push in the right direction. And this he occasionally did.

Father Bruneau sent me a few short lines when I was returning to China in 1924. "Holocaustum tuum pingue fiat" (Ps. 19:3) he ended. This wish did not turn out to be very prophetic in my cases — not literally at least; but the words were encouragement and a comfort. They stayed with me somehow, actually form a part of my little morning rising, stumbling, grumbling, premeditation litany to this very day. Any word from him however slight, was likely to go a long way with me. He had impressed me as having a very thorough understanding of the priesthood and all that related to it. Perhaps I felt a little touched by the unexpected interest, too, in a way. I had no claim on Father Bruneau. There was no particular reason that I knew — except plain charity — why a busy professor in a big seminary should go to any trouble, take time out, for a passing fly-by-night like me.

The two Founders of Maryknoll were themselves Sulpician trained, Bishop Walsh at the Brighton seminary and Father Price at St. Mary's; and this circumstance made another strong link which influenced the students of my day at Maryknoll considerably. Abbe Magnien and Father Dissez, Abbe Hogan and Father Andre and Father Rex, became household names to us as our two superiors plunged into their own seminary recollections almost immediately. A man has to say something when he faces a lot of boys in a spiritual reading period; and a busy man will often fall back on whatever fond memory brings to light, no doubt. I dare say I heard more in one year from Father Price about St. Mary's Seminary than I ever did in all the previous years when I lived so much closer to it. Then, for the contemporary reports on it we had Father Daniel Mc-Shane, of Indiana, himself a seminarian at the time and the first vocation sent to us by St. Mary's; and he supplied in good measure for any possible omissions of Father Price. I can truthfully say that I never met any man who seemed more attached to St. Mary's, was more fond of talking about it, than Father McShane.

There were others, too — many others, indeed, in

152

the course of time. There was Father Robert Cairns, our cheerful little Scotch martyr in the global war, very loyal and very vocal. St. Mary's has been very helpful to Maryknoll in the matter of vocations. And you could climb the high hills and scour the deep seas, of course, without finding any other form of help which is quite so precious. But the big balance of Maryknoll men who passed through St. Mary's are still in the land of the living, I believe and hope; and they will thank me, no doubt, for saying nothing either good or bad in their regard.

I once gave a spiritual reading talk at St. Mary's in a completely unprepared state. Snatching up the breviary for some chance inspiration, my eye lighted on a long quotation from the Book of Tobias which I happened to know more or less by heart already. "Any port in a storm," I thought; "maybe that will help." It did — but in a way not anticipated. With the text hovering in my mind, I worked around to it and then brought it out in what I thought was a telling manner. Some distinct titters and snickers met me at this point. "What, laughing at the Holy Scripture?" I asked myself, ruffled for a split second. Then the saner thought came to my rescue, the grace to see myself as others saw me. "No, you poor idiot," said the warning whisper. "Just smiling a little at what surely sounds like some smug revival preacher in the 18th century. Just too polite to laugh out loud and throw things, as you deserve."

After that I came down to earth, spoke naturally whatever I could find to say, did better. The little talk went off well enough perhaps. So that was another lesson to put with those I learned from Father Tanquerey, Father Bruneau and others. And I shouldn't wonder if it was as valuable a one, when all is said, as any of the lot.

All this relates to a bygone day, to be sure — yes, very much so. I start in some surprise myself to find that I have reached back nearly sixty years in trying to unearth it. Let it go, then, and let it rest; it is over. What will the musings of a man in the sere and yellow leaf mean to the present generation? Very little, no doubt, for time marches on and they march with it. A musty story like this can hope to provoke as much as a yawn, maybe, or a passing smile at most.

Still, Bishop Byrne will not pass out of our lives quickly — nor out of the traditions of Maryknoll and St. Mary's ever, I believe. Besides, the priesthood is ageless. I am still a young priest myself, I hope, when I look at eternity. And because it is one and the same priesthood, yesterday and today and forever, it is linked together in myriad ways over all space and time and circumstance and distance. St. Mary's Seminary was one of the imperishable links in this great chain, as it fell out in my own case. Now I count this as hardly more than a passing trial to St. Mary's. And it was a distinct blessing, surely, to me.

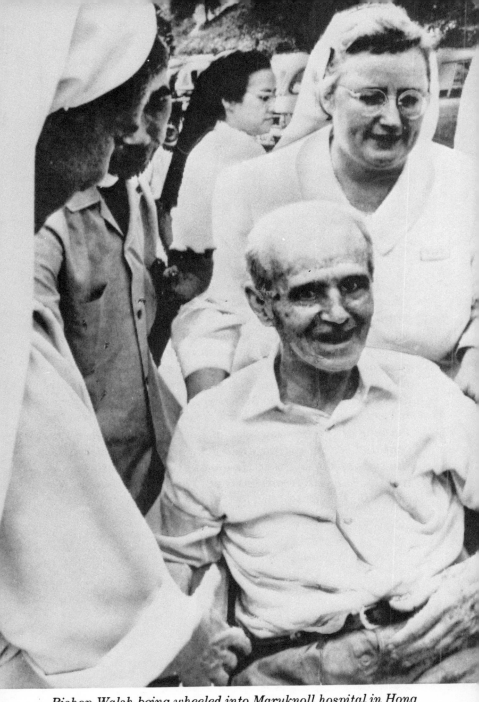

Bishop Walsh being wheeled into Maryknoll hospital in Hong Kong following his release by Chinese Communists

Father Charles Meeus, a young Belgian priest, a Chinese citizen, was a member of the Samists, a community whose members labor under native bishops or papal representatives in mission countries. He was Bishop Walsh's right hand man in maintaining the Bureau and when forced out of China, spent some twenty-five years under a Korean bishop, contracted a terminal disease, was invited to Maryknoll, N.Y., to recover from radical surgery, and is buried in our God's Acre. The founder of the Samists was also a Belgian, Father Vincent Lebbe, an extraordinary missioner, shortly after the turn of the century. He died in China in 1940 following Communist imprisonment. This article is one of a series that appeared in The China Missionary.

Father Vincent Lebbe's Method

The invitation method is one way to make converts. It is a method which has given very encouraging results at various times in a good many places. The method is simplicity itself. It consists in inviting people to lectures on Christian Doctrine which are given in a setting (time, place, auspices, circumstances) gauged to suit their convenience.

The biographer of Father Vincent Lebbe calls this the conference hall method. The name is quite descriptive. However, the invitation feature is the special and essential principle of the method — and the true secret of its success, unless we are much mistaken — so the name here given it is perhaps equally suitable.

Father Vincent Lebbe used this method with great success at times. His experience with it provides a good example of the manner in which it operates.

Father Lebbe was one of the great missioners of modern China. He came to China from Belgium in 1901 while yet a theological student. He acquired a complete mastery of the Chinese language, spoken and written. After his ordination in Peking, he worked in the missions of his Congregation, the Vincentian Fathers, in Peking, Tientsin, Chengting and Ningpo over a period of years and with marked success as an evangelizer. Subsequently he was called to France and Belgium to work among overseas Chinese students. He prompted their

157

interests with great zeal and with very good fruit. After that he returned to China and founded a new Chinese religious congregation, becoming a member of it himself. He died in China in 1940.

Father Lebbe's unusual career was full of movement and variation but certain periods of it were wholly devoted to direct evangelization. The years he spent in Tientsin, 1911 to 1917, constitute the period in which he used the invitation or conference hall method of apostolate. These were among his best years as a convert maker.

One day in 1911 Father Lebbe attended a civic meeting called by the Tientsin Red Cross Chapter. Some emergency had arisen and the object of the meeting was to make provision for it. Father Lebbe made a speech at the meeting and he also subscribed a round sum, in the name of the Catholic community, to the charitable fund which was being raised. Both speech and contribution were welcomed with acclaim. Father Lebbe was impressed with the good dispositions, the receptiveness of the minds he encountered on this occasion. He sought other openings of the kind, making addresses at trade union meetings, builders' syndicate meetings and so on. He was always listened to with great interest.

These experiences led Father Lebbe to experiment with the conference hall method. Somebody gave 300 francs to rent one for a year. A suitable place was found and some little furnishings were installed. Invitations were then issued to a series of lectures on Christian doctrine. The response was prompt and good. Large crowds attended the lectures. Some of the listeners asked for instruction, became catechumens almost right away. Classes were arranged for them. The first conference hall was an immediate success.

Father Lebbe and his helpers then opened other halls here and there in the city, improvising them as best they could. After one year they had nine halls in operation. In all of them converts were made; one hall enrolled 72 catechumens in one month. We are told that once the work was well organized the Tientsin conference halls made at times as many as a thousand converts in one year. The information is fragmentary; but it is evident that some thousands of people were instructed and baptized in the city during the six years when the plan was under operation.

The plan spread around quite widely. "From the experience of Tientsin was born a great movement of conference halls all over China," observes the biographer. "One could not count the conference halls created and opened everywhere," Father Lebbe himself noted, writing in 1916.

There is specific mention of the Taming Mission in this connection, but no other details are given. To what extent the work took hold elsewhere is therefore not clear. However, it is not necessary to go beyond Tientsin for the purposes of exemplification.

The Tientsin work operated essentially as follows:

(1) A hall was rented, borrowed or bought.

(2) The hall had at least three rooms. There was a lobby for a display of literature with some attendants. There was the auditorium. And there was a separate room for private discussion after the lecture.

(3) The lectures were brought to the notice of the public in a variety of ways. "Numerous invitations were addressed to influential pagans," one item states. Notices were put in the newspapers. And some of Father Lebbe's speeches were printed in the form of tracts and scattered around broadcast, at times running 30,000 to an edition. The talks which Father Lebbe gave at public meetings on occasion also served to stimulate attendance.

(4) The lectures were given in the evening after

working hours. Interested inquirers remained after the lecture for discussions and explanations which often lasted far into the night.

Such was the system, simple in essence, involving a deal of hard work in practice, and operating like a charm with respect to fruitful results.

In Father Lebbe's use of the system, however, there are two special additional features to be noted. The first is that the subject matter of the lectures was, in the words of the biographer, "an apologetic placed deliberately on the national and patriotic plane." The second is that Father Lebbe himself, from all accounts, was some kind of a spellbinding orator with unusual powers to sway an audience. The question arises then, as to whether the successful outcome in the case was owing to these unusual factors or rather to the system itself. Or, again, was it perhaps owing partly to both?

The last supposition is probably the true answer. Patriotism and oratory played a part, no doubt, in attracting the people and in holding and interesting many of them at first. These attractions also had some effect in determining the composition of the crowds in the beginning. The people came from all walks in life but included many sorts of notable personalities, we are told, such as the Chief of Police, the Vice-President of the Provincial Chamber of Deputies, the Red Cross Director, mandarins, parliamentarians, scholars, factory owners, industrialists and so on. These types in particular came forward primarily out of patriotism, it appears. There was a reason which made this natural. The year in which the Tientsin effort began, 1911, was the same year that saw the inception of the Chinese Republic. The country found itself in something of a ferment. Patriotism was in the air; the future of the nation was the dominant concern in every mind. Thus the apologetic that was linked up somehow with this motive —

always a strong mode of appeal if not always a wise one — would naturally have great attractive force in certain circles at the time.

A distinction can and ought to be made, perhaps, with respect to the type of patriotic appeal used by Father Lebbe and later reported by his biographer. Apparently, the appeal in this case was on broad lines of principle mostly and had no special connection with, or reference to, any particular patriotic or political movement. There was, in fact, no movement going on at the time; the Republic was established; anything like an actual movement was over. What was left in the hearts of all was a desire to see the country take the new tide at the flood and go on to fortune, that is, to domestic peace, economic progress, national well-being and so on. Nothing more general, less open to question, could be conceived, it seems than aims like these. Moreover, it is well known that Father Lebbe's great method of appeal to non-Christian minds, his own favorite entering wedge, was always the simple principle of esteem for the civilization of China as such, as a past accomplishment and a visible asset in and by itself. This is known because he so declared his own mind repeatedly. One conjectures, accordingly, that the patriotic appeal was usually couched in very general terms, vague enough to be true and harmless both.

As for Father Lebbe's ability as a speaker, it was far out of the common and must have proved a great attraction also. A European tourist who passed through Peking gave an interesting testimony in this connection. He had been taken to a meeting where Father Lebbe was giving an address. "I do not know one word of Chinese, naturally," he said, "as I never was in China before. But I listened to Father Lebbe for about an hour with much interest. Without understanding anything he said, I was greatly impressed by the extraordinary grip

161

he had on his big audience. I could see that his words went home and could feel the response."

From all indications, then, the patriotic or national or cultural appeal and the oratorical performance had their effect — and very possibly a great one — in stimulating attendance at the lectures. That these means brought many people forward, and then went on to increase their tentative interest, is beyond doubt. After that is allowed for, however, it is still necessary to account for the further results in the shape of actual conversions. This ultimate fruit must have come from the system itself, that is, from the exposure to Christian doctrine which was the object of the whole enterprise and to which the original attraction was a mere introduction. Men do not change their religion from love of country; at least they do not enter the Catholic Church with that motive alone because in such a case they simply would not be received. There must be an interest in the doctrine for its own sake; and this cardinal element was the result undoubtedly of the lectures which explained the doctrine. It could not come from anything else.

Again, there were nine halls operating in Tientsin in the course of the first year and others were added, presumably, after that. One supposes therefore that Father Lebbe's assistants must have done much of the speaking in these places and that his own eloquence, patriotic or otherwise, was not a constant factor but an occasional one.

Oratory tinged with patriotism, in short, constituted a very effective form of invitation to tentative inquirers about religion, as the event showed. It is merely one form of invitation among many, however; and the only true essential in such a program is simply that there be some invitation of reasonably good design. That is how the matter appears. An appeal which will somehow reach numbers of people is what is wanted. That and nothing more. It can be very simple, too. Such has been a rather common experience at least, as some other examples of the plan will perhaps tend to show.

Tientsin is a large city, mercantile and industrial. Kaying, in Kwangtung Province, is a small city, mercantile to some extent but not industrial. It is the market and administrative center for a district devoted very largely to agriculture. Merchants and farmers, with the usual sprinklings from officialdom and the professions, make up the population of city, and district both. The people of Kaying are, generally speaking, very energetic and capable. They are also literate to a degree much above the average. This city is another place where the invitation method was used with success.

Father Francis Ford of Maryknoll (later Bishop) became the missioner of Kaying in the middle twenties. He found there a small mission church with several hundred devout, well instructed Catholics to show for a previous forty years of mission work. He added another ten years of his own work. Some converts were made but not very many. That puzzled him, set him thinking. He was at the head of a sizable group of missioners — he did not work alone; and all of the group had been very active. They had made the mission much better known in the city than it ever was before, he thought. And they had made a host of friends and well wishers in the process, as he was persuaded. Friends but not converts; that was the story, so he told himself.

But who were the friends, and where, and how put the finger on them? For the most part nobody knew. Anybody could name a few, of course: the frequent visitors, the personal acquaintances, the rich family across the street, the sacristan's pagan uncle and types like that. But that sort of enumeration would not go very far. And meanwhile what about the unseen and un-

163

known friends, if such they might be called — the numbers here and there who had had occasion to observe the work of the mission for many years, had reacted well to some particular feature of it perchance, had wondered at the fidelity of the Catholic people to their religious duties or had received some other helpful impressions; who, in short, had somehow felt some faint stirring of religious interest in their own hearts which was known only to themselves and to God.

Such people ought to exist and perhaps in very good numbers, Father Ford reasoned. At least enough good seed had been sown, as he believed, to prepare a halfway harvest of the sort. Still, even if they did exist, how was one to find them? That was another matter again, of course. So it was necessary to think about that.

He used the invitation method to find them. He could not knock on every door, interrogate every person in the city to discover who the interested ones were, so he shaped an invitation to perform that work. And he shaped it carefully so that the souls he was seeking in the premises — those of slight interest, busy lives and numerous inhibitions — might find it convenient and easy to respond. The invitation in this case was not intended particularly to create interest, of course; it only sought to capitalize on the dormant interest which was thought to be present already. It consisted, therefore, in a simple announcement to the effect that a series of lectures on Catholic doctrine was to be held at a certain time and place.

What called for the exercise of a little care was the selection of time and place. Also the manner of disseminating the invitation. After some inquiry the time was fixed for November (after the autumn harvest when the people were comparatively free) on several days of the week thought convenient for average people, and at a leisure evening hour (after the day's work was done). A hall was rented in the center of the city which was readily accessible to average people — more so, it was thought, than the mission compound itself (more or less on the outskirts of the city). The invitation was promulgated by means of (1) a pulpit announcement urging the faithful to spread it around by word of mouth, and (2) insertion in the local newspaper.

Between five and six hundred people appeared at the lectures by the time they had gone on for several weeks. Before much longer the majority of them had enrolled as catechumens, so that a catechumenate had to be organized for them, with regular classes of instruction, in the mission compound. Most of the catechumens, to the number of some hundreds, eventually persevered and were baptized.

The first success encouraged the missioners. The program was repeated in succeeding years and was soon extended to other mission stations. It became standard practice in the Kaying diocese. Results varied from time to time, from place to place, naturally. It is not possible to obtain figures, not clear exactly how long the work went on. But the results were good, even quite substantial, on the whole; that much is definitely known.

The supposition that there was a latent religious interest in the hearts of Kaying people, after long years of mission work done under their eyes, and that a well-directed invitation would bring it to light, proved correct, is not surprising indeed — no, not at all; it is rather to be expected. And there are two reasons for this. The first is because a missioner seldom knows what other missioners do, whether in his own mission country or elsewhere, there being no great interchange of information. The second reason is because this particular plan, the invitation system, is so simple and obvious that there is little to discover about it. Lecturing on Christian doctrine, teaching the catechism, is a method that

165

everybody surely knows who knows anything. What is there to discover about a thing like that?

Nothing much, really. The only thing remaining to be known is why such a simple method succeeds. Anyway it is inherently calculated to succeed, presumably, in some cases and not in others. But these are matters, as it happens, which are as pertinent to the missioner's purpose as is the method itself.

There is one antecedent condition which is essential, apparently, for any success with such a method. And there are several little features of the method itself which have their own importance after that.

The prerequisite is the existence of some interest in religion, however slight and dormant, in the hearts of the people to whom the appeal is made. There would be no use, or very little it seems, to try the project where the Church had never been known in any way, where no good seed whatever had been sown, or where it is known definitely for any conclusive reasons that no interest exists at all. Going to lectures on religion is not a popular pastime for its own sake to any extent. If it were the world might have been converted long ago. There must be some little subjective preparation or preconditioning in any case.

Where there is already some little tentative interest to which an appeal may be directed, however, the method is very likely to elicit a response if used with due regard to the remaining problem, which is: How persuade a slightly interested man to go out of his way, to take a little trouble in order to hear lectures? The obvious answer is: (1) make the process as simple and easy as possible for him, and (2) send him an invitation which informs him definitely to that effect. He then knows exactly what he is getting into. He can measure the trouble involved for himself: and supposing the convenience of time, place and other adjuncts have been duly considered, he will find it very little. This is often enough to move him in the right direction; at least it so happened in the cases cited.

The well designed invitation finds the man, knocks on his door and also at his heart. And the tiny flame of interest which is lurking there gets its chance — springs to life.

The following is a complete transcript of the press conference held by Bishop James E. Walsh, M.M., at our Lady of Maryknoll Hospital, Kowloon, on July 16, six days after his release from twelve years of imprisonment in Shanghai. The questions, summarized from about 160 questions submitted by the press, were put to him by Mr. William A. Coleman, director of media relations for Maryknoll.

Hong Kong International Press Conference

Statement by Bishop Walsh: I'm very happy to be free once again. I never thought I would ever see the day of my release. I felt that I would not live long enough to complete my sentence of twenty years, and that I would die in prison. It is a bit hard for me to believe even now that I have been released. I have no bitterness towards those who tried and condemned me. I just could never feel angry with any Chinese. I felt that way almost from the day I first set foot in China in 1918 and it has just grown stronger with the years, even during my imprisonment.

I love the Chinese people.

I must admit that I find it hard to justify the severity of the sentence meted out to me, for I was not a spy either for the U.S. Government or for the Vatican. I came to China in 1918 as a priest and missioner for the purpose of preaching the Gospel of Jesus Christ to the Chinese people and tending to their spiritual and material needs. I can tell you in all honesty and sincerity that I have never spent a day during my 40 years on Chinese soil in doing anything but that.

It should be obvious that from the time of my arrest until my release my experiences have been varied. It hasn't all been sweetness and light. There were periods of harassment and personal suffering. The monotony of daily confinement in a small room for twelve years;

169

waking up each morning and trying to plan how I would occupy my day so as to maintain my sanity and ideals as a priest and missioner to the Chinese people was especially hard to bear. At the same time I'm grateful to Almighty God that for the most part I was treated with basic human dignity and given the basic necessities.

Right now I find myself rather weak physically and I tire quickly. My Maryknoll Superiors have decided I should rest here in the hospital for a few weeks and then return to my homeland. I'm ready and willing to do as they ask. That has been a guideline for me all my life. I'd like to see my brothers and sisters once again and all of my old Maryknoll confreres who have borne the heat and burden of the missionary day with me for so long.

I'm beginning to suspect that many changes have taken place in all walks of life since I last had contact with the outside world. I feel a bit like Rip Van Winkle waking up after a long sleep.

I'd like very much to visit our Holy Father, my superior as Christ's vicar, and hope to do so when I can travel.

I'm more than grateful for all the love and care which has been given to me here in Our Lady of Maryknoll Hospital since I arrived a few days ago. I want to express my heartfelt thanks to the doctors and nurses and to all the hospital staff. I can't possibly answer them all individually, but I want to express my thanks to all those who have sent me telegrams and personal letters conveying their best wishes and joy.

I'm just a bit bewildered by all the fuss and attention that has followed my release. After all I was only doing my duty as a priest and shepherd by staying with my flock.

Question period: Mr. Coleman (C.) — Bishop Walsh (W.)

C. Although you were no doubt very tired on the

Wednesday, Thursday and Friday you were traveling to Hong Kong, were there any particular changes you noticed in Shanghai, Canton or the Chinese countryside since 1958?

W. No, I didn't notice any particular changes. The only changes I noticed were the fact that I spent the night in Canton in a magnificent new hotel of recent construction. I saw from just a general glimpse of the city that it had grown since my old days in Kwangtung. And I also got that impression when I passed over the border. I saw Hong Kong for the first time. I got the impression that it had grown very much also. But it was just a vague general impression that's all.

C. Getting to your trial. What were the specific charges brought against you by the Chinese Communists? This is a three-part question and I'll give you the other two parts also. Were you allowed any defense at your trial? And what form did the trial take?

W. A young lawyer was appointed to be my defense attorney in the trial. The trial was held in the Municipal Court in Shanghai. I forget the street it's on, but it's in the downtown business section; and it was a very large room, with the judges and the judges' bench — about a half-dozen of them — and the prosecuting attorney on one side of the room and the defense attorney on the other and interpreters who translated everything into English; and then there was a large hall and an audience of some hundreds of people in the room also.

C. Did you feel that your defense lawyer did you any good?

W. Why, no. I am sure he was a kindly good man, but he admitted everything and really he condemned me just as roundly as the prosecuting attorney did, saying that everything they charged against me was, of course, true. But that, on the other hand, since I was an old man and some of these things had happened years before

171

that I should be given a little bit of leniency. That is what the defense consisted in.

C. This question has to do with your interrogation. And again it has several parts: What sort of interrogation did the Chinese use against you? How long did this interrogation last? Both as individual sessions and from the time it was first used until it ceased?

W. One year and a half it was. It began the night of my arrest in Christ the King Church. They came in about six o'clock in the evening, they told me I was under arrest, had me eat a bite of supper and then started the first interrogation, which went on for about five hours. This was solely concerned with the financial question about my having assisted a Chinese missionary to bring in some money from Hong Kong for use in Church purposes. And then at eleven o'clock that night, I was taken to the House of Detention, where I stayed for one year and a half. And from then on, the interrogation went on morning, noon and night. Occasionally, they would skip a day. I suppose they would get tired themselves. But it was interrogation in that intensive form for that entire year and a half, from October 18, 1958, when I was arrested, to March 18, 1960, one year and a half later, when I was sentenced to twenty years in prison. Now, the interrogation concerned every possible thing under the sun. Questions about all my own little activities of one sort or another; questions about the great numbers of the people whom I had known in Shanghai, and what I knew about them, and their activities and so on. Questions about everything under the sun, to extract all the information from you that you happened to have in your mind.

C. When you were released, the Communist Chinese news stated that you had made a confession. Did you make such a confession? Were you coerced into making such a confession? And what did it state?

172

W. Well, I confessed two things; one that I had sent a message to a bank in Hong Kong to enable a Chinese friend to import some money from the bank for Church purposes. This was against the law. I admitted that it might be against the law, I didn't know. But, I had actually done this at the request of this Chinese bishop. And it was against the law and at any rate I had done it, because the bishop had requested me to do it, and all I had to do with it was to send the message. He did not have any means to send the message, whereas I was able to send it through the British Consulate, in my personal mail which sometimes the Consul would forward for me with his mail. So that was one thing. That was shortly over, because I confessed that they said it was against the law and in fact I knew myself that the importation of money was against the law. And I really supposed in my own mind that a man ought to be free to send out a message or write a letter that ought not to be against any law, and again I realized that they might consider it to be against the law, so I admitted that.

C. Excuse me, Your Grace, I think that from a number of other questions raised by other correspondents along this same line that specifically they are asking about the charge that you signed a statement admitting that you were a spy. And I think they also want to know the conditions under which that statement was arrived at and signed.

W. Well they made short work of this little financial matter, which was no doubt the real cause of my arrest, and then they immediately began to accuse me of being a spy and they asked me all sorts of questions. I answered them the best I could and that went on for, really, I don't know how long, but I think it must have gone on for about six months. They accused me of being a spy and they said that some friend . . . The evidence that they adduced was that a friend of mine in the shipping business in Shanghai had told me that a submarine was built in Shanghai and that was a state secret, and my listening to that from the lips of my friend constituted me as a spy and, secondly, that another young man who had been a soldier in the Korean War had come to our bureau and had reported to me some facts about the type of weapons and ammunition used in the Korean War. He was a young Chinese soldier who had gone to join the Korean War and he did come to our bureau, but he only spoke the national language, the Peking language, of which I couldn't understand a word. The officer explained that he had told this to a Chinese priest who was in the house with me, and that the Chinese priest had explained this conversation to me in Latin, and therefore I had obtained information about weapons used in the Korean War and that was also a state secret that constituted me as a spy. I explained that I didn't know a single word that this young man said, and as far as the Chinese priest, Father Ho, explaining it to me in Latin, although he spoke Latin very well and I understood it quite well, I explained that Latin is a dead language, there are no words in Latin to describe modern weapons of warfare, and even if there were such, I don't know them and I wouldn't have understood a word Father Ho said or this young man — either one, so what you say is just simply impossible. They said, well, anyhow you did that, so those two things make you a spy. Now that's all the evidence that was ever used to explain to me the things that I had done to make me a spy. And they asked me countless questions about what inquiries I had made around Shanghai, and of course I answered the obvious thing — well, I made some inquiries how to get to the General Post Office, because I had some letters there, and how to find my way down to the French Consulate and how to get to the British Consulate and how to go to Jessfield Park in order to take a walk in the

174

park . . . and a few inquiries like that when I inquired to find my way around the city. I was a stranger in Shanghai. Yes I made many inquiries that way, but I think anybody else would do the same.

C. Your Grace, how often did they try to get you to sign the confession before you eventually signed it?

W. Well this confession that I eventually signed about this spy-business, I suppose they asked me to sign that for a couple of months on end. They'd bring this statement with a few little answers I had given in the interrogation and then they'd wind up with a plain statement that "I admit that I am a spy." I suppose they did that about thirty or forty or fifty times and each time I refused to sign it, and finally one day I got worn out with the whole thing and I finally got suddenly tired of the whole thing that had gone on for months. Every time they changed the statement and would take out the spy business, they'd bring it back the next day with the spy phrase again in it, and so this last time I finally said well, I may have become a spy in the legal sense. I know that you consider all missionaries as spies and it would not surprise me at all. You say that your laws provide penalties for these two things, these two things which you allege that make me a spy. Maybe that's true. It wouldn't surprise me a bit. So, I admit I may be a spy in the legal sense.

C. In their legal sense?

W. Yes, meaning their legal sense, but not in the commonly accepted sense. Well, that seemed to satisfy them, and they brought it back the next morning to me to sign, and they had reduced it down to — "I admit I became a spy in the legal sense."

W. So I thought: well my saving clause — "in the legal sense" — is in there, and I can sign that. That's true if it's understood in the proper sense, so I signed that and that finished with it. I admit I may be a spy in

175

the legal sense.

C. Do you abide by your confession or do you repudiate it?

W. Well, I have no reason to repudiate it if it's understood in the proper sense, but if it's taken to mean that I was a spy in any real, true, or commonly accepted sense, I've repudiated that and denied that a hundred times to them, and I would still do it.

C. This is another three-part question: How were you treated while you were in prison, what sort of meals did you receive, what sort of literature was provided by the Chinese?

W. I was treated very well. The whole time of my imprisonment, apart from this gruelling interrogation process, the treatment was all very humane and good. The meals, food provided was very good and ample. Medical attention was given me the whole time. For quarters I was lodged in the hospital for almost all the period, all but three months. I was one year and a half in the house of detention for the interrogation; in that place you slept on the floor — there were no beds, but you had bed clothes and everything, so I easily got accustomed to that and it wasn't bad. Conditions there were quite sanitary and good also. After that I was put in a cell for three months in the Ward Road Prison — that was a little severe and I had prickly heat so bad it turned to heat boils and the doctor had to lance them and that was a little unpleasant. And then they transferred me to the hospital. For the past ten years, however, ten years of my twelve years in prison, I have been lodged in a large airy room in the prison hospital in the Ward Road Jail. There all the physical and sanitary conditions were very good the whole time. In addition I was provided with reading matter — English books and their own English publications, of course, regularly, Peking Review, China Reconstructs, China Pictorial and magazines like that. And in addition, I remember they brought in to me four of Charles Dickens' novels, four of the best novels written by anybody — Pickwick Papers, Old Curiosity Shop, David Copperfield and Tale of Two Cities. And some other good books, a whole set of Shakespeare, and some other good books, too. After that, they ceased to bring in any more English books, but they brought me Mathew's Chinese Dictionary, which is a large Chinese-English dictionary containing eight thousand Chinese characters, one of the best Chinese dictionaries. But only that, so I've had that for my use for the past six or seven years, so that enabled me to study Chinese, and then in addition, the officers brought me some language study books, a few little books in Chinese with language lessons and English translations, so that I was able to use a lot of time studying the national language.

C. To go back to the period of the severe interrogation, was that all mental pressure or were there any physical beatings?

W. No physical beatings whatever, not the slightest. Just all mental pressure, no physical maltreatment of any sort.

C. Another question. Except for the visit by your brother, did you see any other foreigners from the time of your arrest until the time of your release?

W. Not a single one.

C. Do you believe that your sudden release is in any way connected with the death in captivity in China of the American Hugh Francis Redmond who, the Chinese say, committed suicide on April 13?

W. I have no way of knowing that. I did not know Mr. Redmond personally, I had heard of him before I went into prison. He was arrested a little before I was and I had heard of him at the time of his arrest, but I never saw him or knew him or knew anything about him.

Whether my release had any connection with his death in prison, I don't know a thing about it. They said nothing to me; they merely told me I was released on account of the government policy was one of revolutionary humanism and that I was now an old man and I was almost eighty years old. So on account of my old age, my good behavior, and the government's policy of leniency, I was released. That's all I know.

C. Please describe your activities in Shanghai during the years between the take-over of the Chinese Communists and your arrest. In other words, what kind of activities were you engaged in, in the years just before you were arrested?

W. During those years, the Catholic Central Bureau was suspended by the government after the first year. We were allowed to continue residing in the building and we all just simply went on with our work as best we could. Our clerks were all dismissed. Our work was officially closed by the government, as explained to us by the government, but they said "you can continue to live here" and of course, we were all free then, so we just went on with the work we were doing as best we could. And then, after a year or two, they began arresting various members of our personnel. Father Thierry (French Jesuit), Father Le Grand (the Belgian in charge of our missionary magazine), Father Charles McCarthy (an American Jesuit), and so on. And then one after another they arrested about . . . well we had a staff of about twenty priests working in the Catholic Central Bureau, and at one time or another they arrested about half of them.

C. And you were the last to be . . .?

W. And I was the last to be arrested. And from the time they arrested Father LeGrand, who was really the chief worker in the Central Bureau and who was the publisher of our main magazine . . . the editor of it and all that . . . from that time on, we couldn't do much work in the Bureau. But I occupied myself with two things. First, I had access to the magnificent library that the Jesuit Fathers had at Zikawei, and the Jesuit Fathers told me that I was welcome there to read any or all the books, and they have a splendid library there. I had been instructed by Msgr. Riberi, the Apostolic Delegate, to write some articles about missionary methods of work, so I continued doing that. As a matter of fact, I had more time to pursue that work than before, so I would just go to the library and get some of their books, and get descriptions of old famous missionaries and what they did and so on, take them home and study them, and then write an article describing that. And then I would forward the manuscripts to Hong Kong because I had the impression that Father LeGrand was able to continue his paper somewhere. He had been put in prison for five years, but after that he was released. And so I continued that work, and then along with it there were many people in Shanghai at the time who were in trouble or destitute or had some trouble of one sort or another, some foreigners, some Chinese. They wanted to leave Shanghai, but it was difficult for them to leave. You had to obtain a special permission from the government, and you had to wait for a long time, sometimes to get it and sometimes when they did get it, they didn't have the carfare to pay their passage to Hong Kong and Macao, and I didn't have much means either, but I spent a lot of time trying to help people like that, running back and forth to the British Consulate to try to get them a visa to enter Hong Kong or something of that sort.

    C. Here's another question: While you were in jail — while you were incarcerated — were you aware of the Cultural Revolution in China?

    W. Oh, yes. As soon as that started, they announced it to us in prison and they sent in a team of young people

— they were called a propaganda team — and they took over the whole charge of the hospital, as it appeared to me. I remember the young Chinese engineer with whom I was quartered. I asked him, "What does this mean? These young people come in here, are they going to stay long?" He said, "Oh, yes." "Well," I said, "are they police? "Oh," he said, "they are the revolutionary cultural people, and they have more authority than the police." That's what this Chinese friend of mine commented. I asked him, "That's what's said about them?" And sure enough, they stayed in the prison — they came in May, 1969, and were still there in charge of everything in the prison up to the time I left.

C. One last question. What do you think of the future of the Church in China?

W. I'm sorry to say, I don't know a thing about it. I couldn't get any information at all about the Church conditions, whether of the people in general or the clergy, or the Sisters, with whom I was associated in Shanghai. I didn't obtain a bit of information at any time up to this present minute and I don't know any more than you do.

C. Thank you very much, Your Grace.

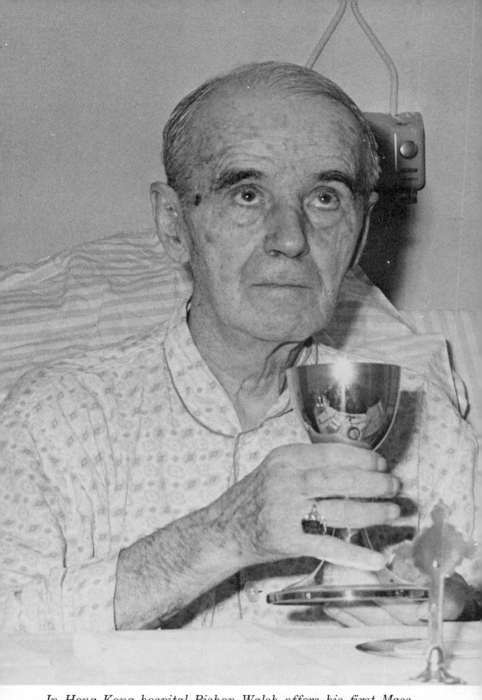

In Hong Kong hospital Bishop Walsh offers his first Mass since his arrest.

On his way back to the United States, Bishop stopped in Rome to tell Pope Paul VI of his experiences. Here the pope helps him back to his wheelchair.

3

Sere and Yellow Years (1970-1975)

On his way back to America from Hong Kong, Bishop Walsh was received in audience by the Holy Father, the drama of which was captured by television for millions of people.

The past five years have been quiet: rest, recuperation and retirement (after a fashion). There have been a very limited number of visits into nearby dioceses, even visits to some of our missions overseas.

The selections in this section represent what Bishop Walsh has said and written on some of these occasions.

September 9, 1970, the Society Chapel was filled to overflowing because it was the official welcome home of and for the Maryknoll Family. Fortunately, members of the Walsh family were able to attend the concelebrated Mass, a very emotional ceremony, partially expressed by many wet eyes and the spontaneous applause — unexpected in those more restrained days.

Thanksgiving to Be Home

Father General, Fathers, Brothers, Sisters and our Maryknoll family and dear friends, on this day, a happy day for me — my reunion with our dear Maryknoll family — I should like to say a little word of thanks in which I hope you will join me — a word of thanksgiving first of all to Almighty God for His grace in giving me what I call a privilege, the privilege of staying with my people in China in their troubled time and also having a still greater privilege of carrying out an elementary feature of my Maryknoll vocation — a vocation that is a real treasure and more precious to me than anything in life and so that it was an opportunity and a privilege to share in my slight little degree the hardship and a tiny bit of suffering in the cause of Him Who took our sins upon Himself and suffered so much for me and for all men. It was a privilege but I thank you also, and very much indeed, for the support that I received from your prayers because while I was supported by my vocation first and foremost, yet I also knew that I had the prayers of our large growing Maryknoll family and I kept recurring to that constantly and it gave me a feeling of security and consolation all through the twelve years that I remained in captivity. So I welcome this occasion to have an opportunity to thank you from my heart for the solace and aid of your prayers during all these years and then I want to say a special word of thanks to Father General himself and to all those concerned in the welcome that I received which I did not expect — a welcome on the part of Father General and our other Fathers in South China and in Rome and in New York again and at Maryknoll and the Brothers also, and particularly, also, of our Maryknoll Sisters who received me on my first entry into the free world — received me into their hospital in Hong Kong and gave me such devoted care for a long time that most of my troubles and worries vanished away in a very short time thanks to their care. So I welcome this opportunity to say thanks to God and to Maryknoll and to all of you and to all in general who helped me by their prayers and gave me such a heartrending welcome on my return. God bless you.

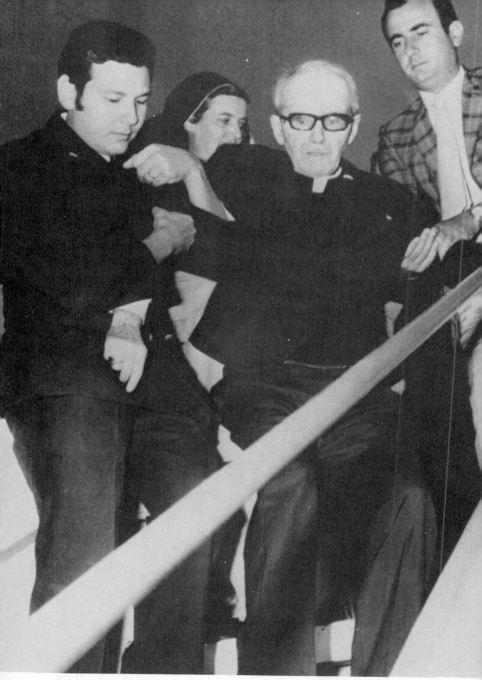

Bishop Walsh being helped from plane on his return to United States.

Over the main entrance to Maryknoll Seminary are the traditional words, "Spes Messis in Semine" — the hope of the harvest is in the seed. This talk was given while the seminarians were having their regular monthly Recollection Day.

Talk to Maryknoll Seminarians

Thank you for the privilege of addressing you on my ordination day.

It's my opportunity to speak to our young students about the priesthood. It just occurs to me to cite my own case, and if my own case is typical, then I should say that the requirements for a happy life in the priesthood are very few and simple, because that's all I had are very few and simple requirements, if I even had that.

One, and the most necessary of all, I think, comes from God, and that's the vocation. "Non vos me elegistis; sed ego elegi vos, et posui vos ut eatis, et fructum afferatis, et fructus vestor maneat; ut quodcumque petierites patrem in nomine meo, det vobis. Haec mando vobis, ut diligatis invicem" (*Jn. 15: 16-17*). (You have not chosen me; but I have chosen you; and have appointed you, that you should go, and should bring forth fruit; and your fruit should remain; that whatsoever you shall ask of the Father in my name, he may give it you. These things I command you, that you love one another). Pardon me for speaking Latin but I am so accustomed to it in my years in Shanghai that I fall into it unconsciously. A vocation from God, a little bit of training from the Church which is God's agency on earth, that is a seminary course such as you're imbibing at present, and then just a little fidelity on your own part. From God a vocation, from the Church a training period, and from yourself a little fidelity, and fidelity to work well, a few simple principles, your prayers, some industry and then charity, especially fraternal charity to those around you.

The seminary course is a seed time. "Spes messis in semine," as engraved on our building here, I think, and it's strange how, to me looking back, it's strange how little seeds dropped in the course of your seminary years, which don't seem to mean much to you at the time, come back and influence you all through your life. Now, I don't remember the theology that I learned here; in fact, like good Cardinal Cushing of Boston, I didn't know any theology and I had almost forgotten the catechism even. But, on the other hand, other little things that you hear from your teachers, from your spiritual director, from your monitor if you have one, and above all from your companions, from your fellow students, they come back to you and influence you and help you all through your priestly life. At least, that was my story and I cite that because, perhaps, it may be more or less typical of those who have a vocation to the priesthood and the missionary life.

One of those lessons that I learned is a simple thing, but one of the very first things I learned at Maryknoll my first year here was in the Dogmatic Theology class, which was taught to me by an old Italian professor, Dr. Berilli. He wasn't a Maryknoller; he had been picked up by old Father General on his trip to Rome. He was a graduate of Capranica College in Italy which is one of the famous theological seminaries there and he was a very good theologian himself, and he taught the philosophy here also to Bishop Ford and Bishop O'Shea and the rest of the class.

At any rate, what I'm getting at is just this little word from good Dr. Berilli — he stayed here as a professor for some years, didn't join Maryknoll, and then left us. He was a very fine man and an expert theologian. Well, I didn't learn much theology from him but I learned one thing that stayed with me for all my life and kept coming back to me all the time, especially when I'd be faced with a little problem or difficulty of some sort. And it was based on a little point in theology lesson that he was explaining to me — I forget what it was really, something about the Passion of Our Lord — and at the end of his explanation (he spoke broken English, he hadn't mastered the English language yet, he had just come from Italy) he took a little picture of Our Lord on the cross out of his book and held it up to me and he closed his explanation by saying, "Look what He suffered for us." Now that wasn't even good English, but that sentence has been in my mind for fifty-five, fifty-eight years and has come back to me a thousand times all through my priestly and mission life, and especially when I was facing some little difficulty or trouble.

It's a seed time. It's strange how those little seeds are dropped into our minds and hearts in our seminary course and they're designed, I suppose, in the divine providence to help us all through our lives. So, this is a time to be receptive. We don't become great scholars or great scientists — at least the rank and file of us don't, a few perhaps are called to that sort of thing — most of us are called to perform the ordinary work of a priesthood which is doing a little bit of persistent work from day to day and especially being kind and helpful to those around us — the people and also our brothers in the priesthood and in our work. There are little seeds of that kind which seem more important than the lessons that I learned, but as I say again I was no scholar.

"Going the whole way for Christ" is one of our Founder's expressions that he repeated time and time again, "Going the whole way, going the whole way, not turning back." Once you pick up the plow, go ahead, go

191

the whole way, go on to the end, persevere. That was Father Founder, Father James Anthony Walsh, that was one of his great expressions, and he harped on that all the time at the spiritual readings. And many phrases of that kind whether from our teachers, or our fellow students keep coming back to a man, I think, from his seminary course. I don't know how to explain that. I only know this is my own case, I cite it, perhaps it's typical, or perhaps it's not. But it was the case with me the things I learned, I learned chiefly from those around me and from our fellow students.

Bishop O'Shea gave a meditation one morning and I remember we had just been given the little cincture with the Chi Rho on it, the two Greek characters representing the name of Our Lord, Christus. He gave a meditation and then he ended up, "Take for your spiritual bouquet the Chi Rho on your cincture, C, H, R, Chi-Rho, take it to mean charity, humility and restraint." Charity, humility and restraint. Well, it happened that restraint was a virtue that our Father Founder had always emphasized. And I never heard anybody else emphasize it, but he. But he did and that became sort of a Maryknoll virtue: restraint. And the old Bishop O'Shea had put these all together and he called it charity, humility, restraint, and gave it to us as a Maryknoll program and a good program for the future Maryknoll missioner. Well, I remember smiling at the time thinking, "That's just like Bishop O'Shea. He thinks he's working in the Navy Yard in Brooklyn still. He makes sort of a pun on this cincture of ours, charity, humility, restraint." So while I smiled at the time, the sentence came back to me for fifty years after that, and often sometimes at difficulties — charity, humility, restraint, when I'd feel perhaps like a little bit the opposite.

Now I'm not sure if that's helpful to anybody but I cite that because it's an example to me of the little things we pick up during our seminary days. It's the receptive time, it's the time of sowing good seed. God is sowing the seed in your hearts and by various means, through the lessons of your teachers, the definite program of training which the Church has given to us, and also through the side remarks of your friends, teachers, monitors and your fellow students, very frequently your fellow students. We can learn a great deal from each other, I think, and those things are very helpful in this formation time. After that all we need to do, once we're launched into the priesthood, all we need to do is to be faithful in a few little things, prayer, of course, prayers, to keep up our prayers. Then to keep up the essential work that confronts us from day to day. Then along with that charity towards everybody, and especially to those around us and close around us and our fellow workers and fellow students, fraternal charity. Those things will take us a long way in the priesthood and that's all that I would know to recommend particularly after fifty-five years engaged in that work, mainly reliance upon God (the vocation came from Him) and these few little principles that will help us to carry out that sublime vocation of preaching the Gospel to our brother men.

Now that's long-winded enough, I think, so I'll subside for a bit.

Cumberland, Maryland, in October 1970, celebrated in a religious and civic manner the return of its native son. During the grand affair, the following observations seemed fitting, especially in view of the special appeal small children have had and continue to have.

Return to Cumberland

Your Eminence, Fathers and Brothers, and Friends.

The most important objects, no doubt, in this world's order are our children.

We pass this way but once, and we pass quickly enough when all's said and done, but the children will inherit this world in time to come, and they do represent our real treasures.

They are our children and they're also God's children. For which cause I bow my knees to the Father of our Lord, Jesus Christ, from Whom all paternity, all fatherhood in heaven and on earth is named. There's a special authority this morning, One God and Father of all.

In short, if our children represent the real treasure, we consider that our whole material world put together is not as precious to us, is not worth as much to us, as one dear little human child. That's our treasure.

And the schools and churches that prepare our children for the work of taking over this world of ours, they are surely our most important institutions, one would suppose.

Because they are God's children, the Church orientates the little minds toward God, the Father and the Son.

And because they are our children, due to take hold

of the work of the world and lead useful lives in the world, the school trains their little minds to do that.

And surely that makes Church and school the most important institutions among all doctrinal endeavors.

Our children . . . our treasures!

And this school consequently represents a treasure house to us that is very, very crucial, vital and important. And all our hearts are with it.

And the efforts of the Christian Brothers to train the children! Surely all our hearts are aware and are with them.

And this is a happy day for me, to see this splendid school, dedicated to that purpose of training and helping our real treasures in their lives in this world. Our dear children!

God bless you.

Recovering his strength, Bishop Walsh visits President Nixon at the White House.

The occasion of the 1970 General Chapter of the Maryknoll Sisters was another opportunity for the Bishop to express his high regard for many whom he had known in South China and for the Sisters in general as they face the new era when their dedication and generosity are challenged by many of the demands of the modern age.

To the Maryknoll Sisters

September 25, 1970, is a very special day, an important and blessed day in the history of the Maryknoll family. One great branch of the family, the Maryknoll Sisters, open their General Chapter on this date.

The delegates will survey the state of their Community, note the good work done, also note the failures that crept in, no doubt, and then they will chart their course for the future. They are to provide for the needs of their growing family, in short. So we invoke the blessing of God our Father in their efforts — God our Father from Whom all paternity in heaven and on earth is named. And we ask the grace of our Lord and Savior on the work undertaken in His name, in the name of Him Whose name is above all names, and we hope that the inspiration of the Holy Ghost will guide them in all their deliberations from first to last.

Every large growing family has some growing pains. Some members make great strides; some make occasional mistakes; some hesitate in doubt, falter and fail. And some even drop out. We must expect a bit of that from time to time. We are human; we are only human.

However, we must also remember that Maryknoll is not merely human. Maryknoll is of divine origin, we believe. Whatever we may be as members, Maryknoll itself — the family itself — has a divine origin. Its

199

whole history shows that. We believe that its founders, all three of them, Father James Anthony Walsh, Father Thomas Frederick Price and Sister Mary Joseph Rogers, all three of the founders of the branches of our big Maryknoll family, we believe that they all had special inspiration from God in making their foundations. And we know — not only believe but know — that the foundation, that these foundations were approved by God's Church, by our Holy Father the Pope, by the Church that speaks in the name of God. This knowledge gives us confidence, and puts peace in our hearts on occasions like this.

God's arm is not shortened. He did not abandon His work. He will not abandon His servants who work in His name. He will aid them with His light and ways. All we need is to trust in Him. And of course, always charity, for "God is charity" as St. John says, "and he who abides in charity abides in God and God in him."

Cumberland, Md., erected this billboard to greet its distinguished native son. He is greeted (below) on his arrival in Cumberland.

It has long been a missionary ideal to become so identified with the people among whom one is permitted to work that he tries to learn their language, their customs, their culture and even their prejudices. It has been said that to become incarnate in another culture is perhaps the most difficult aspect of this apostolic transformation. The following observations, therefore, speak for themselves.

China Impressions

I have been asked to give my news and views regarding China. It is a pleasure to comply with the request, even though I must do so with certain limitations. I am not well informed about recent events in China. My last twelve years there were spent in prison. That is no place to pick up authentic news, of course. And even outside of prison while free it is not easy to know what goes on in China and how and why and when and where. All old China hands will echo that. Rumors, yes, and in abundance. But real news, ascertainable facts, are few and far between, as a rule. There was a saying current in Shanghai that reflects this situation. "Believe nothing that you hear," it went, "and only half of what you see." Most people, including me, found this to be a wise precaution. So my news, especially in respect of present day China, is very meagre.

My views and opinions about things Chinese are something else again. I find that they have changed very little, if at all, in the course of half a century. That probably won't surprise any old China hands, I dare say. I think the impressions of most people who have lived in China will coincide pretty much with my own.

I went to China in 1918 just before the end of the first world war. That was fifty-three years ago roughly. I lived in Kwangtung Province in South China for eighteen years. Then in 1936 I left China and spent twelve years in the United States. And in 1948 I returned to China to spend twenty-two years in Shanghai. That makes forty years in China altogether, just one half of my whole life. I suppose that makes me half Chinese. I hope so.

The first impression made on me by life in China was a surprising one to my mind. I remember it distinctly. It was the remarkable kindness and goodness of the Chinese people in general. I had not expected that. In fact, it almost scandalized me at first, as I recall. How can pagan people be so good without the grace and aid and inspiration of the Christian religion, I wondered. That the few Catholic and Protestant Chinese I knew were very good people did not surprise me. But to find the population as a whole possessed of the same good qualities very largely was a great surprise, though a very pleasant one, too.

The surprise part did not last long, of course. A little reflection showed me that the hand of God was evident in this phenomenon. It meant that He had not abandoned His great Chinese family simply because they did not know His revealed religion. That was no fault of their own. And they were His children. He made them. He loved them. And His Divine Providence had watched over them and kept them good while preparing them for better things. So I concluded after a little observation during my early years in China. And my later experience only confirmed me in this viewpoint. First and last my strong impression was that the Chinese people, generally speaking, were naturally kind and good in notable degree.

"Sz hoi chi noi kai hing tai ya," that is to say, "within the four seas all men are brothers." My first Chinese language teacher cited that old proverb in explaining to us the social customs of the people, the good family life, the kindness and hospitality displayed everywhere and other qualities of the sort. We thought at the time that it was a good description of the popular mentality. And after all these years I still think so at the present day. The Chinese people have always cultivated the social virtues. And that makes them naturally friendly and kind to all grades of people, whether within their own borders or without.

They have their own problems and troubles, of course, as is the case with every nation. They try this and try that and sometimes make mistakes, as most of us do. But their basic attitude is one of friendship and brotherhood. And that makes of them a very good asset for the great human family, the world family, wherein this vital quality is much needed by us all. Such at least is my belief about the common people of China after spending forty years in their midst.

During my first sojourn in China I was engaged in routine missionary work. At the time the country was rather disturbed. It was the war lord period. Local uprisings and conflicts were common. And when they subsided the scourge of bandit groups frequently appeared. There was much unrest. However, we soon got accustomed to the conditions. We found friends everywhere and we made a good many converts. Our work went along very well.

My second period of residence in China consisted of twenty-two years in Shanghai, from 1948 to 1970. For the first ten years I was free in Shanghai, although rather hampered as regards mission work. For the next twelve years I was an inmate of Ward Road Jail. And that brings me to the end of my story.

During my confinement I had no access to information about the Chinese people, except by way of questionable Communist propaganda. And I had no contact with any Chinese, apart from a few fellow prisoners and the various officials and members of the prison staff.

That means, of course, that I am not a competent observer as regards recent events and trends in China. Nevertheless, I retain my original estimate of China's people even after that experience. I am convinced that the general population, when left to their own devices, are among the kindest and best people to be found anywhere in the world.

Bishop Walsh's long imprisonment did nothing to lessen his love for the people of China. At Maryknoll he is always ready to greet Chinese visitors.

The much quoted letter of Bishop Walsh to Father Paul R. Milde, Benedictine of Belmont, North Carolina, again made available in what might be a more permanent book form.

Rosaries in Prison — My Lifeline

My great support during twelve years of imprisonment was the Rosary. I had no religious books and could not obtain any, so it was impossible for me to celebrate Mass or recite the Breviary. I was reduced to whatever resources I might have within myself. Privation is the keynote of prison life. With no facilities on hand except air to breathe and bare walls to contemplate, the situation appears gloomy. There is no place to go, little or nothing to do, and only endless monotony to look forward to. Thus the prospect is bleak.

What to do under the conditions? From long habit the answer with me was prompt and automatic. Turn to the Rosary of course. Fall back on the Rosary. It can be said on your ten fingers as easily as if you had the beads. To say the Rosary one needs nothing at all but time; and now you have plenty of that. So this is really a golden opportunity to say more prayers for the various needs and intentions one has always at heart.

Moreover, it is a way to continue your ministry, come to think of it. You can pray now for all those troubled people of yours instead of just worrying about them all day long. Though deprived of other means to help them, you still have the Rosary.

Prompted by a few thoughts of this nature, I immediately adopted a program for the recitation of the Rosary. For many years previously it had been my practice to say three Rosaries, that is, the fifteen decades, daily; I now increased this allotment to six Rosaries each day with the proviso that I would add as many more as circumstances might permit. As it turned out, I found that there was always enough time for the six Rosaries projected, usually enough time to say a dozen, and sometimes sufficient leeway to complete eighteen. So I cut my cloth accordingly.

As it happens, eighteen Rosaries involve the recitation of 954 Ave Marias (18x53). In my case I had the Maryknoll habit of finishing the Rosary by adding three extra Ave Marias "for all missioners." Consequently eighteen Rosaries with me meant 1,008 Ave Marias (18x56). So whenever I found time for this maximum allotment I thought of it as "my thousand Hail Marys day." And I judged it a day well spent.

It was not possible, of course, to say so many Rosaries except during very dull periods. That amount of prayers will just about absorb all one's waking moments apart from sleeping and eating. Actually I did happen to have a good many periods of the sort from time to time, but more often I was occupied with some little tasks and activities that limited my spare time. Then I had to content myself with less. A dozen Rosaries a day became my customary regime. It was seldom that I failed to say as many as that.

My twelve years of prison life went by without too much difficulty. The experience was not pleasant. Life seemed rather wearisome at times. But I was not despondent at all nor even unhappy. I was not in solitary confinement but was always quartered with another prisoner. That gave me a measure of companionship and was a considerable help. But my great, constant, ever present companion was the Rosary. It ministered to my deepest need by making it feasible and easy for me to occupy myself with one of life's most important and rewarding activities, namely, paying attention to God and communicating with Him in prayer.

The method of the Rosary devotion seemed made to order for one in my situation. Or indeed for any person in trouble. Its fifteen mysteries provided a clear and complete review of the great central truths of religion and the great crucial events in the history of God's dealings with His Universe. Its recitation almost automatically imparted remembrance, gratitude, consolation and hope. And meanwhile no special apparatus, preparation or learning was required. To throw all these treasures open one needed only to enumerate the mysteries, to know the Hail Mary and to have the ability to count up to ten.

In short, the method suited everybody. It was simple enough for any child and yet rich enough to meet all needs. It has met mine all through my life to a good extent, but most of all while confined in durance vile. Then it sustained me when other means were lacking. It came to my aid whenever I felt oppressed by any trouble. It was my never failing lifeline all through my prison years.

Maryknollers who receive their first assignment for duty overseas look forward to and often reflect on various phases of the day when they set out for fields afar. Less than a year after his return from prison, Bishop Walsh shared these thoughts with the young men who made up the 1971 Departure Group.

Departure Sermon

Dear Fathers and Brothers, today you take a great forward step in the fulfillment of your vocation. You set out for your mission fields, for the fields white unto the harvest, as Our Savior described them, where you will have the privilege of preaching Christ to His other sheep. "Other sheep I have," He said. And He ordered His apostles and their successors to carry out that undertaking. "Go ye into the whole world, and preach the Gospel to every creature" (Mk. 16:15). That is the great program Our Lord bequeathed to us. And Maryknoll has taken that program for its own. "To bring Christ's name and grace to all" expresses its purpose and its scope. Maryknoll is dedicated to that work. And so are you.

You departants have already passed many good days and taken many good steps in preparation for this event. You heard the Call — you left everything and responded to it. You went through your preparations. You studied and worked diligently, learned discipline, schooled your character. You learned many good lessons from your books, from your teachers and directors, and from each other. You shared all the treasures and traditions of the Maryknoll family. But above all, you learned your best lesson from God Himself by means of the prayers and the Sacraments and religious exercises that kept you close to Him in your training period. His grace has prepared you to know and understand your vocation. He has spoken to your hearts while here. And now that you are ready to carry out your vocation, to leave for your mission field, His grace will be with you more than ever. You do not go alone. Our Lord goes with you. You will meet Him in the breaking of the bread wherever you go. He will be beside you with His grace and inspiration in all your labors and struggles and needs as you carry out His work.

Yes, God has prepared you. And now you are ready to go forth and make Him a return. "What shall I render to the Lord for all the things that he hath rendered to me? I will take the chalice of salvation; and I will call upon the name of the Lord" (Ps. 115:12-13). That is to say, I will do my utmost to carry out faithfully the holy, privileged vocation I received from God.

Our Co-Founder, Father James Anthony Walsh, had a way of inculcating and emphasizing perseverance and fidelity in carrying out our mission vocation. "Go the whole way for God," he used to say. That admonition was a constant refrain in the conferences on vocation that he gave to the students and Brothers of his day. And it is very good advice, helpful advice, even to the present day.

Go the whole way for God. Do not turn back. Do not be discouraged by a little difficulty. Nor by big difficulties either. You will have problems to solve, hardships to beat, sometimes, but that is part of our vocation. Progress requires effort. And sometimes it involves pain. "Unless the grain of wheat falling into the ground die, itself remaineth alone. But if it die, it bringeth forth much fruit." Remember that. And when things look difficult just keep on keeping on. Persevere in spite of it. Go the whole way. So spoke the Founder of Maryknoll to his family in his day.

Yes, you do not go alone to your field of labor, for God Himself goes with you. And your Maryknoll family

214

will also be with you by its God-given vocation. You are privileged men. For to you is given this grace — to preach among the Gentiles the unsearchable riches of Christ. There is no greater privilege than that among human vocations and occupations. There is no work so important. To preach Christ everywhere is the hope of the world. And now you enter upon that work. You go to take part in it and thus make a return to God for the grace of your vocation. You depart for the missions to find the other sheep for the Good Shepherd, to preach the Gospel to the souls whom He has redeemed by His cross. You are given a cross as a sign of your mission, for we preach Christ crucified. Go, then, with God. And go the whole way for God. That is the wish and prayer of all of us for you on this great Maryknoll day.

The Catholic University in Washington, conferred on the Bishop its greatest award, and it was Cardinal Gibbons who released the young seminarian for incardination in the Archdiocese of Baltimore but service under the banner of the Catholic Foreign Mission Society of America.

The Bishop's reply was brief and concise.

Cardinal Gibbons Award

I am not aware that I ever did anything to deserve such an honor. True, I did spend twelve years in prison in China, and that is something unusual, no doubt. But in my case, the experience was just a routine part of my profession, and therefore, I consider it no great credit to myself. I was a Catholic priest and my people were in trouble. So, I simply stayed with them as all priests should at such times.

Bishop Walsh had the practical experience of begging from parish to parish in the Boston Archdiocese, in the early twenties. Later, he took on the same crusade in New York in the early thirties. He could express himself as one familiar with these matters.

In 1937, when Maryknoll was formalizing its program of promotion, it was the decision of the Bishop, then Superior General, who gave direction to the Society and, fortunately, his decision was born of practical, personal exposure to the necessity of raising funds for his Kongmoon mission.

This talk was given in 1973 to new priests assigned to the Maryknoll Development Department.

On Development

I understand that most of you have returned from the missions and have been asked to work in the Development Department, which we used to call Promotion. I had the same experience as a young missioner and found that the time I spent on Promotion was most helpful to me for my work later on.

When Father General asked me to come home to work on Promotion, I didn't want to go; I asked Father General to look for someone else. I suggested Father Bernard Meyer. My own little place was just beginning and Father Meyer already had his quite in order and doing very well. But Father General insisted and so I came home. I worked in Massachusetts for one year and, later on, spent several months in New York. I look back on that as one of the happiest and most rewarding experiences of my life.

During my time on Promotion, I came to appreciate better the wonderful American people and their dedicated clergy. It was a great pleasure to meet them and, later on, to hear from them when I returned to China.

All this was a great asset to me. Often when I was lonely, I thought of those people back home; and I no longer felt like a vagabond in a far-off land where there were no Christians. I sensed that I was a part of all those good people back home.

Promotion work is one of the best possible ways to

get to know the clergy of the United States. Often, a promoter knows them better than their own fellow-priests. It is also a way of appreciating the solidarity of the Church and of knowing you are not alone in your mission work.

It's hard work to be on Promotion. However, it's simplified a bit because you are always moving from parish to parish and don't have to give a completely new sermon all the time. You just get down a good, simple talk and all those people will appreciate your message.

You will find that you can do a lot of good on Promotion, and when you go back, you will look upon this experience as a great asset to your work. You will be able to understand better your part and your place in Church and the experience will stay with you for the rest of your lives.

Promotion is a good investment for any missioner; you will sense your role as a part of the big Church and feel assured that the rank and file of the clergy and people are with you.

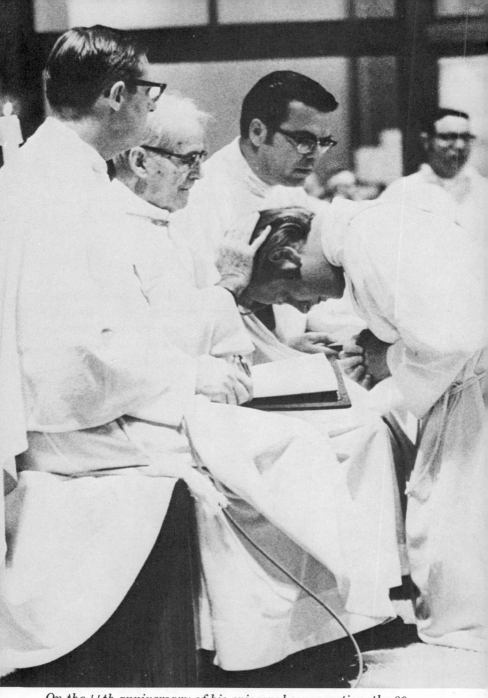

On the 44th anniversary of his episcopal consecration, the 80-year-old Bishop Walsh ordains young Maryknollers.

Another rare appearance was St. Joseph's Seminary, Dunwoodie, N.Y., where our first seminarians, including newly arrived James Edward Walsh, followed some courses. The following brief remarks were addressed to the students, all of whom he met personally.

The Priest, God's Instrument

Reverend Fathers, dear students — to participate in this Mass is like a homecoming to me in a sense. Sixty years ago I was a part-time student here. Maryknoll was just beginning then. It had only a few students, and most of them were in First Year Philosophy class. We had no teachers for Theology at that time. So two of us students, Daniel McShane and myself, who had finished Philosophy and needed Theology classes, were sent here to Dunwoodie.

We attended Dr. Mahaney's Moral Theology class. He was a famous teacher, and I am sure that we profited by his instructions. Daniel McShane was already in Second Year Theology, so he went to some additional classes — Father Albert's class in Holy Scripture; Dr. Mitty's class in Dogmatic Theology, and perhaps others. And Monsignor Chidwick, who was rector then, used to greet us and encourage us from time to time, as we came and went by railway from our embryonic farmhouse seminary at Maryknoll.

All this is long ago and far away now, but I still treasure the memory of it. It was here that I imbibed some of my first notions of the priestly vocation, its scope and its work. Every step towards that great goal has its value, I consider. And I have always felt grateful for the first little steps I was privileged to make here at Dunwoodie Seminary.

So today I am glad to visit the Seminary once again. I am glad to express gratitude for its contribution to me personally in the past. And I am glad also to share some thoughts about the priesthood with its students of today, who will be the priests of tomorrow.

We read in Holy Scripture, "Jesus went about all the cities, and towns, preaching the gospel of the Kingdom, and healing every disease, and every infirmity. And seeing the multitudes, he had compassion on them: because they were distressed, and lying like sheep that have no shepherd. Then he said to the disciples, 'The harvest indeed is great, but the laborers are few. Pray, therefore, the Lord of the harvest, that He send forth laborers into his harvest' " (Mt. 9:35-38).

These words of Our Savior picture the state, the plight, of the human family that He came to save. They have echoed down the ages and they have always brought a response from the Christian people, sometimes a vigorous one, and sometimes a feeble and restricted one, depending on circumstances. This is not surprising. The words outline a great task that was to occupy the Church for centuries and would persist down to the present day.

The Apostles launched out and made a tremendous beginning. Their followers in the early Church made widespread progress here and there. And each succeeding generation added what it could. Whole nations were converted. Whole continents became largely Christian. And yet the great work of preaching the Gospel to all nations still remained unfinished. Half of the world is still outside the fold. And that means that a great proportion of the multitudes in the human family are distressed and lying like sheep that have no shepherd at this very day. So the words of Our Lord describing their condition are still entirely apropos in our own time. And they sound all the more urgent.

Furthermore, this world of ours at present, whether Christian or non-Christian, is a particularly troubled, agitated, divided, unsettled world. Its very progress, although good in itself, has added a lot of unsolved problems to human life. And one result of this state of affairs, one feature of our time, is a human race that is bewildered, bedeviled, distressed and unhappy in very large part.

What is the cure for this? What is the need of the world and its people? Only one thing can ever answer that need in any adequate manner and, of course, it is religion. The struggle is between good and evil, between light and darkness, between sound reason and every work of error and fanaticism. And religion alone can provide the aid humanity needs in that contest.

The fact — the unique and universal necessity of religion — is surely the most important truth of our day. And therefore, the Catholic priesthood, being God's special provision to implement religion, must be the most important and vital vocation open to a man at this or any other day.

This truth is brought home to every priest in the course of his ministry and often in unexpected ways. People turn to him in difficulty and trouble, whether in or out of the Church. His role as a source of help — both spiritual and material — is well and widely known. Surprisingly so, in fact.

Once, years ago in China I was asked by the Head Magistrate of the District to visit a village that had a quarrel with its neighboring village. I was surprised, as the Magistrate was a pious Buddhist. "I am worried about that village," he said, "always in trouble. Please go and talk peace to them. They will listen to you. They know that the spiritual father (their name for priest) likes to help people."

I went. And the net result a year or so later was the

conversion and baptism of the entire village of about five hundred people. And what had led to it? No personal action of mine particularly. The root cause was simply the general impression spread abroad about the Catholic priest — namely, that he is a person who stands ready to help people in their problems and troubles and needs. That is what gave the entry and paved the way to a good success in this case.

Such instances can be multiplied from the history of the priest everywhere. He is the chief agent, the chosen instrument used by God in dispensing His blessings both spiritual and material among the people. That makes him a key figure in the history of the universe. He announces God's Redemption saved the people. He distributes God's multifold charity that helps the people. In short, he is the link that binds and connects God with His great human family, His children, His people. And surely no other human vocation can ever compare in importance with a function, a privilege, like that.

In 1975 Father Bernard Meyer, who was with Bishop Walsh in the first mission band to China, died. The Bishop blesses his grave.

Mount St. Mary's, Emmitsburg, Maryland has recently come into national news because it was the center in this country of the celebrations on the occasion of the canonization of St. Elizabeth Seton. In the vicinity of the Sisters of Charity Motherhouse is a college and seminary established in the early nineteenth century by Sulpician Father (later Bishop) Dubois, staffed by diocesan priests and, in these 1975 days, one of those extraordinary places where seminary enrollment is exploding, a new wing having recently been constructed.

The three Walsh boys followed the footsteps of their father and enrolled in the college (not seminary).

The Mount

"I have lifted up my eyes to the Mountain whence help will come to me."

These words of the Psalm come back to me today as I renew my association with Mount St. Mary's College. They often occurred to my mind down the years, in fact, and served to remind me of all I owe to the old Mount. My indebtedness has been considerable — I have received help from the College in many ways throughout my life and I am well aware of it. These benefits would make a litany. Good lessons learned in college days, good guidance from my teachers, strong lifetime friendships formed among my schoolmates and fellow alumni. And then, the first little seeds of my priestly vocation. I believe these are some of the Mount's gifts to me, and I am grateful for every bit of it.

I was never in the seminary here — my vocation declared itself a little later, but I always felt it had its beginnings in the strong Catholic atmosphere that pervaded the whole establishment here in my student days. And if so, I could never thank the Mount enough for such an aid. For to me that vocation is, of course, the most precious thing in all my life.

Many years later, in strange circumstances as it happens, these same words of the Psalm came back to me with greater force than ever. And then they sang in my heart for a long time. 1960 was the Golden Jubilee year of my graduation class at Mount St. Mary's. At the time, I was imprisoned in China, and I had been given a sentence of twenty years. I was not unhappy — I was content to be there as a part of my vocation. In many respects, however, the outlook was rather bleak.

Then one day, to my great surprise, I was informed that my brother, Judge William Walsh, had come to China to visit me. Soon after that he was ushered into the prison and we had a visit together. And after a few words about our family affairs, one of his first actions was to take a gold Rosary out of his pocket and hand it to me.

"This is a present from Mount St. Mary's," he said. "It is a souvenir of the Golden Jubilee of our class of 1910. It was given to all the surviving members of the class, and as you could not be present at our celebration the college authorities asked me to take this Rosary along to China and give it to you."

At that point the presiding prison officer intervened and confiscated the Rosary. "This matter must be referred to a special bureau," he said. "Such articles are usually against regulations, but I will consult the authorities, and see if it can be given to you later on." Actually, I never saw the gold Rosary again until I was released from prison ten years later. Then it was finally restored to me.

But the confiscation did not matter much, really. The thought behind the gift was the important thing. The Rosary had brought me a message. It said to me, as if in plain words almost, "The Mount remembers. The Mount thinks of me, and Mountaineer friends will pray for me." It was like an insurance of prayers. That is what it conveyed to me, and prayer, of course, is always the greatest need of a man in my situation. Thus, this thoughtful gift was a very practical help and a real comfort to me during the long weary years I spent in prison.

So small wonder that the familiar sentiment often re-curred to me — "I lift up my eyes to the mountain and help will come to me." Yes, help actually did come to me at that time with that gift from Mount St. Mary's and I'm happy to express my gratitude for it now.

I also wish to thank the College authorities for the award of the Dubois Medal. It was conferred on me while yet in prison, I understand, and now is given to me in person. Frankly, I do not know just how I came to deserve this distinction. I went through some strange experiences in the course of my mission work, it is true, and among them was a period in prison. But that was nothing extraordinary — it was just because I wanted to stay with my people and share their troubles, and every Catholic priest, of course, does that. It's a principle with us, a part of our vocation. Nevertheless, I appreciate this award because of its source. It comes from the Mount and that makes it precious to me. I thank the donors.

And in conclusion I should like to make a wish for Mount St. Mary's College. I hope that God will bless the college richly — and that He will enable it to carry on its academic work in that same strong and inspiring Catholic spirit that has always characterized it.

One of the Bishop's relatives was a Visitation Sister in Wilmington, Delaware, and on a recent occasion — 1973 — speaking to the community, he remarked about his prayer life in prison.

Summing Up: Time to Pray

I don't mind telling you that during my twelve years in prison I was not unhappy a single day. I dreamed — well, first I woke up one morning and found myself in prison. I had been taken there the night before — handcuffed, surrounded by six guards. When I woke up the next morning, I thought: "This is what I've dreamed of — time to say all the prayers I couldn't say while I was working."

I had time to pray for my family, for my friends, for people all over the world, everybody under the sun. And I knew you were praying for me during those years. God put us here on earth to help each other. The best way to help people is to pray for them. That's why you're here. Keep it up. I felt that I was being helped during those years by your prayers, by the prayers of my friends, and, I hope, my own. Prayer is so powerful. I am a living example of what prayer can do.

Since his return from China, Bishop Walsh largely spends his days in prayer.

Colors in the Air

by

Michael Eckers

To my parents

Dale and Gladys

Whose life together
is the inspiration for this book.

FOREWARD

September 1944

<u>Over Germany</u>

As he peered through the rubber eyepiece, the ground below passed under the crosshairs of the Norden bombsight. He followed the railroad line alongside the canal and when the refinery buildings came into view he flipped the toggle switch. Hearing the familiar tick-tick-tick of the bomb release switches, he sat up straighter and flexed his back and neck to loosen the tight muscles. The final run from the *IP* to the *AP* this time seemed like a milk run, they didn't even have to take any evasive turns. It was important for the pilot to fly straight and level while the bombardier entered the final data into the bombsight. He thought it just a little strange but chalked it up to the relentless pressure the 8th Air Force and *RAF* had been putting on the Germans. With the Brits area bombing at night and the Americans' precision work by day the enemy couldn't be getting any rest.

"Bombs Away, Captain", he said into the intercom.

"Well done, Weldon", he heard in reply followed by a few chuckles. I'm sure they enjoy that one, he thought. For his fifteenth mission, this one was turning out alright. He felt out of place in the nose of this aircraft. During the pre-mission briefing his own crew was held at the base with needed repairs to the "Lucky Lady"; he'd been reassigned to another crew and plane for this one mission. It was the first time that had happened just before the mission began. He was content with the thought that he was getting closer to the last one and then, home. At this point in the war, completing the required twenty-five missions was not easy. The odds were pretty good you'd be shot down before then.

He was enjoying the sunlight in the nose of the Flying Fortress as the squadron began its turn back toward their base in England; he had the best seat for a view. At that moment everything changed. The ugly black puffs of the flak bursts were directly ahead and right on their level. Somebody on the intercom shouted, "They've got us zeroed in this time." "Keep your eyes open for *bogies* up above this crap and keep this channel clear; use it only for calling out the fighters." The second voice was the pilot's, the only one he recognized. He's from Pennsylvania, he thought, no.... Connecticut. Then the left outboard engine was hit hard; the bomber started a sudden diving left turn, centrifugal forces pinning him to the bulkhead. "Got to get to the escape hatch"; but his vision was already going crazy, starting to blur and go dark at the same time.

He woke up falling, no idea how long he'd been out. The plane was spiraling down below him and he saw two other specks that were probably crewmen. As he watched, it seemed like slow motion; the plane *auguring* in. He couldn't see any more bodies getting out or any chutes open. A sudden panic seized him as he checked for his own parachute. With relief he felt its weight on his chest, right where it should be. Pulling the ripcord he was jerked up hard; no, not up, just down slower. He might have laughed at his mistake if this wasn't so serious. He was a good 150 miles inside Germany and heading toward the ground where everyone was an enemy.

He could see farm fields beneath him with a small patch of woods maybe a half mile to the west and for one fleeting moment, Dale imagined the farmlands of Minnesota. Pulling on one of the chute risers, he tried to side slip in that direction. He realized he wasn't going to make it far enough, but it was the best chance of getting under cover before dark. With the silk map and small compass he had hidden on his uniform, he had a chance, a very small chance, to get back to England. Now he could see two men running from a field to where he was going to land. If I had a gun I could shoot them from here, he thought. That would not endear him to others that might show up later. He could identify them as an older man and younger boy, maybe not even in his teens yet. They were both carrying pitchforks and were ready when he hit the ground.

"Hande hoch, hande hoch." They motioned with the pitchforks for him to put up his hands. He had to release the parachute harness first; thinking, perhaps, he was reaching for a gun the older man jabbed him in the butt with the pitchfork. That took any thoughts of fighting it out from his mind. He raised his hands as the pain in his backside nearly made him faint. He thought of Shorty, his bride of just over a year and how much she would miss him; he had heard the horror stories of what civilians did to downed airmen.....

Chapter 1
September 1941

<u>Minnesota</u>

"Hey, Shorty....would you like to go to the pavilion at Lake Harriett this Friday? The Andrews Sisters will be there; I think Gene Krupa's playing, too." Dale turned off the engine of his 1932 Ford and hopped out, over the door that he seemed to never use. Although he was studying electrical engineering at Dunwoody, his friends in the auto repair class liked to tinker with the Roadster while Dale was in class. He considered it 'one of those advantages of going to school'. Many of his friends from high school were either working or joining the armed services.

Talk of America getting involved in the War in Europe had been increasing lately. President Roosevelt said that as the 'arsenal of democracy', the United States had an obligation to help other nations fight the tyranny of dictatorship. Quite a few folks thought he was trying hard to pull the country into a war between Germany and England. A couple of months ago, back in June, Hitler's German army had invaded Russia. People in the U. S. were pretty divided about whether we should help fight against a country that was at war with Communists and our old enemy, the British Empire.

Dale and Shorty, whose real name was Gladys, didn't think too much about the madness of the world; though there was more than enough of it to go around. They had been dating since before graduation, which to other people meant about six months. Shorty was living with a family in The Park, working as their housekeeper. Right now she had just returned from a job interview at the school district; trying to get a position as secretary to the Administrator. She was pretty much 'all business' as her close friends would agree. Gladdy, as she preferred to be called by everyone but Dale, had come up to Minneapolis from the country a year earlier to finish school and to make her future. She was a serious student and took all the business courses available. Living with the family of a successful store owner helped her make connections that would allow her to move up. What she hadn't planned on was meeting Dale.

Dale Weldon was not nearly as serious a person as Gladdy; he had a fun loving streak that was known to run in at least one of the family in every generation. His father was not like him, having been a soldier in the Great War and a more serious man. His mother, it seemed, had passed the more carefree genes down to him. She had been an American student in Paris when the Germans invaded; not this time, but back in 1915. She volunteered as a nurse and was actually an ambulance driver for the Expeditionary Forces when she met Dautin, Dale's father. They had been drawn together like the opposite poles of a magnet. Now they had two sons; Dale and his brother Don, who was four years younger and already a state level wrestler. Don planned on becoming an accountant after he graduated from high school in 1945.

Dale agreed to go on to technical school after graduation in part to appease his parents but also to learn a skill that would prove useful if the country did, indeed, get into the War. He had in mind to become a pilot or some other position that would be exciting. He did not want to be in the infantry like his father, or his grandfather, or even his great, great, however many there were, grandfather. He knew of the family's history of soldiering; he just didn't really want to be in the infantry unless he had to.

"Dale, I'd love to go! Hey, can I fix you a sandwich; I haven't eaten yet and I'm famished after that interview. I think I've got a good chance at the job; Mrs. Baston said I'd be great and I already know nearly everybody else at the offices. If I don't get this one, I'll probably have to look for something in Minneapolis and I'd hate to have to spend the time on the trolley every day, not to mention the cost."

"Thanks, hon; I'd like something to eat. I've got to get out to the range and help Don." After the quick lunch, and a 'not-too-quick' thank you kiss, Dale headed out to the gun range on the edge of town. He and his brother both worked there, setting up trap and skeet and doing whatever else needed doing. This time of year was pretty busy as men practiced their aim before duck and goose season. The two brothers loved to hunt pheasant, but didn't get much time for it until later in the fall. Both would rather walk and hunt than sit in a cold, usually wet, blind waiting for birds to fly in. Working at the range had a couple of big advantages; they could shoot all they wanted and were both good shots.

"Hey, Don, let me give you a hand with those." Dale hopped out of the car and trotted over to where his brother was unloading boxes from a truck. "Man, these got here just in time; you know this Saturday's going to be a busy one. It seems like every week the Gophers are playing away, we're up to our ears in shooters."

"Yeah; I sure wish I could get to see them play just once this year. It's Bruce Smith's last year of college and I'd like to watch him run just one time." Don was four years younger than his brother, making him all of 15. He was the one that loved sports; he'd practically hug the radio every time he had the chance to hear a football game, especially if the University of Minnesota Gophers were playing. Don was on the high school wrestling team; he was the only freshman to make the squad. He enjoyed the work at the gun club with his brother. It gave them time together and he got to do plenty of lifting; cases of shells were pretty heavy after the first dozen or so.

Dale nearly spilled the beans about a surprise, but caught himself just in time. Their dad, along with the boys' uncles, had gotten tickets to the college football championship game in two weeks; the Gophers would be playing their close rivals, the Wisconsin

Badgers. The Gophers already had four championships in the past 10 years and were expected to win again. He could not imagine how excited Don would get when he found out they were going to the game.

"How many guys are we expecting to have this Saturday; did Ernie say anything about it?" Dale knew that Ernie, the club manager, would have told his brother. Even at his young age Don helped Ernie plan these events, he had a head for numbers and figuring out how much of everything would be needed; shells, *clays*, cleaning supplies for after the shoot. Ernie relied on both boys to make sure the gun club ran smoothly. Now that Dale was going to Dunwoody and was busier, he naturally used Don more and more.

"Oh, he said we have about 50 signed up so far. Of course there will be quite a few that just show up, always are. I suppose we'll go through close to 4,000 shells and a couple of thousand clays. You and I ought to get a fair number of tips, too." Don smiled and knew that they would do well in that department. Once the men started shooting and had a couple of beers, they would loosen up the change purses and share with the boys working.

Dale replied, "That would be swell. Shorty and I are going to see the Andrews Sisters on Friday and I could use some dough. I'm going through nearly $2.00 a week in gas to and from school and that doesn't include driving around on dates and such."

Chapter 2
November 1941

<u>Minnesota</u>

"Man, what a game!!! Can you believe it? I mean, who would believe the Gophers could demolish a team like that, really... 41-6; boy, can that Smith run!!!" Don was absolutely beside himself with excitement as they left the stadium for the walk to the cars. He, Dale and their dad were riding with Uncle Ben and their cousin Dick. Uncles Bob and Roy were in the second car with Dale's cousins Bobby and Ray. They had all just watched the University team manhandle the Wisconsin Badgers for the national football title.

On the way back to the car, Dale walked with his dad, deep in conversation. "You know, pop, joining now would guarantee me a spot at cadet training and I wouldn't end up as a ground pounder if this thing in Europe gets any worse; which it probably will." Dale was considering joining the Army Air Corps Reserve as a potential pilot trainee. The program was a rather new one; it would allow him to continue in school and not report for active duty for up to a year, plenty of time to finish his schooling. After he reported, he would be in line for a spot in pilot training right away.

"Son, you know I'm not against this idea as much as I'm for it; I just need to talk it over with your mother. She should have some say in it as well. I understand the threat the Nazi's are to America and I'm worried about Japan as well. There's a lot of saber rattling going on and Roosevelt, as hard as he's trying, cannot keep us out of this war indefinitely. We'll talk to mother when we get home; for now, let's savor the Gopher win. The past ten years have been easier to deal with when we've had a great football team to enjoy going into each winter."

After dinner, Don was in his room studying when the subject came up again. Esther was also understanding about Dale's desire to finish school and saw the Reserve program as a way for him to do it. It would afford him the chance at becoming an officer as well, a big advantage for the future. She was most concerned about how Gladdy would handle the news.

"Have you told her about this yet?" She saw Dale shake his head. "Well, when you do, tomorrow, be sure to remind her that we are her family, too. We'll be here no matter what may happen in the future. For now, I think we should pray for protection over all of us, especially our son that's soon to be in the military. Dale, would you please get Don down here to join us?"

The next morning Dale drove Gladdy to work, picking her up at the Hoigaard's home where she was boarding. On the way, he pulled the car over to the side of the road and told her of his decision to enlist. Holding his hands, Gladdy told him she had known something like this was on his mind; he'd seemed a bit distracted the past week or so. She also said that she was convinced they would both be alright in the future. No matter what, she knew things would work out. Dale was impressed with her cool, unperturbed attitude. When he mentioned this, Gladdy threw back her head and laughed, "You know, I've been praying about us, you and me, and this whole mixed up silly European war for quite some time. Now, you get this car in gear or I'll be late for work, and you'll be tardy at school young man." Gladdy seldom passed up a chance to remind Dale that she was a whole month older than he was.

Two weeks later, on December 7th, Japan attacked the United States.

Chapter 3
Early 1942

Minnesota

In the days following the entry of the United States into the Second World War, recruiting offices in the Twin Cities, Minneapolis and St Paul, were overwhelmed with men volunteering for service. The Marine Corps kept their offices in downtown Minneapolis open around the clock for several days, signing up the men lined up on the street outside the building. There was no talk of whether the US should fight; now the issue was how soon it would be over.

The army and navy of Japan were running wild all over Southeast Asia and the Pacific Ocean. Within weeks of the attack on Pearl Harbor cities and islands like Singapore, Hong Kong, Manila, Wake Island, Guam and Corregidor became household words, always spoken with the words defeat, loss or retreat. The men who had fought there were not just guys from somewhere else; nearly a hundred men in a National Guard tank unit from Brainerd were fighting and dying in the Philippines.

To Dale and Gladdy the war was not so far away now. Dale had received another letter from the Army Air Corps Reserve; he was still allowed to finish his schooling at Dunwoody before reporting for cadet training. He was in his final classes, studying electrical engineering. This meant he'd be leaving the beginning of June, just a few months away. For him it was not encouraging to be reminded of the continual defeat of the Allied forces. It seemed that everywhere in Europe and Africa the Germans, allies of Japan and Italy, were enjoying victories over British and Russian troops. Only in the skies over London had the Royal Air Force held their own, downing *Luftwaffe* planes at a ratio of nearly two-to-one. Hitler had been forced to postpone an invasion of Great Britain in the spring of 1941; two months later the German army had invaded the Soviet Union. It seemed that the *Wehrmacht* and the Japanese Army would meet in India in a very short time, one driving from the east and one from the west.

Three of Gladdy's sisters were now in the area as well. Still in high school, they seemed to be enjoying their newly found volunteer jobs as hostesses at a USO hall in Minneapolis. These were dances supported by local businesses and individuals to help welcome military men and women to the city. Since Fort Snelling was a place where many new soldiers came through on their way to various training sites around the country, Minneapolis and St Paul were well stocked with people in uniform. Providing them entertainment when they were off duty became a big business, helping to make the Twin Cities a top spot for music. Big name bands and singers like the Andrews Sisters, Spike Jones and Tommy Dorsey would provide the music. Gladdy's sisters would dance until they could hardly stand up on Thursday evenings as a way to help the soldiers pass the time. One of them had told Gladdy of a friend that had bruised her lips as part of a Semper Fidelis Club. It was a group of girls that would send off newly enlisted marines with a nice kiss at the train depot. Before too long all three were dating servicemen; one sailor, one soldier and one marine. They liked to joke that Dale rounded out the bunch as a future airman.

Chapter 4
June 1942

<u>Minnesota</u>

The concert had ended with a nice slow version of Glenn Miller's "Moonlight Serenade", one of their favorites. Dale and Gladdy had enjoyed every second of the dance, holding each other close and not too tight. She looked up at him when the music faded with tears in her eyes, knowing they only had a few short days together before he had to report for active duty and training at an airfield in Texas. He had gotten the letter a week earlier reminding him of his obligation as soon as school was over. He finished his last class and graduated yesterday. They walked outside hand in hand to the railing looking over the calm waters of Lake Calhoun. They could hear the sound of a loon calling to its mate, a wonderfully hollow, haunting lilt that struck both as somewhat sad. Dale nervously took hold of both of her hands, looked deep into her eyes and stumbled through the words he'd been rehearsing all day.

"You know, we've been, well, together for quite some time. I was wondering if you'd like to….uh….what I mean is…would you care to…ooohhhh." Taking a deep breath and twisting his neck and shoulders to lessen the stress, he finished. "What I want to say is….I love you and want to marry you. What do you say?"

Smiling and with a short giggle, Gladdy kissed him and gave him a big hug. She had been waiting for some time to hear this; Dale was always holding his feelings pretty much to himself and she knew how hard this was for him. Fighting an urge to prolong his obvious anxiety waiting for her answer, she nodded and told him her own good news.

"Yes, darling, I will marry you; but not right away. I found out today I'm starting a new job next week and I think it best if we wait until you're through your pilot training anyway. We can both start saving up and when you get some leave, I'll take vacation and we can have our honeymoon when we're not both starting something new; I mean, besides a life together."

"That's swell; I don't even have a ring yet anyway. Let's go soon and pick one out so I can buy it when the Army starts paying me, OK?"

"Fine, dear. We'll tell your parents tomorrow and announce our engagement the next day. I've known you were the man I wanted to marry since we first met, you do know that?"

"I've always known it would happen, I just couldn't figure out the right time to ask. Now with me going away for awhile and all…well, I wanted us to be as close as we can be while we're so far apart."

Three days later, Dale was driven to Fort Snelling by his father. Once all the paperwork was done there, he'd be sent on to Ellington Field in Texas for primary pilot training. His father had wanted to take him and have an opportunity to say goodbye alone. Some neighbors donated a few extra gallons of gas for the trip; since rationing began it was not easy to even drive across town without careful planning. As they pulled into the parking area at the fort, his dad turned to him.

"You know, son, this is no small thing you're doing here. I probably should have talked to you about all this before, but it's not easy to bring back to mind all the memories….some are pretty bad. You're going to be defending the rights and freedoms of more than just your country. Remember your neighbors, your friends, family…..remember that you're even fighting for Gladdy

13

herself. I want you to know how proud I am of you and how all of our ancestors down through the generations are smiling at your patriotism, as corny as that sounds. My father told me these words just as his father told him; keep your head down and come back to us. I know you think this is just a few months of training; with the army, you never know. You might not be home for a very long time. Write often and we will do the same; God be with you and protect you. This will be my daily prayer." With that and a firm handshake, his dad was done.

Dale climbed out of the car with a sudden lump in his throat like he'd just swallowed a lemon or something. Up ahead he could see a soldier pointing to others where they were to go. He headed that way....

Chapter 5
July 1942

<u>Texas</u>

It was hot. The sun blazed down and seemed so big and close he wanted to reach out and touch it. Dale had been in hot weather before; Minnesota was known for its heat and humidity this time of year. This was very different; more like a furnace that seemed to be boiling the brains in his head at the same time it was frying his feet in his shoes on the concrete runway apron. He and the other cadets had been standing here for nearly an hour in the scorching Texas sun. It wasn't just the sun either; most of these men had never seen so much dust. Every time the faintest breath of a breeze promised a little cooling it left another layer of dust that caked to the skin and left all of them thirsty, itching and downright miserable.

"Man, if this is the Army Air Corps, you can keep it. This is not what I left Maine for. I joined to sail through the cool skies, not to stand in the desert like the French Foreign Legion." Phil Harris was a tall, lanky kid with blond hair. He was from Kezar Falls, a small town in the woods near the New Hampshire border. He was one of three other cadets that shared a room with Dale.

"This isn't so bad, Phil. I remember once when I had a shoe actually stick to a tar road back home, pulled my foot right out of it and nearly lost my sock on the next step. 'Course Nevada's just a bit warmer than here this time of year. The dust isn't nearly as tasty as in Las Vegas either. I remember how the dust would change color depending on what part of Hoover Dam was being built; sometimes gray cement dust, other days it'd be brown dirt

15

dust." Jack Hale stood a few inches over five feet with dark hair and eyes. For his small size, he was about the loudest person Dale had ever met. If Jack were to whisper, it could probably be heard two counties away. His father had been a foreman on the dam when it was constructed; some said it was the biggest thing made by man since the Great Wall of China or the Pyramids of Egypt.

"Quiet in the ranks, no talking." Sergeant Blain, their drill instructor, was an anomaly. He was a fun loving, laughing type when not in uniform; when he put it on, he became a no-nonsense, by the book soldier. Right now he stood in front of the company, ramrod straight. The cadets could see that not one single speck of dust was daring to land on him. There was not the least little hint of sweat either. They marveled at how he could stand there and look like he just got dressed. They couldn't even get out of their barrack rooms without sweating buckets in this heat.

They heard it before they saw it. The sound of four Wright engines, perfectly synchronized, was one that would become music to their ears in the future. As they squinted into the glaring sunlight, the speck began to take shape as an airplane, but one unlike they had seen, except in pictures. The B-17 came in, touched down at the far end of the runway gracefully, like a 20 ton ballerina. None of these cadets had seen one; they couldn't resist the impulse to cheer as it rolled up and stopped in front of the formation. Even Sergeant Blair felt the surge of pride at its sight. This "Flying Fortress" was a thing of beauty; to the enemy it would become the beast, carrying its load of death and destruction to those who would try to take away freedom.

This was what they had signed on for; to learn to fly this enormous machine and take this war to the gates of Berlin and Tokyo themselves.

"Well, Miss Ady, I see by this letter of introduction that Mrs. Baston considers you to be a most capable and hard working young woman. She says you have abilities that go far beyond those required at your present position. You understand that we are a new agency here in Minneapolis, one that has a lot of work to do in the defense plants being built to win this war. President Roosevelt himself feels that the country has to break through long held ideas about women and others entering the work place. I sincerely hope you take this work seriously and will labor diligently."

Frank Rarig was the new director of the War Manpower Commission, whose job would be to ensure that area employers understood and complied with the government's desires. The Great Depression in the 30's had made it very difficult to get jobs in manufacturing if you were anything but a male and white. With so many men entering the military, the need for new workers in defense plants far outweighed the number available. The Commission was formed to help women and others get these jobs; though they faced an uphill battle with many business owners.

Gladdy's new position would be to go out to the plants, speak with the owners and convince them it was in everyone's best interest to open their hiring to include women and others. She felt able to do this, provided she could get in the door in the first place.

Over the next few days, Gladdy assisted Mr Rarig and the rest of the staff in setting up an office in the old milling district along the river opposite the campus of the University of Minnesota. The entire staff shared a former dorm building, made available because of a decline in enrollment at the university. By the middle of July visits were being scheduled to factories and other businesses that were getting the new defense contracts. Some, like Honeywell, had been around for quite some time and were very amenable to the new hiring policies. Others, such as

Northern Pump Company and Munsingwear, grudgingly agreed to hire some women but practically refused to hire anyone but whites. Since there were no enforcement policies in the executive order creating the Commission, the staff could only make recommendations at this time. Mr Rarig and the others realized this kind of change could not come overnight but were convinced their work would lead to vast improvements.

To Gladdy all of this was one big adventure. Though she took her job and its responsibilities very seriously, there was that part inside her that enjoyed the looks and attention her presence caused when she visited a plant. In representing the federal government and speaking of the desires of the President to leaders in business she was careful to never reveal her age; Gladdy acted and dressed as though she were nearer to thirty than to twenty. No one needed to know she was only a year out of high school; let them think she had already finished college and had years of experience behind her.

Chapter 6
September 1942

<u>Texas</u>

"Listen, son. You really ought to feel some relief or gratitude that the Air Corps isn't just sending you packing to a maintenance school to be a mechanic or worse. The chance to continue officer training as a Navigator or Bombardier is about the best that you could ever hope for considering..." Major Walther was sitting at his desk as he continued to look over Dale's records. He continued, "Your knowledge and aptitude at math and science are quite impressive; at the same time, we do have rules about reporting incidents like this and paperwork sometimes seems to rule over common sense. You failed to note the damage to the aircraft before you signed for it. The damage was properly noted by the next pilot trainee. How do we know, except for your word, that you didn't cause the cracked frame spar?"

Dale knew he was *fubar* on this one; he hated the thought that someone else had really caused the damage and was still getting to fly. When he checked out the PT-19 training plane to get in a few more hours flying, he had noticed a slight crack but it seemed like nothing bad enough to report. Soon after he landed, another cadet had signed for the same plane and made a note of the damage. By regulations, it was now Dale's fault. He had been called into the Major's office and was now learning what consequence would result from his oversight.

"Sir, it's always been my desire to become a pilot. If the Air Corps sees fit to allow me to remain an officer candidate in another position, so be it. I really do want to fly."

19

"I know you do, Cadet Weldon. As a Navigator or Bombardier you'll be flying, though it will not be in command of the aircraft. You know, I'm a Bombardier myself. I like to think that the pilot's job is to get me to where I do the really important part, delivering the goods on the enemy. Isn't that what we're here for?"

Dale thanked the Major for his understanding and the second chance. He reported to another office and received his orders; he was to be at the Bombardier school for training in two days. Training there would last about two months. The school was located in another part of the same airfield so there would be no travel time. Dale knew the hardest part would be to write Gladdy and his folks with the disappointing news.

My dearest Shorty,

I've just discovered the Air Corps' sense of justice. I made a mistake in judgment about a plane I checked out to fly. Because I didn't mention a minor crack in part of it before I flew I'm being held responsible for the damage. It's a rule they have here so we get used to the military way of doing things. As a result I've been reassigned from pilot training to become a bombardier. Lucky me; I still get to become an officer but won't be flying anymore, except as a passenger. The CO here was good about it, all in all. He explained that my new job will be to deliver the goods which is what air warfare is all about, I suppose. My new school is right here but now I won't be coming home until probably Christmas. A little disgusted with the whole thing right now but I'll leave it in God's hands, He knows best. I don't feel it is my fault but I am willing to accept the reassignment since I'll remain an officer candidate. On a more pleasant note, I picked up a ring here and will be sending it with a friend who is going home to Minneapolis next week for a short leave. I've given him Mom and Dad's address and he will deliver it there. I hope you like it as much as I do; it's very much like the one we looked at before I left for the Air Corps. Write as soon as you get it. With my love and kisses (lots of kisses), Dale

Minnesota

The whistles she could probably get used to; it was the looks from the men in the plants that bothered her the most. The first few times it seemed alright but now it was getting downright uncomfortable. At times she felt like they were undressing her with their eyes as she walked past. This situation was nearly intolerable; as she entered an assembly area, work literally stopped as the men stared at her. The manager that was giving her the tour was a guy in his fifties with thinning hair, too much stomach and a mousy, pencil thin mustache. His name was Lou and, as he explained it, Gladdy was a perfect example of why women shouldn't be allowed to work in the plant.

"You see, little lady, the men here are all about work. Until something distracts them, that is. And I'll tell you, you are some distraction, yessir...."

"Lou; may I call you Lou, Mr Nesterman? I don't see, nor have I seen since my arrival here, anybody working. Maybe, just maybe the problem isn't that I'm here; could it be that if more women were around, they would no longer be a distraction? You know, sir, with the war going the way it is right now.... why, I'd expect the Army will be calling up a large number of your employees anytime. Who are you going to replace them with and still keep up your production?"

"Well, I'm sure the front office knows about things like that. I'm just a floor manager; I don't do the hiring, just some of the firing." Lou let out a real belly laugh at his own joke. "Now, missie, if you're done looking around, I think the boys got work to do. What say we go back into my office and talk some more about this?"

That was about the last thing Gladdy wanted to do. She'd had enough of Lou and his circus of whistling wolves and gaping monkeys. She explained to him that she needed to speak to the business owner again before she returned to her own office to write her report. She managed to thank him, though it made her stomach turn and the words nearly caught in her throat. Lou escorted her back across the assembly area and on to the front offices. The chorus of lewd remarks and whistles were stopped only by the shutting of the door behind them as they left.

"Mr Harris. I'd like to thank you for your time today and for the attention your manager here, Lou, has shown me. I have enough information, I think, to draft my report. The only final question I have is to verify what I've observed. You have no women working here and no one of color?"

"Well, Miss Ady, we do have Frank. He was here when my company bought the building a few years ago. He knows where most of the pipes and wires and things are, sort of our facility expert. I believe Frank is a quarter, or is it an eighth, I forget... anyway, he's part redskin, Indian, you know... Anyway, we don't need anybody here that would, you understand, upset the pot? We're all good men here and mighty proud of it, too."

Gladdy smiled. Inside she was about ready to explode. This was the fifth defense plant she had visited and the first that was this bad. Sighing, she got behind the wheel of the car and started it. She wasn't quite sure she wanted to do the follow-up visit to this place. Maybe she could convince Max to do it. He seemed to be willing to help her, at least he offered to every day. Yes, she thought as she drove through Minneapolis back to the office, Max is a nice guy; he'd help her out if she asked him.

Chapter 7
October 1942

<u>Texas</u>

With his right hand raised, Dale repeated the words along with nearly a hundred fellow trainees. The solemnity of the moment with the bombsight on the table in front of them, secured by armed guards and under the cover of a canopy, caused him to realize the importance of the job that could be his.

"Mindful of the secret trust about to be placed in me by my Commander in Chief, the President of the United States, by whose direction I have been chosen for bombardier training...and mindful of the fact that I am to become guardian of one of my country's most priceless military assets, the American bombsight...I do here, in the presence of Almighty God, swear by the Bombardier's Code of Honor to keep inviolate the secrecy of any and all confidential information revealed to me, and further to uphold the honor and integrity of the Army Air Forces, if need be, with my life itself."

There was a hush when they were finished; the sound of the Texas wind blowing across the runway being the only thing heard. The Colonel in charge of the school stepped forward and ordered the men to form into their classes. For the next two months, Dale would get to know his classmates very well. They would sleep, eat, drill, learn, practice, stand guard, pass and fail tests, together. It was expected that those who mastered the math involved would help those who didn't get it; assisting one another was as

23

important as your own individual ability. Teamwork began right here and continued throughout the rest of your time in service.

Classes in the science of dropping bombs from a moving aircraft 20,000 feet in the air accurately on a target no larger than a baseball diamond relied on math far beyond what most of the cadets had ever learned in school. Calculus, trigonometry and algebra were followed by studies in electricity, air density and aerodynamics. Each type of bomb the Air Corps used had to be studied and a cadet had to know the process to arm every one and how each would fall. The Norden bombsight they would use was the most secret device ever made for the American military. It was a type of analog computer that determined the exact instant the bombs were released after all the variables were entered into it by using a multitude of knobs and switches. Dale was glad he had studied well at Dunwoody after high school; it was a big advantage for him and he was able to help the other cadets in their studies all along the way. Not that any of the training was easy for him; he only had to work a little less than others. The most difficult task was putting all the information in the bombsight itself; one mistake and the bombs would fall far from the target. This could mean a second, or third trip to the target for a squadron of planes; flying hundreds of miles through enemy fighters and anti-aircraft fire to hit a factory again because a bombardier had made a mistake the first time.

Any spare time Dale had, and there wasn't much of it, was spent writing home to Gladdy or his family. His brother Don was doing very well as a wrestler this year at school and was ranked third in the state in his weight class. Dale wished he could be there to cheer him on; he always enjoyed watching Don in action. His dad was still working at the Minneapolis Tribune newspaper running a printing press, though he was putting in more hours since there was a shortage of trained press operators. Dale had received a letter from his dad describing the work Gladdy was doing to open up the hiring of women and coloreds in the defense plants; he had said he wished she could get some help for the Tribune as well. Dale's mom was, as usual, very busy helping out with scrap drives for aluminum, paper and rubber; she was also working at a local USO giving out coffee and sandwiches to soldiers, sailors and airmen passing through Minneapolis. Dale knew this was work she really enjoyed doing and he appreciated the mothers who did the same thing down here in Texas.

One Friday evening Dale and three of his classmates were rewarded with passes to go to town for a few hours. They road a bus into San Antonio and found a restaurant; after each had enjoyed about the biggest steak any of them had ever seen, they went to a movie and then stopped by the USO before heading back to their base. It seemed to Dale that every other person was in uniform, like schools of fish in a large pond. He decided to stay on base in the future and save his money, though the steak was awfully tasty. When he got back to his barracks, he wrote a letter to Gladdy about his evening out.

My dearest Shorty,

Well, I finally got a pass for a few hours off the base. I went with three other guys into San Antonio; it's an interesting place but dusty, just like everything else down here. Had a steak the size of Texas and took in a new movie, *Casablanca,* with Humphrey Bogart. It wasn't the same without your shoulder next to me to put my arm around. One of the guys I went to town with has a brother in the Marines. The newsreel before the show was about the fighting there on Guadalcanal. Even though there will be some danger on our missions, I'm sure glad I joined the Air Corps. Those boys are fighting the jungle AND the Japs. We stopped by the USO for coffee and pie; guess what song was playing? "Jukebox Saturday Night", one of our favorites. I sure miss you and me at Malcoff's or the deli on Lake Street. The ladies at the USO reminded me of what Mom is doing back home. They all seemed so happy to be serving their boys. I think I'll stay on base from now on; the evening cost over $10 for the bus, steak, movie and all. That's money we'll need once we're married. Did you get the ring yet? I've not heard from you in awhile and Dad's last letter didn't mention it arriving. I'm sure you're busy as a bee getting jobs for everyone in Minnesota!

Training is going swell; the stuff I learned at Dunwoody is really paying off now. I'm actually glad I'm not going to be a pilot. This is more exciting and uses much of what I've learned. Tell Don my next school, in January, will be in gunnery and the word here is that we get to shoot all the shotguns we want to while riding around in the back of trucks! That ought to get his goat a bit. Tell him also that I'm proud of my little brother and how he's doing at wrestling. I'd really like to see him at a meet, but I suppose the season will be over by the time I get home again.

How's Dad doing? Is he having to work more since so many guys are off in the army? You would not believe how many men there are down here in uniform. Hey, I'd better close for now; "Light's Out" just sounded. . Write when you can.

My love to all,
Dale

Minnesota

"Hey, Lou wants to know when you're coming back to his plant? He said all the boys are working too hard and need a distraction. They seemed to really enjoy your last visit, Gladdy." Max chuckled as he delivered the message from Lou. He set the papers on her desk as he took off his coat and hat and hung them on the stand near the office door.

"Well, I sure don't miss Lou or the other jerks working with him. You know he asked me to come into his office to 'talk over' things? The nerve of that guy! Anyway, he won't be so glad to see me again after his boss gets the report I'm filing. They have only ONE *minority group* employee? Their janitor is half Ojibway and only works there because he knows where all the water pipes are located. I could almost scream when I think of how many defense plants there must be like that one!"

26

"Listen Gladdy. You can send me to any of those places you don't like. Besides, you're so much better at the paperwork and reports than me. Maybe we can work together to get these inspections done. Would you like to talk about that someday at lunch?" Max tried hard to hide the excitement he felt as he spoke with her. For weeks now, since Gladdy came on staff at the agency, he'd been working up the nerve to ask her out on a date. She was so pretty and slim; Max often imagined dancing with Gladdy to Moonlight Cocktails or some other nice tune. Then, maybe on the drive home...

"... I really can't. I bring my lunch every day, you know. My fiancée and I are saving our money for marriage. He's at bombardier school right now, in the Air Corps; I do miss him so. Anyway, I'd be happy to trade typing for visiting places like Harris Manufacturing. I don't mind compliments, but those men only had one thing on their minds."

Max was jerked back into reality by her words. He knew he'd have to go slow if he ever wanted to have a good time with Gladdy. So many of the girls he'd known since the war started were the same; buy them dinner, go dancing and then it was 'sure, why not, we might be attacked by the Japs next week anyway...'. Gladdy was so different; she had a classy way about her that drove Max kind of crazy at times.

"Well, the offer of lunch covers a sandwich here as well as something at a diner. I just thought we could compare notes on some of these plants and maybe come up with a way to get them to agree to hire more women and negroes, you know."

"I guess that would be OK. Maybe some day next week; this one is too filled up with visits and paperwork anyway. Remind me Monday and I'll pack us both a lunch."

"That's more like it. Now about Harris Manufacturing..."

Chapter 8
January 1943

<u>Arizona</u>

Dearest Gladdy,

I got your letter a few minutes ago. I have no idea what happened to Fred Qualley or the ring. I cannot believe that he would stiff me like that; keeping the ring when he promised to deliver it to Mom and Dad. I'd like to think I'll run into him again during this war; if I do I'll really let him have it! I am happy for you in your work back there. It sounds like a lot of responsibility; I hope no one is taking advantage of your abilities or love of paperwork. I don't know anybody that enjoys a typewriter as much as you. Don't wear down your fingers too much, leave room for a new ring on one of them (ha-ha). Life here is more of the same. Reveille, roll call, breakfast, march to class to learn about the guns and ammunition we use and then out to the range for practice. You know that's my favorite part. We stand in the back of a truck and while we're being driven all over the desert, *clay pigeons* are being launched from the sides of the road. Don would have the time of his life out here at gunnery school. I've fired hundreds of rounds of fifty caliber bullets and maybe a thousand shotgun shells already!

I'd better say goodbye; I've got to help another cadet with a bombing problem. He was allowed to pass bombardier training but needs more practice so I've been assigned to work with him. He's a good kid from Wisconsin so we talk a lot about fishing at Lake Pepin and how much we don't miss the snow.

Love, Dale

"Weldon, come on! Our barracks has been challenged on the range by our next door neighbors. Don't let us down, now... you know nobody comes close to you. You are the shootingest man I've ever seen!" Webster, Webbie to the other guys in the barracks, was a fine shot as well. He and Dale always placed at the top of the list, it was common for both to score 50 out of 50. The two of them would be hard for anybody to beat.

The four men, two from each barracks, mounted up in the back of the trucks and off they went, to the shouted encouragement of their classmates. For a solid hour they were bounced around, their drivers trying their hardest to upset their aim. When they had returned to the barracks area, Webbie and Dale had a confirmed score of 97 out of the 100 targets thrown. Their competition came in a close last with 95. The Officers' Club was a noisy place that night as the losers bought the beers. Dale settled for two, but Webbie was carried back to his bunk after his ninth! Dale heard him get up a half dozen times during the night going out to the latrine.

The next morning their instructors reminded them, quite loudly, that it was alright to "let loose" every so often, but to remember the deadly seriousness of their jobs. After their classroom time, they were further encouraged by a five mile run around the base. Dale was thankful he'd only had the two beers; Webbie and some others got back from the run mighty late indeed. Officers or not, they were still in the Air Corps!

Six weeks of gunnery training went by quickly. Dale then spent another six weeks in classes on basic navigation so he could work at that job if the need arose. This involved learning how to get accurate position fixes by using the stars at night or the sun during the day, just like sailors on the sea. He learned how to plot a course by compass and clock and other skills that would get a bomber "home" if the Navigator was killed or wounded. This was part of each man knowing more than his own job as a member of an air crew. It was late March when Dale finished his classroom instruction and went home for a short visit before his next phase of crew training. He was looking forward to spending most of his time with Shorty, though he also missed his family and friends. Maybe there was a way he could satisfy his desire to see everybody before he left again.

Chapter 9
March 1943

<u>Minnesota</u>

"Max, I've got to stop having lunch with you. You've been spending entirely too much money on me and, besides, there's someone coming here today I want you to meet."

In his imagination, Max figured it was Gladdy's mom or dad. He hoped he was getting along well enough by now to 'meet the parents'. He felt sure that his slow approach to her was going to work after all. He'd seemed content to smile and be nice and for the past couple of weeks she had even agreed to go out to lunch with him instead of always eating at their desks.

Later that morning Gladdy came in to his office arm in arm with an Air Corps officer. "Max, this is Lieutenant Dale Weldon, my fiancée. We'd like to invite you to our wedding; it's tomorrow evening in The Park at the Lutheran church on Excelsior Boulevard at 6:00 pm. I do hope you can make it. I know it's short notice but Dale has to leave the next morning for more training."

Max was stunned to say the least. A wave of depression swept over him as he managed to stammer out a reply. "Uh, hello Lieutenant. It's been a real pleasure working with Gladdy and all. I'll try to make the wedding, have to check my schedule and work out transportation. You know, I tried joining the Air Corps myself, but something's wrong with my balance, some inner ear thing they said. Anyway, now I'm doing my part here for the government." Coming face to face with the trim, smart looking officer made Max feel very inferior; he was angry with his own inability to qualify to wear a uniform. He was also surprised with the level of jealousy he felt toward Dale. He told himself that someday he'd show he was better than this flyboy. Max walked out of his own office mumbling to himself.

"Rather strange guy, I think. Anyway, dear, where would you like to have lunch? I spoke with your boss; you don't have to come back to work until next week. I don't know where we'll spend our wedding night; still working on that. There are not any rooms available in The Park, maybe downtown Minneapolis will be better."

"Don't worry about that one, darling. When I got your telegram I met with Mrs Hoigaard. It seems the family is going to be away for awhile beginning today. She insisted we spend the night at their home and their driver will bring us to the train station so I can see you off properly this time. I know it's a short honeymoon, but when you finish up this air crew phase training, or whatever you called it, we can take some time and go someplace special. How long a wait will that be, another eight weeks, right?"

The next 24 hours sped by, filled with preparations for the ceremony. Dale picked up another ring and asked Don to be his best man. Gladdy's sisters and their boyfriends were attendants. Her boss, Mr Rarig, agreed to give her away and they were lucky to get the high school music teacher as organist. Dale's folks were wonderful, helping out with other details; the USO ladies offered to serve a light dinner as a reception and Dautin made sure the announcement made that day's paper.

Everyone seemed to have a good time and all said Gladdy was stunning in the dress she borrowed from a good friend. It was made from a silk parachute her husband had brought home; he was in the *Airborne* and had somehow managed to obtain one. The next morning Dale and Gladdy arrived at the Milwaukee Road train station in the Hoigaard's 1938 Rolls Royce Phantom III, driven by their chauffer. Bystanders stopped and gawked as the car pulled up, expecting some dignitary to step out. When an Air Corps Lieutenant emerged, several were laughing and pointing. Gladdy got out as well and the two newlyweds gave a pretty good performance with their goodbye kiss. Dale was not the least bit flustered by the applause.

South Dakota

"Lieutenant Weldon, I'm Pat Collins; we'll be together in the nose. Lieutenants Bob Gracy and John Wooster over there are pilot and co-pilot. We have the next couple of hours to get acquainted before the enlisted crew arrive. What say we head over to the Officers' Club; might be a bit more comfortable."

Dale appreciated the easy, outgoing manners of Lieutenant Collins, the navigator. He imagined it wouldn't be difficult at all getting to know this guy well before they actually flew in combat. The next eight weeks would give all four officers the chance to come together as a team, along with the six enlisted men that would complete the B-17's crew. These would be the flight engineer (also the top turret gunner), the radio operator, ball turret gunner, two waist gunners and the tail gunner. Together, all the men would have a single mission; to fly the bomber to the target, deliver the payload and return safely to their base. When you added in other factors like mechanics, weather, anti-aircraft fire and enemy fighters it became a huge challenge. A crew had to fly 25 missions before their tour of duty was done and they could rotate back to the States. The average crew survived seven or so missions before they were killed or shot down and captured by the enemy!

That afternoon all the officers talked about themselves to get to know each other. Bob Gracy was from Wisconsin and had studied engineering at Madison. John Wooster grew up in Oregon and had worked as a logger before his acceptance to pilot training. Pat Collins, from Tennessee, had graduated from high school in 1942 and was accepted for navigator training a few weeks later. The oldest was their pilot, Gracy; he was already 22 and was considered the "old man" in more ways than one. As pilot, he commanded the whole crew. Dale and Bob Gracy were already bantering each other about the football rivalry between the Gophers and the Badgers. In fact, Bob had also been at the championship game back in 1941; he was one of the linebackers on the Wisconsin team!

About two hours later the enlisted men arrived. Dale made notes about each man; name, where he came from and interests or hobbies. He knew they would all have to get to know each other well to survive later. All the men were sergeants, though none had been in combat. The flight engineer, Bud Hooper, and the tail gunner, Frank Haskill, were from California. The radio operator's name was Ben Murphy; a freckle faced red head from New Jersey. Don Wilson was the ball turret gunner from Georgia; short in height but probably the strongest of all of them. The two waist gunners were Harley Spike out of Maryland and Henry Schultz who had once played trumpet in Glenn Miller's band; he grew up in Pennsylvania.

It was curious that all of the officers were married and all of the enlisted were single. Of the ten men in the crew, six were still nineteen and only the two pilots were old enough to drink off base. Dale also noted that Harley and Henry both had the same initials and shared the same birthday! Bob Gracy suggested that they name their aircraft the "Lucky Lady" in honor of the officers' wives. No one seemed to disagree; after all, he was the plane commander.

The next day they got to meet the "Lucky Lady"; a B-17 that had seen thousands of miles, all in the United States. With a training pilot on board their first flight together was a six hour orientation, getting to know the particulars of flying together and working as a team. Part of this initial flight took them over the Black Hills and Badlands of South Dakota. The desolate beauty of the land below impressed all of them; most of these boys had never been more than a hundred miles from their homes before the Air Corps. Now they were seeing just how big and majestic their country really was.

The crew of the "Lucky Lady" would log more than 20,000 miles before they finished their final training and prepared to head over to England to join the Eighth Air Force in its battle against the Luftwaffe.

Chapter 10
May 1943

<u>Minnesota</u>

Max strode into the office as Gladdy was hanging up the phone; he noticed the troubled look on her face. As he hung his hat on the rack he turned and, in his most sympathetic voice, said, "Everything OK on the home front?"

"Well, it's just that Dale's folks are both not feeling well today and said I really ought not to come over for supper. I was planning on seeing them this evening; we get together every week to compare letters we've gotten from Dale. Plus, I miss a real home cooked meal; I just can't match an oven with a hotplate in a dorm room." Gladdy managed a weak smile at the last line; inside she felt a little uncomfortable at resuming lunches with Max a couple of times each week. Right now she was also feeling quite lonely with Dale gone and none of her own family available to visit.

"Hey, we could go after work and grab a bite to eat down on Hennepin Avenue. Maybe even a show afterward?" Max knew he'd not get the show, but maybe she'd settle with the lesser offer of dinner.

"Max, you're such a dear. You know I can't go to a show with you. Just this once, I am feeling a little shut in.... just a quick dinner?"

"Sure. I'll call and get a reservation at this place I know; that'll save time if we don't have to wait for a booth."

Though he walked out of the office, Max was practically skipping inside. He had followed his plan of "lying low" after Gladdy's wedding and hadn't even mentioned lunch for a couple of weeks. Then it was once, followed by two in a week, now dinner out. He felt quite proud of himself and his ability to win her over. The rest of the afternoon at work went by quickly for him as he gazed out the window and softly whistled; no time now for foolish paperwork.

As Max and Gladdy were walking down Hennepin toward the restaurant a humming, buzzing sound could be heard, getting louder in the air. Looking up, the two stopped and stared as a flight of six huge aircraft flew over. It was not the first time Air Corps planes had used Minneapolis as a turning point in training flights from the air bases in the Dakotas, but it was seldom enough to capture peoples' attention. Everyone on the ground stood, pointed up and then began to cheer and applaud at this little air show.

Gladdy's heart leapt in her chest as she knew, she just knew, that Dale was up in one of those planes! She thought of herself down below, with another man, going to dinner and she absolutely wanted to cry. How could she be so selfish to think of her own fun when her husband was having to work so hard?

"Max, I have to go. I can't have dinner with you, or lunch again for that matter. It's not fair to Dale. I'm sorry."

"Hey, wait a minute. You think he wants you to lock yourself up like some nun or something? This is just dinner with a friend, nothing more. He'd understand; you were supposed to be at his folks' place and they're not feeling well. So you went for something to eat with a co-worker, so what?"

"Nothing more; you're sure you can do this? I've heard most guys don't settle for 'nothing more'. Let's have dinner and then you drive me straight back to the office so I can get home. Deal?"

"Now we're talking. The restaurant is right here; we'll be out and you'll be home before he even lands, wherever that is."

Max opened the door and put his hand on her back to guide her in. He felt the instant tightening of her muscles and then felt them relax. Smiling inside, he tried hard not to show his eagerness.

"I don't believe it! Gladdy, what on earth are you doing here?" The voice was all surprise and excitement; it belonged to Golda, her younger sister. "I start working here and who do you suppose is my first customer? My own sister! Did Donna or Vivian tell you to come here tonight? Honestly, I've not been working for fifteen minutes! What do you suppose are the chances in this?"

"I had no idea you got a job here. I haven't heard from Donna, Viv or you for that matter, since the wedding. I suppose you're all pretty busy with school and all?"

"Yeah, gotta finish this last year. Viv's got one more, though. Hey, I saw Don this morning; he says his mom and dad are pretty sick. There's quite a bit of flu in the school at Park, too. Listen, I'll be back in a minute to get your order. First, you have to introduce me to this good looker here."

"Oh, Golda this is Max, a guy I work with. Max, this is Golda, one of my sisters."

"I'm glad to meet you. We're just here for a quick bite after a hard day's work. I've got to get your sister back so she can get home for some shut eye before tomorrow."

As Golda slid by in the crowded aisle, she whispered "Dreamboat" in Gladdy's ear. Max didn't hear what she said but immediately noticed the blush that came to Gladdy's face. Dinner went by fast, Max managed to softly touch her hand a couple of times when they looked at the menu. As nice as the meal was, Gladdy was distracted by the entire event. As Max dropped her off at her car, one feeling overwhelmed her; confusion.

In the Air

"Pilot to Navigator....good job, Collins. We're dead on with the Foshay Tower right on the money. Now we'll come right and it's on to St Louis. Bombardier, any words as tourist guide over this fair city? It sure looks nice down there with all those lakes."

"Bombardier here... the round one directly below us is Lake Calhoun and Lake Harriet is just to the right. There's a nice pavilion there with big bands playing every Friday night. Care to land? Tonight's probably Tommy Dorsey or Benny Goodman. We just passed over where I lived; I wonder where my ""Lucky Lady"" is right now..."

"Well, Lieutenant, after the poor honeymoon you gave her, she's probably out on a date with some 4-F'er, or worse....a sailor." The voice sounded like one of the waist gunners, Harley or Henry; Dale could hardly tell them apart on the intercom.

"Can the chatter.....Let's make this last one our best flight yet. I'd like to land within a minute of our scheduled time, although if we had a couple of real bombs, it'd be tempting to drop them on Memorial Field down there. What do you say, Bombardier?"

"Not on your life, Skipper. That place is holy ground after what the Gophers did to you Badgers!"

"On to St Louis and then sack time!" Gracy knew just when to stop the kidding. The crew had gotten real close these past weeks; they knew what all the others had to do in practically any situation. It was bound to pay good dividends when they got into combat. The other pilots were behind them in a good, tight formation. Bob Gracy was a natural pilot and his commander had noticed right away. In fact, it seemed like everyone on the plane were at the top in their positions.

Hours later they had come in right over St Louis and had made a practice bomb run on a factory there. Dale was glad when the instructor in the last plane had said over the radio, "Well done, lead plane. Your Bombardier put those eggs right in the pickle barrel. If this had been a real mission, you could scratch one Kraut factory!"

"Pilot to crew....looks like Weldon buys the first round tonight."

When the planes had finished their final approaches and touched down back at the base, everyone was in a great mood, although a bit tired. At their debriefing, they answered the intelligence officer professionally; this was one more part of a mission they needed to get used to. Right now questions about how many enemy planes did they see, or whether they counted the parachutes coming out of a destroyed bomber didn't carry the weight they soon would. They knew the importance of being alert and paying attention to every aspect of the mission. All in all it had been their best flight to date. It seemed nothing had gone wrong.

"Lieutenant Gracy, a word if you please." Dale looked up and saw their training commander speaking to the pilot. A few minutes later, Gracy was back with a huge grin on his face.

"It seems gentlemen, that we have finished here. After this last flight, the commander says we're ready for deployment. Only hitch is, we won't have time to say goodbye to anyone. After a good night's sleep we fly tomorrow for Maine and pick up a plane we have to ferry across the Atlantic to England. When we get there we'll be assigned to a squadron as a replacement crew. The best part is we get to stay together!"

Minnesota

"Gladdy, there's a call for you." The knocking and voice at the door startled her just as she was falling asleep. She got up and put on a robe. The phone was down the hall from her room in the college dormitory.

"Hello, this is Gladys." She was curious who would call now.

"Long distance Operator, one moment please..."

"Gladdy, are you there? It's me, Dale."

"Darling, what time is it; where are you? Are you here already?"

"Honey, I'm afraid I won't be home for awhile. It might be a long time. We're leaving tomorrow for Europe. I had to call, we really aren't supposed to but Gracy said those of us married guys owe it to our wives. Gladdy, I love you so much. I hate to have to say goodbye like this...."

"My love, it's not goodbye, only so long. I love you too and I'll pray for you every day. Write me as soon as you can. I thought of you today when I saw six bombers fly over downtown. I know it's silly, but I felt you were looking right down at me."

"Keep that feeling; it WAS me! We flew over Minneapolis and St Louis and then back. I was thinking of you the whole time we were over the city. I'll write as soon as I can post a letter. I love you with all my heart."

"I love you too, darling. I'll pray for you every day. I love you more than anything else. I'll tell mom and dad everything."

"I have to go now, honey. We only got a minute each. I hate this damn war; I count the days until we can be together in peace, you and me. Goodbye."

With that there was a click and Dale was gone. Gladdy felt totally alone. She knew what she had to do. Running back to her room she got dressed and looked at the clock. Midnight; doesn't matter, I'll wake them up. She walked to the parking lot and started the car. Driving across the river she took the road past Dunwoody,

41

where Dale had studied before the war. Her eyes began to fill with tears.

Dautin and Esther were worried when they heard the knocking at the front door. Dautin opened the door as Gladdy wrapped him in a hug and started crying on his shoulder. Esther stood behind him, fearing for the worst.

"Oh, dad, he's gone. Dale's leaving in the morning for Europe somewhere. He has no idea when he'll be back."

Dautin held her close for a minute, until her sobbing quieted down a bit. "Now, now....you knew this time would come. Mother, would you please put some tea on? Gladdy, come in to the kitchen, come on... we'll have a cup of tea and talk."

Gladdy spent the weekend with the family. Don was great at working to cheer her up, telling her funny stories of what was going on at the high school. Donna, Golda and Vivian showed up Saturday afternoon and took Gladdy and Don out to go roller skating. Gladdy was feeling much better, especially after the family went to church on Sunday. She had not been attending since she got the new job; she made excuses about not being able to find the right church downtown. She made herself a promise that it was time to find one; she needed God's strength now more than ever.

Chapter 11
June 1943

<u>In the Air</u>

"Can you imagine Lindbergh flying all this way alone? The boredom is enough to drive me nuts!" Hooper, the flight engineer, eased down out of the upper gun turret and stretched his back. Standing between the two pilots he could look out and see more than just the sky. "You know, sir, looking up isn't much worse than your view. But you do have the ocean, too."

"You ought to be happy we're not flying over your ocean, Hoop', said Lieutenant Wooster. "That one would take at least one stop to refuel and there aren't many islands in the middle of that body of water."

"Bombardier to pilot. Skipper, if you look out at about fifteen degrees relative, there's a convoy down there heading east."

"Thanks Weldon, we see them. Looks like about twenty ships with five, no, six escorts. Log their position and the time, navigator. With radio silence, we'll just report their location when we land." Gracy turned to Wooster and said, "John, can you take the controls? I've got to go take care of business and check on the crew." With that, he slid out of his seat and headed to the back of the aircraft, threading his way carefully through the bomb bay. He noticed the radioman was already trying to tune in to hear any radio traffic between the ships below. Murphy gave the pilot a thumbs up as he went by. The two waist gunners were lying down on some spare parachutes trying to get a few winks, without success. They both waved to Gracy as he continued to the "outhouse" next to the rear wheel well. Closing the lid when he was done, he was thankful they weren't at a higher altitude. It was tricky enough not to miss the hole with the plane's motion; it would be worse with urine freezing on the deck, too. He squatted and crawled to where he could just touch the rear gunner. Haskill was startled a bit when he was touched, having just dozed off. He waved over his shoulder, letting Gracy know he was fine.

On the way back, Gracy saw that Spike and Schultz were both looking out one waist gun window. Plugging into the intercom he heard the tail gunner's excitement, "...the hell. One of those ships down below just blew up, I tell you! Two of the escorts are changing course, too. Man, oh man, is that a fireball; must have been a tanker. Those flames are reaching up and up! Must have been a Kraut submarine that got her."

"Skipper, do you want me to circle back and have a look?"

"Negative. We've got their position and time. Nothing we can do anyhow; we're not to deviate from our schedule."

When he got back to the cockpit, Haskill returned to his turret saying, "Forget anything I said about boredom. I'll take this flight over being on one of those ships any day!"

The rest of their time in the air passed without further incident. The crew landed the plane in Scotland and, the next morning, flew it on to the staging area in England. There Gracy turned the plane over to a ground crew and reported in. He had been a bit nervous on the flight over; this plane was brand new, but he'd rather fly one he was familiar with. He wondered if they would receive another new one when they got a squadron assignment or some shot up, old wreck.

The rest of the crew was waiting when Gracy walked into the mess hall. Collins, the navigator, greeted him. "Powdered eggs and Spam; welcome to England."

When the crew of the "Lucky Lady" arrived in England, the war had been going on between the Axis and the British for nearly four years. Although the German Luftwaffe rarely made an appearance in English skies anymore, their army was still in France, only miles away across the Channel. Royal Air Force's Bomber Command was beginning to take the war to Germany, hitting the city of Dusseldorf with nearly 800 bombers in one night. The strategy of the RAF was known as area bombing; planes would fly individually, in a long stream stretching for hundreds of miles, coming in alone dropping their bombloads on a target city. The belief was that by hitting an entire city, the factories and the homes of the workers would all be destroyed, affecting production and morale together.

The American strategy was daylight precision bombing. This involved formations of planes flying together to afford greater protection against Luftwaffe fighters and striking against individual factories or railyards, inflicting maximum damage through pinpoint accuracy using the Norden bombsight. So far the Air Corps had launched limited raids against targets located mainly in occupied territories of France. Part of this was caused by the lack of range of escorting fighters, the 'Little Friends' as the bomber crews called them. Without fighter escort, the formations of bombers were at greater peril of suffering damage and loss at the hands of the experienced German fighter pilots.

Elsewhere in this 'world war', the Allied armies and navies were just beginning to turn the tide of victory from the Axis. Stalingrad, in Russia, had been a turning point in the East when the Soviet army defeated part of the German Wehrmacht after long months of deadly house-to-house fighting. More than 1.5 million casualties were suffered on both sides in this battle, including over 90,000 German prisoners of war; of these POW's less than 6,000 lived to return to their homes after the war. In the Pacific Ocean, Japanese forces had been driven off of Guadalcanal Island by the Americans and had also removed their troops from Kiska, in the Aleutian Islands, part of Alaska. The Japanese Navy was still very powerful and controlled most of the central Pacific and Indian

Oceans. The fighting in North Africa had just ended the month before when, in May, Allied armies had forced the surrender of the last German forces in Tunisia.

In England, American air and ground forces were arriving in great numbers in preparation of an invasion of Europe everyone knew had to happen before the war would end. When the Battle of Britain ended, Winston Churchill had said it was "not the beginning of the end, but the end of the beginning". The industrial potential of the United States was being realized as planes, ships, tanks and other weapons of war were beginning to arrive in astounding numbers.

Chapter 12
July 1943

<u>Minnesota</u>

The evening air was cooling down and made the water seem even warmer than it was. Gladdy, along with Golda, Donna and two of Dale's cousins had spent the afternoon at a beach on Lake Minnetonka. They were planning on getting some ice cream on the way home to The Park. It was a relaxing end to a rather hectic week at work for her.

Max had seemed on edge and grumpy, not responding in his normally nice way when Gladdy told him she couldn't have lunch with him the day before. When she thought a bit more about his attitude, the realization hit her that he had become increasingly short and testy in the past several weeks. He continued to press her to join him for dinners and lunches more often; she had agreed to lunch only once a week. He seemed to resent her explanation that there was more work to do now than ever and she needed the lunch time to keep up with the reports and surveys on the ever increasing number of new war plants being built and staffed. Real progress was being made in hiring and things seemed to be working out well.

Mr. Rarig, her boss, had picked Gladdy over Max to be a sort of liaison with a group of British RAF Officers who would be arriving for a tour of the Honeywell plant. The tour was of a new facility that was turning out parts for a new method of bombing. Rarig had told her it was "all hush, hush; you know, secret and all that. I figured that since your husband is a bombardier, you'll be the one to accompany them and show them a bit about the hiring and

47

everything we help with." Gladdy had thought it was sort of nonsense; what their agency did was not directly impacting the production of anything. However, she thought it would be infinitely more interesting than all this typing of reports. Max had not reacted well when he found out; he figured Rarig didn't pick him because he was 4-F and not fit for military duty.

The ice cream shop in Minnetonka Mills was still open and Gladdy had one of the best chocolate malts ever. It was a sweet treat she counted as a reward for the hard week. She and Don went for a walk through the neighborhood around the folk's house to enjoy the cool air. As they walked, Don noticed a dark car following them slowly, with the headlights off, a few houses behind. He was more curious than afraid and told Gladdy to keep walking. Don stopped and bent down, pretending to tie a shoe. The car came up just a bit closer and Don jumped up and ran toward it, in the street. The car lurched forward and swerved, actually trying to hit Don, who jumped out of the way at the last instant. Gladdy had turned at the noise and screamed when she saw the car nearly hit him. The car sped up past Gladdy; she couldn't see who was driving in the dark, but when the car turned ahead the driver braked to slow down. She noticed the left brake light didn't come on.

"Don, are you OK?" Gladdy ran up to her brother, who was sitting on the grass rubbing a knee.

"Yeah, sis, I'm fine. Hit my knee on the curb, it'll be alright. Did you get to see who that was? I think he was really trying to hit me. I only wanted to see who it was."

"Do you think we ought to phone the police from dad's house? I mean, things like this don't happen here, only in the movies. I wonder who on earth that was and what he wanted. I saw a hat on his head, but couldn't make out his face in the dark. Come on, let's get home. I'll be honest, this really scares me."

After the police had gone, Esther and Don went up to bed. Dautin and Gladdy sat with the last of the tea in their cups. "So you have no idea who might have been in the car? I wonder, with the work you do; having access to all the new war plants in the cities, you know. I don't want to make this scarier than it might really be, but..." Dautin was usually very level headed; Gladdy could see this was really bothering him.

"I'm sure I'll be OK. I'll tell my boss about it Monday and see what he thinks. I cannot believe some sinister foreign spies would trail me in The Park of all places. I mean, all I do is monitor hiring in these places."

"But, honey, don't forget that you GET IN to all those places. You see things you may not even know anything about, but you do see them. Look, forget I'm saying anything; it was probably some friend of Don's spying on him or something. You go on to bed; I'll clean up and see you in the morning. Good night."

Before she went to sleep, Gladdy took pen and paper and wrote about the evening's event to Dale. She downplayed most of it so he wouldn't worry; he certainly had enough on his mind fighting the war anyway. Her sleep was a bit restless; she couldn't get the picture of the car with the burned out brake light from her mind.

Monday morning Gladdy went in to speak with Frank Rarig. He seemed genuinely concerned with the story of the car. He made careful notes of everything she said and when Gladdy finished, he said he would look into it himself. Though a bit puzzled by this level of concern on his part, she felt relieved having told him.

"Now, let's see... oh my, the time. You and I have to get to Honeywell; we're to meet those RAF boys I was telling you about. I'll drive; why don't you grab a notebook and pen, OK?"

They arrived at the plant some 20 minutes later and met Group Captain Wallace, appointed by Churchill himself to coordinate technology sharing between the RAF and the Air Corps. A Group

Captain was equivalent to an Air Corps Colonel and Wallace was, in his fifties, fit and dashing in his uniform. His clipped accent was pleasant to the ear and his face brightened noticeably when Frank Rarig introduced Gladdy as the wife of an Air Corps bombardier.

"Splendid. I'm very pleased to meet your acquaintance, Mrs. Weldon. I trust time spent touring these factories will be pleasant and productive for the both of us."

"Thank you, Group Captain. It's an honor for me to be of assistance, in my small way, to the mission you and my husband share. Anything we can do to bring all our men home soon is an endeavor worthy of tireless effort."

"Well said, indeed, madam. I trust your command of language transfers equally to your writing? I admit that most Americans I've had the pleasure to speak with use a minimum of variety in their speech."

Both shared a laugh and another when they saw Frank trying to digest what they had just said. Gladdy was thankful for the studying she had done under the watchful eyes of those like Ethel Baston; people who felt language was an art form.

"Well, I can see I'm leaving you in good hands, Gladdy. I've got to get back to the office; when you're done here, call Max. He can come over and drive you back then. So long, Group Captain."

Chapter 13
August 1943

<u>England</u>

"OK, listen up. Because of the fine job we've done these past weeks, we're going to be one of the lead planes in training other newly arrived crews over here. I know we came to fight and I'm told we'll get the chance, plenty of them in fact, in time. Right now we have a different job to do. Let's get it done right so we can join in the real fighting we're itching for."

The groans and gripes of the rest of the crew took a minute to subside. Dale and Pat Collins were quiet, but they felt just like the others. They had joined up to get into action. They had both been through more than a year of training already; now the thought of training others instead of dropping bombs on Germany 'stuck in their craw' as Pat put it under his breath.

The Eighth Air Force was in a sort of transition; squadrons had been sent to the Mediterranean Theater to assist in the pre-invasion softening up of Sicily, the next stepping stone to Italy. Other squadrons, those containing B-24 Liberators, had taken part in a mission to bomb the oil fields of Ploesti in Romania. Those units equipped with B-17 Flying Fortresses combined to hit Regensburg and Schweinfurt in a double punch. The raid was nearly a disaster with 60 Flying Fortresses being lost out of 376 that were sent on the mission. Reorganization of the groups and squadrons was necessary by the end of the month. Additional training for newly arriving squadrons and the increase in the number of airfields used by the Air Corps required that some crews be made available as instructors.

Bob Gracy and his crew became a part of this new concept. To form up squadrons of twelve planes into groups of thirty or more in the air, often in the fog of England, and then form into ever larger groups before setting off for Germany, required strict adherence to flight plans. Each bomb group, consisting of four squadrons, had a very specific flight pattern and area in which to form up; gaining altitude and avoiding collisions with other aircraft. It could be nerve wracking work. On occasion two planes would come together in a huge fireball in the clouds, killing all 20 crewmen in both. Along with improving pilots' skills, Dale and Pat worked with squadron bombardiers and navigators to improve their abilities. Often targets were not visible due to cloud cover or smoke made by the enemy to hide factories. The use of ground radar and homing beacons were experiments allowing for 'blind bombing'; this worked better for the RAF and their area bombing than for the Air Corps' individual targets.

The bottom line was that the crew was getting plenty of flight time, but none of it counted toward getting them home in the short term. Only combat missions were counted in the 25 needed to rotate back to the States. All of them understood the importance of what they were doing; it wasn't a question of ignorance. What bothered them was the idea that this dangerous flying they were involved in would not get them finished earlier.

Chapter 14
September 1943

<u>Minnesota</u>

There's something irresistible about the unattainable; in this case it was driving Max crazy. He was beyond reason with the feelings he had for Gladdy. Focus on his work was nearly impossible of late. He had made a mistake a while back and knew he couldn't do something so stupid again. He could not understand why she refused to even go to dinner with him now. He'd tried being nice and polite and patient. As he looked at himself in the mirror he vowed, 'Not next time'; and he knew there would be another opportunity.

The RAF officers had nearly completed their tours of the various plants in the area. Max himself hadn't really given thought to how many new factories there were. Gladdy and that Group Captain had been together, smiling and joking with each other as they were lead around by plant managers and owners; while Max trailed behind like some forgotten servant. His only duties seemed to be keeping track of the employment numbers and reminding the managers of their responsibilities in reporting to the Commission on time. The idea that this was his job escaped him. All he felt was jealousy over the attention she paid to the funny talking, snooty, uniformed Englander. Tomorrow night things would change, yes sir. He and Gladdy were to drive back to Minneapolis after touring the new ammunition plant being built down near Farmington. Max had already driven the route a couple of times and knew just where he could pull off the road, stop the car and .....

"I say, Max. Do you have the numbers you chaps keep track of for this project for the past few months? I'd appreciate having them so we can plan on what we'll need to start up a similar work back in Wales."

Max brought himself back into the real world. Fumbling through his briefcase he pulled out the file on the plant and said, "Sure thing. I've got them and I'll get you copies tomorrow before we leave for Farmington." Nothing but a forgotten servant, that's all.

That afternoon Gladdy sat in her dorm room reading a letter from Dale. It explained his predicament and feelings about not being in combat and the impact it would have on the time they would be apart. He also said he finally got up to London and had picked up 'a few things' that he would be sending in a package for her and thanked her for the treats she and his mom sent. He wrote that the cookies had arrived all broken into crumbs but the crew enjoyed them immensely in bowls of fresh cream the ball turret gunner had gotten from his English girlfriend.

She put down the letter after reading it several more times. She thought of what she would write to Dale the next evening after the final tour with the Group Captain. She had enjoyed the time with the RAF people more than any other work she had ever done. Turning out the light she slipped under the covers and thought of her husband as she fell asleep.

The ground area of the unfinished new ammunition plant was immense. Several large farms had been bought by the government for the site. It used to be some of the finest land around; some said the price paid was far too low and the former owners were taking the buyer to court in protest. The plant was already months behind its construction schedule and no one seemed to know if it would ever actually produce anything. Group Captain Wallace was amazed at the imagined cost of it; he was more astounded at the ability of a country to spend that much and, perhaps, get no return for the money. He had been told about the plant and wanted to see it. Frank Rarig relented even though his

Commission had no work to do there yet. The construction companies did not fall under his authority, but as a favor to the State Department, he sent Gladdy and Max down as escorts.

A few hours later it was time to leave and return to Minneapolis. Group Captain Wallace suggested that they all meet later that evening at the St Paul Hotel for dinner in the restaurant there. He said it was his way of thanking Gladdy, and Max, for their assistance and kind hospitality during the mission. He let them know that Frank and the others that worked at the Commission office would be there as well.

Gladdy and Max got in his car and led the way. As the sun went down and sky grew darker, Max began to drive a little faster and the headlights of the other car became dimmer in the mirror.

"Max, would you mind slowing down just a bit? I don't think the Group Captain's driver feels as comfortable as you do on our roads; I'm sure he doesn't remember the way back by himself." Gladdy tried hard not to let her annoyance with Max come through in her voice. These past days he had been acting more and more in ways that made her feel uncomfortable in his presence.

"Hmmmph" was all she got as a response. Max turned sharply onto a side road as they passed through Rosemount. "I know a shortcut."

"Max, stop the car. The other driver does not know any such shortcut. You're beginning to scare me with your driving." Gladdy was not kidding; he was frightening her badly.

Max sped up just a bit and made two more turns; Gladdy didn't have any idea where they were. She was really concerned now and slid over, right up against the passenger door. "I just want time to clean up before dinner", Max said. "This will get us there faster." He knew she probably didn't believe that, but he needed just a few more minutes before he was at the place he wanted.

He turned onto another road, passing through the stop sign at the corner and throwing dirt and gravel as he skidded just a bit in the turn. Gladdy knew he went around the corner that fast so she wouldn't try to leave the car at the stop. A red light came up from behind and a siren began to sound. Gladdy let out an audible sound of relief.

"Don't say or do anything and I won't hurt you." Max looked over at her with a face so determined, so full of anger, that all she could do was nod her assent.

The officer walked up to the side of the car as Max rolled down his window. The brightness of a flashlight filled the front seat of the car. "May I see your driver's license, sir? You're going a bit fast, just went through a stop sign and your left brake light is not working."

Gladdy turned to Max and cried out, "It was you!" She opened her door and got out as quickly as she could. The officer stood up, dropped his flashlight and went for his gun. Max stepped on the gas and the car sped away, throwing gravel behind; the policeman had his gun out, running to his car. He got in and radioed the car's description to the dispatcher in Rosemount. Gladdy didn't move; she felt frozen to the spot where she stood. The officer got back out of his car and said to Gladdy, "Stand where you are." Noticing the bewildered and frightened look on her face, he asked "Are you alright miss?

England

At that precise moment Dale woke up. He lay for an instant and listened to his heart beating fast. Thinking it must have been some dream, he got up and went to the latrine. Afterward, splashing water on his face, he couldn't get the feeling out of his mind; something's happened or is about to. He went back to his bunk and laid down, unable to sleep. Joe Collins woke up, "Man, it's still hours until wake up call; try to get to sleep."

56

"Sorry, Joe, I've just got this funny feeling like something bad just happened. I don't know what it is. I'll be OK in a minute; go back to sleep."

Dale hadn't shaken the feeling as they were eating; powdered eggs, some kind of oatmeal porridge and a sausage that Joe was convinced was not made from any animal he could think of.

"Hey, I've got it. Maybe we'll find out today what squadron we're going to get. It's been too long since we started this gig. I bet we're going into action; come on, that's what it is. Look, we missed the raid to Regensburg and Schweinfurt; that's OK 'cause it was a bad one. But the RAF just leveled Hamburg and we're still not flying against the enemy. This is really starting to get to me."

"Starting to get to you? You've been grousing about this for quite awhile. I'm sure Gracy is letting the *brass* know we want in on the action. We'll get our turn; what we're doing here is important. I just don't like being away from the States without feeling like I'm a real part of this thing."

Gracy stuck his head in the mess door, looked around and saw them. He walked quickly over with a grin on his face. "OK you two, listen up. We're finished with this squadron in a few days; probably have two more flights practicing forming up. I just got the Colonel's promise that one more, only one more, squadron and then we join that one when we're through. I guess he figures we'll give our best to the group we'll be flying with over Germany."

"Well, a yippee yahoo for that! It means we'll have our first real mission under our belt before Armistice Day. I think I'll have another of those 'mystery meat' sausages to celebrate." Collins had a way with words.

Minnesota

"I'm Frank Rarig; you called and said you needed to see me?"

The police sergeant nodded and led Frank back into a detective's office. Gladdy was sitting with a cup of coffee in her hands, looking quite shaken up. The detective stood up and extended his hand.

"Lieutenant Withers, Rosemount district. You must be her boss? Thanks for coming down, I know the late hour and all. We need you to verify her identity; her purse with everything in it, apparently was left in the car." Withers proceeded to fill Frank in on all that had happened, based on what Gladdy had told him.

Frank was shocked. "Max? Max did that? Do you have any idea where he might be now?"

"No sir. We've put out a state wide alert for him and the car. He'll show up eventually. In the meantime, if everything Mrs Weldon has said is true, and I believe it is, he's still a threat to her."

"Lieutenant, if it's alright with you, I'll take Gladdy home. She's welcome to stay at my house; my wife's there and we'll see she's safe for tonight. I think, given the circumstances, I'll make a call to the FBI if you don't mind; this does involve foreign military personnel and my boss will want the Bureau to know about this."

"Frank, what about the Group Captain. When Max was driving crazy, we lost their car. Have you heard from them at all?" Gladdy was thinking with her business mind again.

"I called the St Paul Hotel as soon as I heard about this; you know, to explain why we wouldn't be there. I was told by the front desk that they were back at the Hotel, but didn't actually speak with Wallace. Lieutenant, you have my home number; will you please call me if you hear anything more? Do you have a phone I could use now?"

A few minutes later Frank and Gladdy were on the road back to his house in Mendota. Frank was still puzzled about Max and his

58

behavior. Gladdy opened up and told him all about Max pestering her about dinners out and the night in The Park with Don and the mysterious car.

"I was scared nearly out of my mind with what was going on. Then the policeman stopped us; when he said the brake light was out, I knew. It all came in a flash and I had to get out of the car. I could cry when I think of what he was planning; I did cry in the police car. I'm still feeling frightened over this ordeal."

"Gladdy, you've been through too much for anyone tonight. I'll have my wife settle you in the guest room and make sure the office is safe when we arrive in the morning."

When they arrived at the Commission office the next day, two men were already there waiting for them. Gladdy knew, without first hearing an introduction, they were from the FBI. To her it was like a scene out of the movie 'Public Enemy Number One' or something.

"Mr Rarig, Mrs Weldon; I'm Agent Roberts and this is Agent Kline, Federal Bureau of Investigation. We have some new information about last evening."

"Certainly, gentlemen; a cup of coffee while we talk?" Frank motioned to his secretary and the coffee was there in a minute.

Agent Roberts told them that Max's car had been found parked at the edge of a bluff overlooking the Mississippi River near the Ford assembly plant in St Paul. It was a spot used by 'jumpers'; people killing themselves. That was not all the news, however. When Frank had first called the Bureau a warrant to search Max's apartment was obtained. Agent Kline had found copies of handwritten notes about the war plants the Commission visited; notes that went far beyond employment statistics. There were also photographs; Kline had found Max's briefcase. In it there was a hidden camera that could be used to take pictures without anyone knowing.

59

"Mr Rarig, we have reason to believe Max Brenner may be working for a foreign government. There's enough evidence to charge him with espionage. Is there anything he's said, or done, that would lead you to believe he might be involved in something like that?"

"No, nothing I can think of at the moment. I'll have his personnel files brought in and copies made for your investigation. I can think of nothing he's done or said; it's hard to imagine the guy involved in anything like that."

Gladdy was completely shocked by the revelation that she may have been working with a spy all this time. A shiver went down her spine when she recalled the events of the last day. What was going through his mind?

"We'll have the river below the Ford plant dragged. Most of the time if bodies are found, they've been miles downstream according to the police." Agent Rogers was talking. "Mrs Weldon, is Mr Weldon aware of what's happening? We'd like to speak with him if that's possible."

"My husband is in the Air Corps in England. He's a bombardier over there and I'm not quite sure how to get hold of him. We write each other nearly every day, but I haven't seen him since the day after our wedding in March."

"Well, I sincerely hope he's fine and you'll have a happy homecoming one day. You may want to tell him about your own part in this war when you see him. If Max is connected with foreign powers, he faces a death sentence. That is, if he's still alive."

"You mean, you don't think he killed himself?" Frank had to sit down; all of this was getting to be a bit too much.

"Well, if I wanted to throw someone off my trail, it's the first thing I'd try." was Roger's response. "If he's really doing this, and I think he is; he won't be back to his apartment. He'll know we're watching it. My guess is he's contacted whoever he works for and will lay low awhile. Just the same, we need to make sure Mrs Weldon is safe. Is there anywhere you can stay that Max doesn't know about?"

Chapter 15
October 1943

<u>England</u>

"Lieutenant Gracy? The Colonel will see you now."

Gracy walked into the Group Commander's office, snapped to attention in front of his desk and saluted. Colonel Bowman returned the salute and put him at ease.

"Pleased to meet you Gracy. You and your crew have done a fine job up to now; I have faith that you'll be as successful with the 615th Squadron. After you lead them through their indoctrination here, you'll become part of it yourself I understand. Glad to have you with us."

"Thank you, sir. I know my crew will agree with me; we're itching to get into this fight. It's been a bit hard to watch others fighting while we've been here. We'll do our best, sir."

The officers and aircrews had begun arriving the day before. The ground *echelons* and support units would be following in about a week by troop transport ship. They were stationed at a small village called Deenethorpe, northwest of London. Training for the aircrews would begin as soon as possible. The 401st Bomb Group was made up of the 612th, 613th, 614th and 615th Squadrons; they had been trained in Great Falls, Montana, before crossing the Atlantic.

The men in the Group came from all across the United States; gunners who had just graduated from high school, mechanics that learned their trade by working on their own jalopies back home. One pilot had been a barber; another had actually worked as a bush pilot in Alaska Territory, flying hunters and mail to remote lodges in the wilderness. There was a lifeguard on a southern California beach who was now a bombardier and a former racing jockey flew as a ball turret gunner.

After the weeks spent perfecting formation flying, the Group was ready for their first mission. The officers were awoken at 0400 by that soon to be familiar flashlight in the face. Breakfast was at 0430; real eggs with sausage and warm bread. You got real eggs in the mess hall when a mission was on. Briefings began at 0500 with the pilots, navigators and bombardiers all instructed on time sequences, headings, weather patterns and all the other details they would need to know. Today's target was the port of Bremen in northwest Germany.

The lead plane, flown by Colonel Bowman himself, took off at 0800; by 0900 sixteen planes of the twenty assigned for this mission were in the air. Four planes failed to make it off the ground; one rolled just off the runway during taxi and managed to trap another piloted by the 615th's skipper, Major Seawell, behind it. There was a collision in the air as a B-17 from another group came up beneath "Fancy Nancy" and cut off the ball turret, killing the gunner. The aircraft were both able to land, but were damaged too badly to ever fly again, creating a ready supply of spare parts.

As Dale sat with Pat Collins in the nose of ""Lucky Lady"", he couldn't get a song out of his head. They had been invited to a dance the night before and a Royal Navy band had been playing. Their rendition of "Doin' the Jive" was great; if he closed his eyes, the music was Glenn Miller and the singers became the Four Modernairs. "Clap your hands, and you swing out wide; do a Suzy Q, mix in a step or two, put it all together and you're doin' the jive..." He enjoyed the music but ached inside, missing Gladdy. Dale had to work hard at focusing on the mission right now.

"Fighters at two o'clock level, looks like they're swinging in to take us in the nose." This was the top turret gunner and his words were punctuated by the staccato of his guns as he opened fire on the enemy. Several minutes later there was, amid the calm voices and barking of the guns, a high pitched "Yahoo, I got me one"; it was Wilson, their own ball turret gunner. "Well, I guess all you Yankees owe me a beer." The bomb run was full of flak, but nearly all of it came up short and well below their own altitude. All in all it was, as they would come to describe it, "eight hours of pure boredom punctuated by several minutes of absolute terror".

The Group lost no planes to enemy action that day. There would not be too many more with so little cost.

Chapter 16
November 1943

<u>Minnesota</u>

The table was set, every inch taken by dishes. It was built for six but there were ten place settings today on the dining room table alone. As everyone came in and sat, elbow to elbow, someone joked it was well they were all right handed; there would be no room for a southpaw. As host, Dautin asked a blessing on the food.

"Thank you, Lord, for the bounty you provide for us. We thank you as well for your protection and watchful care over our loved ones. Be with Dale and all the other boys as they are in foreign lands fighting to maintain our freedoms. Let them all know we are thinking of them as we celebrate this day of Thanksgiving. Amen"

As Gladdy looked up she saw a tear on Dautin's cheek. She took hold of his hand and gave it a squeeze to thank him. Dale's folks were hosting a large part of the family this year on the holiday. It was a joy to see everyone; with the war and gas rationing, visiting was a special event in itself. Gladdy's sisters were here, along with Dale's aunts, uncles and the cousins not old enough to be in the military. The variety of food was amazing, considering there was a war on; wild goose, duck, venison accompanied by mounds of potatoes, cabbage and carrots. There was hardly room for the pies and other desserts.

After the meal, the men and boys retired to the living room and talk soon turned to remembering the football game they had gone to at the University of Minnesota back in 1941. It seemed like ages ago, not a scant two years. Now Dale, Dick, Bobby and Gladdy's own brother Bob were scattered around the world fighting the enemy in Europe and the Pacific. The tide of war was turning; 1943 had seen horrendous fighting, in the air above Germany, on the ground in Italy and on the ocean and islands of the Pacific. Just a few days before, news that the Marines had landed on Tarawa and Makin Islands was released; the combat was ferocious with more casualties than anyone could imagine. A neighbor of Dautin and Esther had learned yesterday that their son had died when his ship was torpedoed by a German submarine. Every person at today's dinner was aware of at least one person they knew being killed or wounded in the past couple of months. All of them were also sure that 1944 would bring an invasion of Europe in France or the Low Countries to gain control of the continent from the Nazis.

Dale had often written to Gladdy of life for him in England. He told her of the double-decked busses in London and the different sounds of the train whistles. He did not write of the missions he had flown, nor did he mention the friends he had seen die as other planes around him blew up in huge fireballs from direct flak hits, or those that slowly spun down towards the earth as they were shot up by German fighters. Those were details of his daily life he would not share with her. She did not need him to tell her, either; she had seen one of their high school classmates when he returned from the air war. He was a gunner in B-24s assigned to a different Group and had come back after only four missions as a mumbling, drooling mess who screamed and tried to hide at any sudden noise. It was commonly known as 'shell-shock', though it had a longer medical name. His mother had asked Gladdy to visit him at the Veteran's Home because they had been good friends in school; she had hoped he somehow would improve at the sight and touch of a friend. He was the only survivor of a plane blown apart by flak over France; the plane had disintegrated around him. He was found and rescued by a trawler off the coast, floating in his *Mae West*, his head and hair still covered with the insides of another crewman. Gladdy did not need Dale to tell her of the horrors he was seeing up there; when she wrote him of seeing their friend she only mentioned that he was wounded. Now she prayed for Dale and his safe return constantly.

A couple of weeks earlier Gladdy had moved in with Dale's family when she was told by the FBI that Max had been found; his body washed up on shore down river from the Ford plant. They identified him through papers found on the body and felt the case was closed and Gladdy's life could return to normal. She wondered if 'normal', in 1943, was having your true love away risking his life day after day while you tried to stop looking over your shoulder all the time.

England

"Give 'em each a double shot, Doc. After what they saw up there they probably deserve more, but you know the Army." The Major strode purposefully away after saying these words to the medic that was dispensing the brandy ration at the beginning of the post-mission briefing.

The crew were quiet, each barely able to control his emotions. One wrong comment and they all would have 'gone off'. Pat Collins, their navigator, was in the worst shape; he was still shaking and hadn't been able to change out of his flight suit yet. It was stiff with the blood of one of the waist gunners, Henry Schultz.

The briefing officer took a little extra time getting ready to write down all the details. Every one of the crew lit up Lucky Strikes, even the ones who didn't smoke. "Alright, let's get going with the report" he said, after he had shuffled the papers around long enough.

Bob Gracy began; "We took off on time, formed up and had no problems until the 'little friends' left us just before the Kraut border. Then all hell broke loose. Me-109's and Fw-190's were everywhere; so many it was useless even calling them out on the intercom. Where we were positioned we actually had it a bit easier, maybe, I don't know.... Anyway, a swarm, maybe six or seven fighters concentrated on "Betty's Boop" right alongside us. It seems like a cannon shell must have hit the bomb bay or something; she went from a plane to nothing but a flash and debris in an instant. The explosion was so violent I had a hard time controlling our plane for a second. Then another '17', I don't know which one, flew through the fireball and came out the front side with an engine already smoking and the entire nose missing. That's when I saw the bombardier, or maybe the navigator, fall out with no chute on." Bob dropped his head and sighed.

John Wooster continued. "That's about the time a '190' came in on us from straight ahead. The top turret was blazing at him when he dropped down; I thought we were going to collide; don't really know how we missed. Well, he went down smoking and the ball turret reported the pilot had bailed out. Things were quiet for a minute or so when a Messerschmitt came in from below. I could feel his rounds hitting our belly and heard a voice on the intercom. I called the ball turret gunner but got no answer. That's when I told Collins to go aft and see what was up."

Gracy took up the story again. "Collins went back there and found Spike and Schultz all shot up. Spike was picking his own hand up off the deck; Schultz had one arm blown clean off and the other was barely attached. Collins tried to get Schultz's suit off so he could, you know, treat his wounds. The kid bled to death right there; maybe twenty seconds. Collins got Murphy, our radioman, to help put a tourniquet on Spike's arm and bandage him up. Then he plugged into the intercom to tell me what was going on; I told him to check on Wilson, the ball turret gunner, 'cause I hadn't heard from him. Well, Collins opened the hatch to the ball turret and.... there was nothing there. Nothing. I don't know if he was killed by the fighter or fell or what.... he's dead, for sure. You know they don't wear a chute in the ball. Man, oh man; what a mission."

The briefing officer looked at Collins; normally the navigator would speak after the pilots. Pat was just staring through him with a vacant 'I'm not here' kind of expression. Dale took over the debriefing. "We got to the IP alright, didn't fall out of formation or anything. I tried to open the bomb bay doors; they were stuck shut. When I got back to them to try and force them open I could see they were all shot to pieces and couldn't be opened. We landed with the full load; it's a miracle none of the bombs went off right there, or on the landing. The rest of the mission went by in a blur; we had a little flak. Otherwise nothing to report."

When they were done; the squadron flight surgeon came over and told them they were being stood down. They were not to fly until he was satisfied they were alright. No one complained or said a single word. Dale thought to himself, "Fourth mission and we've already lost three crewmen. How are we going to make it to twenty-five?"

Chapter 17
December 1943

<u>Minnesota</u>

"Hi, Dad. I thought you might like some company and a ride home tonight. I've got one of the Commission's cars for the weekend; I have to go tomorrow and visit a war plant in Minnetonka out by the lake. Hop in; we can surprise Mother by getting home early for once."

It was not often that Gladdy had the use of a car now that gasoline rationing was tightening up a little. She even had to schedule two, sometimes three, visits in a single day to help conserve fuel. Some things were getting harder to find 'than a hen's tooth' as her own family would say. She yearned for a new pair of silk stockings, even a nice pair of nylon would do. One of the girls she worked with used leg paint in attempting to look dressed properly. Gladdy had taken to wearing slacks on days she visited the plants; that served two purposes. First, they were easier to keep clean and, secondly they helped keep down the comments and whistles of the men. Besides, dressed that way she looked like one of the ever increasing numbers of working women in the war plants. Business owners were finding many benefits in having them in the workforce; attendance and productivity were up a great deal in those facilities hiring women and minorities. Apparently there were advantages to having workers that actually wanted to be employed! Why, even her old 'buddy' Lou Nesterman, the manager at the first plant she had visited, was happy at the increased output of his department. He actually seemed much nicer to Gladdy when she visited the plant, though he still tried to get her to 'visit his office' every time she showed up.

She was more relaxed now, having put the entire 'Max affair' as she called it, behind her. Living with her in-laws was pretty convenient; a good home cooked meal each evening and someone to ride with on the trolley to and from work on most days. Dautin had been able to change his schedule by an hour just so they could commute together. He was such a considerate, loving man. She was so thankful to have a loving and caring family. Don especially went out of his way to help her; he said it was his duty in helping the war effort. Gladdy knew he had a strong desire to be a part of the real fighting; he was still too young and she could sense it grated on him.

Her own sisters were all engaged now. Vivian, the youngest, had snagged herself a sailor, though he was away in the engine room of a destroyer out in the Pacific somewhere. Donna also had chosen the Navy to supply her with a fiancée; Golda had held out for a Marine. She didn't know it but her boyfriend was getting ready to go ashore with the First Marine Division at Cape Gloucester in the invasion of New Britain. Gladdy had received a letter a few days earlier from her brother Bob. He was just arriving in England when he wrote it; Gladdy was sure there was little chance of him running into Dale. Bob was a sergeant in a machine gun company in the Third Army.

That Saturday, Gladdy brought Don with her as she drove out to the new ammunition plant in Minnetonka. It was not easy getting Don inside; until the production manager showed up and recognized him from the gun range. It was like watching two old friends as they went off on a tour while Gladdy attended to her business, collecting data and interviewing some of the new hires. On the way back home she was thinking how swell it was that her life was returning to a more normal pace, even with the feeling that 1944 would be a hard year of fighting for the entire country. Right now she planned on making the most of this Christmas with as much family as was still around.

That evening Dautin and Esther joined Don and Gladdy as they sat to listen to a few favorite radio programs. There was a special Christmas broadcast with music from Glenn Miller, now an officer in the Air Corps, and his military band. Word was out that Captain Miller would soon be taking his music to England to entertain the increasing number of American troops there. The mixture of military tunes and traditional Christmas favorites was nice to listen to as the snow fell outside and the wind blew. Esther had made a large pitcher of hot chocolate, a real treat now, and buttered toast sprinkled with cinnamon for dunking.

For the first time Gladdy, or Don for that matter, could remember, Dautin spoke of his time in France during The Great War. He spoke of the excitement of the young Americans arriving to win the war that France and England had been waging against Germany for so long. Without going into detail, he even told stories of life in the trenches. Don prompted him once again, to tell of how he had met Esther over there.

"Well, let me see. It was in early August of 1918 and we had just launched an offensive against the Boche, the Germans. It was 'up and over', out of the trenches and into that stretch between our lines and the enemy's; through the barbed wire, over and through all the craters from their bombs and artillery shells. I had gone about fifty yards when a shell landed just ahead; it exploded with a kind of 'whumfff' sound and a gray cloud of what looked like smoke. It wasn't smoke. I reached for my gas mask when I got hit by two machine gun bullets, one in each leg. Well, there was no standing around after that, I can tell you. I went down like a sack of potatoes and only reached my mask and got it on after taking one breath of that terrible stuff. My mouth, throat, eyes and lungs were burned; not enough to kill me but it sure put me out of action for a couple of weeks. I was brought to a French hospital with my eyes wrapped shut. For the first week all I remember was the angelic sound of this one nurse's voice when she would speak to me or read me a letter from home. I couldn't wait for the bandages on my eyes to come off; I so wanted to see the face of that angel. Well, sir, the day arrived and the voice was there

72

speaking and telling me to wait a few minutes after the doctor unwrapped my eyes before I opened them, to get used to the light. Her voice grew quiet as the light flooded in, even through my closed lids. Finally I opened my eyes and there was this mule faced, old hag; I tell you she was a fright to see! Your mother had moved to another bed just before that moment and another nurse, an old French woman, had taken her place. Well, I was shocked to say the least; I thought it might have been better to have breathed in more of that gas. A moment later this other nurse turned from the soldier next to me and asked if I could see anything yet. Recognizing that angelic tone once again, I turned and there she was; more beautiful than I had even imagined. The rest is history, including you and your husband, our first son. And you, too" he said as he roughed up Don's hair with a smile.

It was the most wonderful story Gladdy had ever heard. She hugged Dautin hard around the neck and gave Esther one for good measure. Somehow the cocoa and toast tasted even sweeter after the story.

<u>England</u>

"OK, so who's it going to be? One of us has to tell Wilson's girlfriend about him. I had to write the letters home on him and Schultz. I'd really appreciate someone else going out to the farm to find and tell her." Gracy was rubbing his head as he said it. As pilot, it was his responsibility to do these things; writing letters notifying families when a crewman was killed or wounded.

"Heck, Gracy, Dale and I'll go out there. I don't think Pat's in any shape to do it anyhow." So it was that Dale and John Wooster, the co-pilot, found themselves on bicycles on this cold, wet, foggy English day; they were trying to find the farm where Alice Wender lived with her parents. Alice had met Henry Schultz at a community dance weeks earlier and the two had hit it off immediately. Alice would send little things along with Henry when he returned from visiting her; things like a couple of sausages made from real hogs, or a meal of mutton and a few fresh

73

vegetables, mainly potatoes. It was usually just enough for each man of the ""Lucky Lady"" to have a bite; more of a tease than real relief from the army chow. All of the guys appreciated her thoughtfulness, though. Without anyone else finding out, they had even arranged for her to get a short flight in the plane one day. Gracy made sure everyone understood that this would <u>never</u> happen again, no matter who the girl might be or how pretty she was!

They found the farm on the third try; the first two had given them directions they could hardly understand, let alone follow. It was a mud colored frame house with a thatched roof; two smaller buildings were nearby. Smoke was curling out of the chimney and the cold mist was letting up as they rode to the door. A small, bent over man answered; his hands were three sizes too big for his body and he had the look of many years of hard work to him. "Name's Wender. Can I help you blokes?"

"Yes sir, I hope so. We're wondering if Alice is at home? We're part of the aircrew with Sergeant Schultz."

"Come in, get out of this wet. You can dry by the fire while I get Alice." There was just a hint of friendliness in his voice but his expression didn't change at all.

A few minutes later Alice had come in and their duty was over. Dale was relieved that John had done nearly all the talking; he wasn't sure how he would have told her. It helped that she seemed to guess the purpose of their visit when she saw them. She cried softly as they told her, sparing her the details. They left her with some of his things; a set of sergeant chevrons, a photo of the two of them and all the money they had found in his foot locker. Schultz was a pretty accomplished poker player and they felt Alice and her family could put the dollars to good use.

The ride back to the base took less time with the sun breaking through the overcast and Mr Wender's instructions on how to get there directly. Back in his room, Dale immediately penned a letter to Gladdy about the whole episode.

Dearest Shorty,

This is a letter I never want to write again. Two of our men, Schultz and Wilson, were killed on our last mission and another, Spike, is badly wounded. I'm fine as are the rest of the crew. We were attacked by German fighters during our flight to the target and made it back to base alright, except for those three. We've been ordered not to fly for a short time, maybe a week or so. John Wooster and I just got back from having to tell Schultz's English girlfriend about him; probably the hardest thing I've ever been a part of. Darling, please don't let this worry you too much. I know you realize the dangers over here are very real but I feel, I know, I'll be coming home in one piece. I don't know exactly how it is, but I KNOW IT'S TRUE! Bob, Pat, John and I are going up to London for a few days to blow off a little steam, as Pat puts it. I'll be careful, as always, and will be sure to let the English *birds* alone. I listened to the Andrews Sisters yesterday singing "Don't Sit Under the Apple Tree" and it made me think of you and how much I love you. You, and I suppose Mom, Dad and Don, are the reasons I'm over here doing what I'm doing. When this job is done and it's safe to come home, I'll be the first in line to get there. I miss you. Give my love to everyone there and a big hug for Mom. Save a few for yourself.... Love, Dale

Chapter 18
January 1944

<u>Minnesota</u>

"Mom, would you like some more help tonight at the USO club? I think I'd like to tag along and pour coffee or hand out a doughnut or two." Gladdy was a little anxious to do something to keep herself busy. Esther was glad for the help, which also came with a ride as Gladdy drove her government car.

The evening was a fairly typical one for the USO. A fine local dance band was warming up when they arrived at the club; the music put a spring in the step of the ladies as they set up serving tables and chairs around the dance floor. Hot chocolate, plenty of coffee, piles of donuts and even a couple of donated cakes gave the place a real party atmosphere. As the club opened, one older lady mentioned to another that it was funny how the line leading to Gladdy's hot chocolate station was so much longer than anyone else's.

"Just wait until they hear she's the wife of an officer. That line will disappear faster than the Invisible Man getting undressed. That's the truth for sure."

Gladdy was pouring hot cocoa into cups as fast as she could when Golda, Donna and Vivian walked up. All three were laughing at the sight of their sister surrounded by soldiers, sailors and marines. The three waded into the throng and began to take some of the pressure off Gladdy by asking the men to dance, several at a time. A short while later more young women showed up and Gladdy was able to sit down and take a break to the

76

amusement of the older women. By the end of the evening she had also danced with dozens of young servicemen, politely informing each that she was, in fact, married to an Air Corps officer.

Christmas and New Year's had not been the festive interludes they once were. Most of the family had gone to Uncle Roy and Aunt Min's place for dinner; with so many of the boys not there it had turned into a quieter party than anyone anticipated. The same held true for New Year's Day when the men gathered around and listened to the Rose Bowl football game. Because of the war related travel restrictions the Big Ten Conference team could not go to Pasadena for the game. It was played between USC and Washington; the Trojans beat up on the Huskies, winning 29-0. The few who listened on in Dautin's living room were not at all enthusiastic about the game or conversation in general.

In addition to attending church regularly, Gladdy had determined to help with the war effort in more ways; besides helping Esther at the USO she was on the neighborhood committee organizing another scrap drive. These were not as successful as the early efforts of 1942 when Minneapolis and St Paul had held huge city-wide contests which resulted in tons of rubber, metal and paper being collected. Now a good effort might get a couple hundred pounds of paper and four or five tires along with a few boxes of crushed cans and scrap metal. It did, however, remind folks that there was a war on.... as if people needed a reminder. Pretty much everything from butter to tobacco were rationed, using a myriad of confusing stamps and coupons. Because Gladdy worked for the government and drove to the various war plants, gasoline was not a big problem. She did not smoke or drink so those items weren't missed either. Like many other younger women, she also found it a bit easier to maintain her slender figure; there wasn't a surplus of things to eat to put on much weight.

Work was what kept her busy. With the war plants humming at near capacity and new ones coming on line, her responsibility of monitoring the staffing was becoming enormous. The Federal Arms plant up near Anoka, built during the First World War, was expanding and turning out huge amounts of ammunition. Their workforce alone had more than doubled since Pearl Harbor. The Commission had two new monitors working alongside Gladdy, but the work load was ever increasing. Some days she found herself at her desk typing up reports hours after she should have left for home. Dautin and Esther expressed concern, often, that she was going to wear herself out; Gladdy smiled and said it kept her "mind off other things".

Chapter 19
February 1944

<u>England</u>

"Lieutenant, these are the new guys. Sergeant Ron Adams, waist gunner, Sergeant Bill Williams, ball turret and Sergeant Tom Banks, waist gunner. Men, this is Lieutenant Dale Weldon, our bombardier. You wouldn't happen to know where Lieutenant Collins is by chance, would you? I'd like our new gunners to meet all the officers before we go up in the morning for our first flight with them." Gracy had three new men in tow that all looked like they were about 17 years of age.

"No, sir; the last I saw of him was noon, at chow. You might try the chapel; he's been spending more and more of his free time there, Captain."

"Thank you, Lieutenant. Men, if you'll follow me."

Dale was concerned for Pat Collins, their navigator. Since the last mission, when they lost the three gunners, Collins had not been his light hearted self. He had become grumpy, irritable and short with people. Everybody seemed to think it was pretty normal and that he'd come around with the time off of flying that they'd been given. That mission was three weeks ago; the Squadron had flown eight times since then. It was nice not facing the flak or the Luftwaffe, but it also meant they would be here longer before finishing their tour of 25 missions when they could rotate back to the States. Most of the crew was ready now to resume their duties and get flying again. Now that they had new men to replace Schultz, Spike and Wilson, Dale knew it would only be a few days at most before they were back over Germany.

Pat Collins was, indeed, in the chapel. It seemed to be the only place he could find any peace of late. Even the sound of the B-17's on the flight line warming up was enough to make him break into a cold sweat. This morning he woke up shaking, his hands clenched into tight fists and found himself chewing his own tongue. He didn't want to let the others down by reporting to sick call; that would make him seem, somehow, like a coward or a mental case. He prayed that God would give him back his courage and be able to function normally in the air when they flew. On his way out of the chapel, he saw Captain Gracy approaching with three enlisted men he didn't recognize. A cold chill went up his spine and he felt his hands start to clench. He forced himself to relax enough to keep walking.

"Lieutenant Collins, hey Lieutenant, over here. You preoccupied or something? I want you to meet our new gunners, Sergeants Adams, Williams and Banks. They'll be joining us tomorrow morning; we've been given two practice flights to get our heads together again before an actual mission. We'll be going up after the Squadron leaves, right around 1030 hours. I just hope the "Lucky Lady" hasn't been mistreated by the other crews while we were stood down. See you tonight at the Officers' Club, Pat?"

"Don't think so, sir. If we're flying in the morning, I'd like to go over a few things and then get some sack time. I'll see you at briefing."

As Collins walked away, Gracy watched him and shook his head. He was glad they were allowed a couple of practice flights. He wasn't feeling good about his navigator; he would have to keep a close eye on him.

The next morning the sky was clear and the sun felt warm; the first such day since before Thanksgiving, if you asked anybody. The crew assembled at the briefing room and headed out to their plane just as the last of the other Flying Fortresses took off on their mission for the day; they would bomb a factory in Dijon, France. The "Lucky Lady" took off on time and Gracy ran everyone through drills as they flew northwest over Scotland and back. Everything seemed alright, the navigation was 'spot on' and the practice bomb run was near perfect. They met up with another B-17 and had a chance for a bit of formation practice on the way home. All in all the flight was a good one and the new gunners seemed to settle right in to their jobs. Gracy decided that another practice would be a waste of time; he wanted to get back home as much as anyone else. Several days of fog and rain followed, canceling missions until the weather cleared. Word came a mission was on the next morning. Gracy made sure all of the crew were on base early that evening to get plenty of sleep.

"Sir, wake up, Lieutenant. Mission today, breakfast at 0600, briefing at 0645. It's 0430 hours right now, sir." The light in his face was a reminder that they were really flying today, on an actual mission. Dale was up and on his way to wash the sleep out of his eyes in a moment. He glanced over at Collins; Pat was lying on his rack, staring up at the ceiling.

"Didn't sleep a wink all night. I'll be alright though; I've had enough shuteye the past weeks to last a long time." Pat managed a smile at Dale as he swung his feet out of bed and started to stand up. Dale noticed that Pat's hands weren't shaking, he seemed fine this morning. Relieved, Dale headed to the latrine out back. Breakfast was a welcome return to real eggs; three weeks of powdered ones were enough for a lifetime. The men were careful not to drink too much coffee and cautioned the new gunners about it. Having 'to go' at altitude was a challenge; you could freeze certain anatomical parts you might want to keep. The whole crew seemed eager and ready to fly; Gracy and Wooster noticed the attitude and smiled at each other.

"Roger, navigator, changing course to zero nine five degrees." Gracy looked out the window to his left; there was "Doolittle's Doughboys" alongside and a little behind, right where she should be. He had forgotten how magnificent the view of several hundred bombers spread out ahead and above you was; one of the few things he'd miss. Wooster looked over at him and saw his face; then looked out and up himself. They shared a short nod and smile; words were of little use between them right now. They knew what each other felt and didn't need to share it with the crew.

"Fighters, two o'clock level; looks like three ME-210's. I'm on them." It was Bill Williams, the new ball turret gunner. Already the guys were calling him 'Bill Bill' because of his name. The sound of his twin .50 caliber guns and the shaking from their recoil was soon joined by others as the swarms of Luftwaffe fighters came in. The next few minutes were perfect examples of what would not be missed by any of them in later years.

"Bill Bill, you got him! Look at that sucker come apart. Whooooeeee! Left waist to pilot; sir, that '210' just blew up back and below us."

"Pilot to tail gunner; can you confirm that, Haskill?"

"Yes, sir! That's one gone Nazi. The pilot bailed out, his chute just opened....oh, oh, his chute's on fire. Bye-bye, Fritz."

"Ok, ok, let's get back to business. Keep calling out the fighters; good job Williams. There's flak ahead so I think we'll be done with the Luftwaffe for awhile."

The flak was heavy, but mostly below the formation; sometimes it was like that. Other times it seemed they had your altitude locked in good and you could get out and walk on the stuff. The rest of this mission went like a textbook for the "Lucky Lady". The same was not true for "Doolittle's Doughboys". On the return from bombing the aircraft plant at Leipzig, the enemy fighters again jumped the formation. Two FW-190's swooped in on the plane together and set two engines on fire. She dropped out of formation and Haskill narrated their demise.

"Tail gunner to pilot. Sir, the plane next to us is falling back and is trailing smoke from both outboard engines. She's flying level and I can see guys bailing out. There's one, two, two more, five, six......seven, I think...yep, that's eight chutes. Holy Hanna, she just lost both wings, folded right up. No more chutes, sir. Just the eight."

"Pilot to navigator. Pat, note that in the log book. Eight chutes from 'Doolittle's Doughboys'."

Each of the men in the "Lucky Lady" wondered who the other men had been; imagining one was a person in his position on the plane. Even as Haskill counted the chutes, he was convinced the tail gunner had not been able to reach an escape hatch in time. They had no way of knowing the pilots had flown the plane straight and level so everyone else could escape; sacrificing their own lives to save the rest of the crew. They also worried how each of the eight who had bailed out would be treated when they landed in Germany. They knew of the threats by the Nazi leaders that downed airmen were gangsters and criminals and deserved to hang.

Everyone was quiet the rest of the flight back. After they had debriefed, Gracy bought them all a round of 'pints' at the local pub to celebrate Bill Bill's first kill.

Chapter 20
March 1944

<u>England</u>

He should have been home, relaxing with his sweetheart after a weekend celebrating their first wedding anniversary. Instead he was 25,000 feet up in the thin, frigid air over France on his way to Berlin; the worst, most heavily defended place in the entire Nazi Fatherland! Dale went over the wind speed indicators and listened in as the radio operator tuned to the weather broadcast from England. Pressing the headphones tighter to his ear, he could just make out something about gale force winds expected over the continent.

"Pilot to bombardier and navigator. We received a recall signal; winds are too strong for the assigned target. We're to head to the secondary. Navigator, plot me a heading."

Dale glanced at Pat Collins who was already looking at the map and figuring a course change to Cologne. Dale tried to remember what the meteorologist had said about seven-tenths cloud cover over most of Germany. He figured they would be bombing by radar; all he would have to do was toggle the bombs when the lead ship dropped hers. At least that took some of the pressure off of him.

"Bandits, four o'clock level. Coming out of the clouds. Six, no seven of them; they look like Me-109's." It was Tom Banks, left waist gunner calling out the enemy fighters.

"OK, let's do this right. Easy on the triggers, short bursts. We've got a lot more flying to do; let's not use all our ammo early on." This was Hooper, top turret and flight engineer. He had become sort of an "old man" to the other gunners. He was the only member of the crew with three confirmed kills.

The enemy fighters buzzed by, guns blazing, cannons showing a slower blink as they fired out the nose of the plane. Dale could hear bullets hitting the side of the plane as he fired the right cheek gun that Collins normally used; Pat was still working on their new target course. Suddenly a cannon shell exploded between the two of them; it was a blinding flash followed by chaos. Dale felt something rip into his right thigh and his left arm went numb as he fell to the deck. He tried to look over to Collins but everything started to go black, like ducking into a pool of warm, dark water.

He started to come around; felt himself being lifted and carried through a very tight place. The disorientation was the worst. He didn't really know if he was facing up or down, right or left. Then hands were all over him, feeling under his sheepskin coat and pants. He was cold, so cold. His left arm felt like it was asleep but the pain in his right leg more than made up for it; that sucker was awake and screaming. No, he thought, that's ME screaming!

Hooper was looking down at him with a strange half smile on his face. "He's coming around. I think he'll make it. Sir, Lieutenant Weldon, sir.... you've been off oxygen a few minutes, sir. That kraut shell cut your lines. I've fixed your hose and plugged back in your heated suit; you'll be a bit warmer soon. It looks like you took a hit in your leg, but I don't think it's broken. Your left arm is really swollen and bleeding a bit, but no break in it either, sir."

Dale blinked hard, squeezing the fog from his brain. His eyes focused a bit and he tried to talk but the throat microphone wasn't on. Hooper bent down to try to listen. "Collins, how's Pat....Lieutenant Collins?"

"I'm afraid he's gone, sir. You'd be, too, if your arm hadn't been caught in the ammo belts on that gun, sir. That cannon shell ripped open the nose pretty bad; both pilots are having a hell of a time keeping us in the air. We're dropping down so we can all go off oxygen and start throwing shit out to lighten the ship. That Kraut got in one good shot before the plane next to us smoked his ass. At least I got to watch him die." Hooper had that half smile on his face again.

The "Lucky Lady" would have to live up to her name on this mission. They were still deep inside enemy territory and were flying on three engines. Gracy and Wooster were weaving from cloud to cloud and thanking the Lord for the awful weather. The high winds that had slowed them down on the way to Germany were helping them home now. As long as no more fighters showed up they should make it back to base.

When they could take off their oxygen masks Dale learned from Hooper what had happened. The enemy shell had exploded and torn a hole in the side of the plane's nose, which opened further because of the speed the plane was moving. No one was sure but it probably sucked Pat right out the hole; Dale had been tangled up in the ammo feed belts of the machine gun he was firing at the time. The plexiglass nose of the plane had also been shattered causing the front end of the aircraft to bend to one side knocking out one of the inboard engines. Hooper and Ben Murphy, the radioman, had managed to get Dale out of the nose and jettison the bombload. Getting rid of the weight helped them continue flying; it also lessened the risk of them blowing up when they landed. Now they were alone, limping along toward home on the three engines still running.

The two pilots, now physically exhausted from fighting the plane as it constantly tried to turn to the right, managed to land her safely. Hooper got out of the plane, knelt on the paved hardstand and kissed the ground. An ambulance took Dale to the base hospital while a multitude of curious onlookers stared at where the front end of the plane used to be. When he later saw pictures of it, Dale was stunned and amazed that he had survived. The doctor took a piece of metal about 4 inches long out of his right thigh. He said it was 1/8 of an inch from cutting his femoral artery; Dale would have bled to death in a minute if it had. His left arm was badly bruised but would heal quickly. He should plan on being ready to fly again in about three weeks. He was looking forward to finishing his tour of 25 missions, if only to honor his crewmates that had already died.

At the end of the first week, while he was enjoying a meal of a hamburger and ice cream, Dale was approached by a nurse. She quietly told him he had visitors and she was to clean him up a bit. He didn't have a clue what she was talking about.

"I say... perhaps it would be worth a pranging just to have some of that ice cream. You don't know me but we have a mutual friend; I should say she's a much better one of yours, however. My name is Wallace, er, Group Captain Wallace of the Royal Air Force. I had the distinct pleasure of being assisted by your wife on some factory tours last year in Minnesota. Nearly a year ago as I recall; she's a remarkable woman. When I looked you up I had no idea you'd just been wounded, not too seriously I hope?"

"No, no sir, not bad at all. Be up and about in a couple of weeks and back giving *Jerry* some more medicine. Let me get this straight... you worked with my wife, Shorty? Sorry, Gladdy; I guess only I call her Shorty."

"Yes, yes. It was after you had already headed this way. She has quite the responsible position back there, working for your, uh, Uncle Sam." The Group Captain had a pleasant smile and reached out to shake Dale's hand. "I suppose part of this is official business as well. Before we chat a bit longer, your General asked if I would care to give you this..." He reached down and placed a Purple Heart on Dale's pillow next to his head.

Minnesota

"No, honestly Frank, how could you even suggest I accompany the Group Captain on another tour? You remember all that happened last time. He'd probably think I'm some drippy American dame who screams and cries at the drop of a hat or something. No, I can't do this assignment. Use Bob or Alice; they both know the factory situations as well as I do now. Besides, I'm not in the mood to entertain anybody right now. Remember, I've got a husband lying in an English hospital on an airbase near some town called Deenethorpe that I can't even find on a map! Do you have any idea how maddening that is?"

"You through? Got it all out of your system? Huh? You sure, or are you just nodding 'cause you've got more building up inside? OK, here's the scoop. Group Captain Wallace, or as he's called now since his promotion, Air Commodore Wallace, is arriving in three days and insists, not requests.... insists that, where is that telegram....that 'Mrs. Weldon be assigned to assist in this endeavor if it is at all practicable', whatever the hell that means. I looked up that word and it means you're it. You'll meet his plane when it lands at Wold Chamberlin Field Thursday afternoon. And try to show the Air Commodore everything he wants to see; he's the equivalent of a General now."

Gladdy left Frank's office as though she were more than a little upset. Once outside, she smiled. The time she had spent with the Group Captain had filled a need for excitement she had inside herself. It wasn't that she was attracted to him, goodness, he was more than old enough to be her father. No, it was the quiet, commanding strength he had; it flowed from him like some kind of cologne. He had never been the least bit flustered or bothered by anything that had happened on his last trip. She was already anxiously awaiting the arrival of his plane.

That evening she explained to Dautin and Esther that she wouldn't be able to help at the USO for awhile and may be working late more often because she would be playing tour guide to the English again.

"I don't believe it. Why does a car have to stop working right when the owner has to start?" Gladdy was so mad she nearly stomped her foot as she said this.

"Don't let it get to you, honey. I'll talk to Dwight; he doesn't work on Thursdays and has a "B" card. It's not like your "X" permit but he can get gas when he needs it. I can drive you to meet this English officer and I'm sure he'll have a car there for his own use anyway."

"Thanks, dad. You're a sweetheart." Gladdy planted a kiss on Dautin's cheek and, maybe it was her imagination, he actually seemed to blush just a little.

They arrived at the airport. Dautin offered to drop her off but Gladdy insisted that he stay and meet the Air Commodore. Dautin snorted just a little about 'officers and gentlemen' but seemed willing to stick around. They were able to park near the runway, next to an army staff car with American and English flags on the front corners. A few minutes later a large two engine plane, Dautin said it was a C-47, landed and taxied up to where they were parked. The door opened and out stepped four men and a woman, all in RAF uniforms. Air Commodore Wallace smiled and tipped his hat to Gladdy as he strode over.

"Good day, Mrs Weldon. I trust you've not been waiting too long?"

"Not at all, Air Commodore. Sir, may I introduce you to my father-in-law? This is Dautin Weldon; dad, this is Air Commodore Wallace."

"Sir, it's an honor to meet you. Welcome to Minnesota; I guess for the second time. I hope your business here is safe and productive. Anything we can do to help get a twist on the *Heinies* is alright by me."

"Mr Weldon, I've not heard that term since The Great War. You Yanks loved to call the enemy Heinies then. I was told it referred to always seeing their, um, backsides when you went at them. Any truth to that?"

"Well, we sure saw them skedaddle at Soissons in the summer of 1918, that's for sure."

"Soissons? That was a hot spot! I was a very young Lieutenant in the Royal Flying Corps serving as an aerial observer with the American First Division at that time. Were you there as well, by chance?" The Air Commodore was enjoying this conversation immensely. Gladdy was standing there with a growing pride in these two men who had already contributed so much to the freedom of others.

"Absolutely, until I got shot and inhaled a snootful of mustard gas, that is. I met my wife in a French hospital there, too. Say, what are the odds the two of us were on the same battlefield then and here together now? I've half a mind to ask you over for dinner so we could talk some more. Do you think you might have time for that during your stay here?"

"I should enjoy that very much. What do you think, Mrs Weldon? Might we find a time to impose on your husband's parents for a meal at some point?"

"Certainly, sir. My instructions are to be as helpful as I can be. I'm sure we'll find the time for a visit."

"Splendid, splendid. Catching up on the past will be most welcome. By the by, I nearly forgot to mention....I ran into someone you may possibly know last week in England. You wouldn't by chance have a close acquaintance bedridden and being stuffed full of American ice cream in Deenethorpe, would you?"

"Dale? You've seen my husband? Oh, Commodore, do tell me; is he alright? I mean, how badly injured is he, really? He wrote that it's not too bad, but part of me thinks he says that so I won't worry."

"Well, why don't you ride in my car with my adjutant and secretary; she happens to be my daughter as well. Your father can drive my other two aides, if he doesn't object. We can talk on the way to the hotel your government has us staying in and Mr Weldon can tell them a few more tales of The Great War; I'm sure they're tired of hearing mine."

Chapter 21
April 1944

<u>England</u>

"Weldon, you're cleared to fly. I don't see any reason why keeping you grounded would be a benefit to the Air Corps."

"Thank you, Doc. I'll be checking in with my pilot right away and see how many missions behind them I am. Would you let the other folks here know how much I appreciate their attention and kindness?"

The doctor nodded and Dale was out the door. The leg was still a bit stiff but he knew that would work itself out with the walking he'd be doing. His left arm was fine; the bruising had gone away as had the tingling in the hand. He felt confident that he'd be able to perform all his duties as well as before. As he walked across the base toward the officers' quarters to look for Gracy, he glanced at the Chapel. A sudden flow of emotion swept over him as he thought of Pat Collins; possibly still alive when he was hurled out of the plane and tumbled down toward the hard earth below. He could not imagine the terror felt as the ground rushed up at you and there was no parachute to open. He physically shook his head to clear the scene from his mind. About ten minutes later he found his pilot talking with another officer Dale didn't recognize.

"So in this crew we function as a very tight knit group. We get to where we know just what all the others are thinking in a situation. Up there it's the only way to survive. Excuse me a sec. Hey Weldon, good to see you up and about; you've made quite an

92

improvement in just the past few days. When are you flight ready?

"Hi Gracy. The doc just cleared me for duty. I can go up again any time. I wanted you to know first; just in case you'll need me tomorrow. Any word on a mission?"

"Good timing. Dale, this is Fred Hoyle. He'll be our navigator for awhile. We've had two since you went into the hospital; I'm pretty sure the Squadron is using us as a sort of training crew for the new replacements. It'll be great to have you back in the nose. We've had to fly different planes, too. "Lucky Lady" was out of action nearly as long as you; we just got her back a couple of days ago. We hit Schweinfurt yesterday; it was frightful how bad the flak was. They said it wasn't like the first time there, but it was bad enough to have several wounded in about every other plane that made it back. Anyway, word is we get another day off then we'll probably be flying again on the 17th or 18th."

"Yes, sir. Well, I'm ready. I think I'll take time tomorrow to run through the simulator; it's still on base I think. I'll go check now; might have time to run a mission or two to get the mind back in the game. Say, Fred; where you from? You've got kind of a familiar face."

"I'm from Sioux Falls in South Dakota. I know Bob here is from Wisconsin; where are you from?"

"Just outside Minneapolis, right between the two of you. Nice meeting you; where have they got you settled in?"

"They've got him in with you, Weldon. He'll be in Collin's spot." said Gracy.

"Fine. I'll see you there later. Gonna go check out the simulator."

Two days later they were in the air, on their way to Oranienberg. The Lead Plane had to abort with mechanical problems so the

93

Deputy Lead took over; his plane was not equipped with radar so the bombs had to be dropped visually using the Norden bombsight. With the target totally socked in by heavy cloud cover, the secondary target was chosen. It was a factory in Wittenberge and the bombing was dead on, more than 90% of the bombs dropped within a few hundred yards of the target.

"Man, it is a beautiful sight to see all those high explosives land in that small of an area." This was said by Haskill, the tail gunner. Because of his position, there was nothing to block out what he could see behind the plane. He always bragged about having the best view of what they came to do. The others would tease him about never knowing where they're going.

Maybe because of the change of target, or just sheer luck, there were no Luftwaffe fighters seen and the flak was incredibly light and well below their flight path. Dale was just glad the mission went off well; he didn't want to face a really tough one his first time back.

When the "Lucky Lady" returned to the base at Deenethorpe, Dale spent a few quiet moments in the nose; the new nose that had once been part of another aircraft. It had been, perhaps, from a plane that had crash landed or had some other part destroyed but the nose was intact; ready to be used on this plane to continue its own life. Dale sat and stared at the navigator's desk, only an arm's reach away. He thought of Pat Collins, who had never actually sat at this desk, but at one exactly like it in this same aircraft.

Minnesota

"I must say, Gladdy, your in-laws are wonderful. The way your mother made us feel so at home and the stories your father told; I could listen to him all evening. He took me from laughing to crying and back again too many times to count. Thank you, as well, for the kindness and patience you've shown all of us during our time here. My father has not had an opportunity to relax and be led

94

around for quite some time. His duties in Washington and London have been too much of a strain on him. With me getting married this summer; well, part of me feels almost like I'm abandoning him."

"Kim, you can't let yourself feel that way. Why, with his position and influence, I'm sure he won't have trouble finding another secretary. He will, however, have to get used to not calling her 'daughter of mine'. Perhaps 'Leftenant so-and-so' won't have the same ring, but he'll get used to it. It has been a real privilege for me to show you around for the past weeks. If you or your father happen upon a certain American airman back in England, do give him my love, won't you?"

"That, and a kiss on the cheek, if it's not too forward of me. The pictures you have of him would make that a real pleasure I'm certain. I'll make a point of looking him up to make sure he's flying straight and level and report back to you, ma'am." Kim smiled and gave Gladdy a hug before climbing into the staff car. The Air Commodore had just finished saying his goodbyes to Dautin and Esther. As he strolled down the sidewalk toward Gladdy, standing by the car, he waved and tipped his hat to all the neighboring houses. He had noticed them staring out between the curtains in their windows.

"Good God, Mrs Weldon. I shouldn't be afraid of any of the *Hun* sneaking around here; the good people living nearby would spot them in an instant."

"Thank you for that report, Air Commodore. I'm sure they've never seen an official staff car with a British flag flying on it before; particularly in The Park. Thank you so much for your visit. I do hope it was a fruitful one and will help bring the war to a conclusion soon." Gladdy reached out her hand.

"Madam, I assure you the pace of development of the weapons and other equipment I've seen these weeks will ensure that Hitler and Tojo will soon join their fellow sewer rat Mussolini. I'd prefer

95

your American custom to a handshake if you don't mind. One simply cannot get enough of these fine, allowable female hugs." With that he put his arms around Gladdy and squeezed, completely taking her by surprise.

"Why, why th-thank you Air Commodore. I look forward to seeing you again sometime in the future. Good flying, sir and may God watch over you everywhere you go."

"Thank you, Gladdy, for the patience you've shown this old man in his drudgery of a job. I've given my address to your father-in-law. I do think Dautin and I enjoy so much, speaking together about old times and everything. I should like to hear from your father again, you know, from time to time. You can expect a package for him soon; I'll be sending it to your office. If you would see that he gets it on his birthday, please?"

"It would be my pleasure. Goodbye."

At that the Air Commodore got in the staff car and it pulled away from the curb. Gladdy walked back in the house, where Esther was just finishing up washing the dishes and Dautin was next to her drying and putting them away.

"Here, Dad. Let me help do that."

"Not on your life. I intend to have this job for years ahead; no one is going to pull rank on me yet." He smiled and asked her to pour one more cup of coffee.

Don came down the stairs, having changed from his suit and tie back into more 'normal' clothes. "Man oh man, those uniforms were so cool. The stories; that one guy, Flying Officer Lewis. Did you catch his one about taking on two Heinkel bombers at once over London? Gosh, I'd love to do that kind of flying."

"Maybe, young man," said his mother, "but you don't hear stories from all those hundreds of RAF boys that didn't make it. There

96

are certainly other positions in the military safer than being in the air."

"Still, I can't wait to tell the guys at school tomorrow about this visit. An Air Commodore; that must be like next to Prime Minister or something!"

"Well, Air Commodore Don Weldon; would you mind, awfully, sir, taking out the trash?" Dautin couldn't help ribbing his son, snapping to attention and saying this in an awful, overboard British accent. All four of them laughed as Don went out the door with the garbage.

"Mom, Dad, if you'll excuse me. I want to write Dale a letter before I turn in. I could fill an entire book with the past few weeks and I haven't written more than a couple of lines at best."

"Sure, honey. I'll wake you in the morning for breakfast before work. Sweet dreams." Esther wiped her hands and gave Gladdy a nice, warm hug and kiss.

Chapter 22
May 1944

<u>England</u>

"Hey catch this on the radio."

"This from the BBC. Supreme Allied Headquarters reports this morning that the Soviet armies in Crimea have forced the surrender of vast numbers of Germans. News of the collapse of Nazi resistance in the Black Sea area comes shortly after our own combined force of RAF and American bombers have attacked Germany's capital Berlin for two straight days."

"You know, this thing has got to start getting easier. The 'Rooskies' are sure pounding the Krauts on the ground over in the east while we're hammering their towns at night and industries during the day." Dale, Gracey and Wooster all listened politely as Fred Hoyle spoke.

Gracey answered first, "Fred, I know the past two days have been long ones; plenty of flak and bandits. What have you got now, four missions done with another twenty-six to go, being a new guy you've got to do the new thirty mission requirement? Dale's got ten, oh right, eleven under his belt; John and I each have seventeen apiece. I'd like to think the war will be over before you hit your thirty and rotate home. I'm pretty sure the Luftwaffe has enough left in it to make the rest of us stay here flying for awhile, yet."

"Yeah, I don't even like to think of the next eight. You know, one of these days we'll be flying 'milk runs' over France; the invasion has got to be just around the corner. There are so many Americans over here now this British Island will sink soon!" John Wooster was not one to make a joke; he felt in fine humor today, being able to soak in some of this rare English sunshine.

The four of them were lying in a warm, sunny spot; sheltered from the breeze by a couple of equipment shacks. The sun on his face made Dale so sleepy, he kept dozing off until his own deep breathing would wake him up. He tried to imagine laying on the grass near a lake, his fishing pole held lightly in one hand. The sound of a hundred or more Wright Cyclone engines warming up on the B-17s was just not quite the same as the faint buzzing of dragonflies...

"Mail call...."

Fred jumped up and shouted over his shoulder as he ran, "I'll see what we all got."

"Now that's what I like; a junior officer who knows his station in life." Gracy and Dale both laughed out loud. Yes, John must be in a very good mood indeed.

When Fred returned with a handful of letters and a package for Gracy, attention turned to reading news from home. Dale received two letters from Gladdy and one from his folks. So far he'd gotten 27 letters from her since getting to England with two that still hadn't shown up. Gladdy numbered each envelope; it was what nearly everyone did so you knew which to read first.

Darling,

I'm writing this at the end of an evening we all spent with Air Commodore Wallace and his group. Don't be surprised by visits from more Brits as I asked them to look you up if any of them have a chance. The past few weeks have been a fast paced run of plant tours, dinners and a few sight seeing escapades thrown in for good measure. Please forgive me for not writing more; I've been burning that candle from both ends and the middle!

Mom and Dad hosted a dinner tonight for the lot of them. She really outdid herself in the kitchen and I'm sure they are all sleeping now as they fly back to Washington. You can imagine what six hungry men and three women can do to one of her pot-roasts! I got to know Wallace's daughter, Kim, pretty well while they were here. She is my age and already a Lieutenant in the RAF; advantage of having a high ranking father, I suppose. The Air Commodore and Dad hit it off right away, not more than five minutes after they all landed at Wold Chamberlin they were like two old chums talking about their experiences in The Great War. Seems they both were in the same battle sometime in 1918 or something. Anyway, I keep having this queer feeling that somehow all our lives will continue to be linked together.

How are you, my darling? I pray all the time that God heals your body and keeps your mind clear and your heart all mine. Kim is certainly evidence of how cute the English ladies are and the men kept talking of how 'the Yanks' were taking all the women over there! You better mind your manners, mister! I have eyes watching you now. I love you and anxiously await your return. We still have a honeymoon to finish! Write when you can and tell me about the area and people where you are. I've tried and tried and cannot find Deenethorpe anywhere on a map. Frustrating to say the least!

I love, love, love you with all my heart,
Shorty

Minnesota

Gladdy and Don shared the back seat of the car. Dautin and Esther sat up front for the drive; they had been on the road just over an hour. Making their way south from The Park they had crossed the Minnesota River at Shakopee and followed winding roads to the east and south through Northfield across the Cannon

100

River with the ruins of the flour mills along it. They entered the area of the Big Woods; some of the only old-growth forests left in the southern part of the state. Up to just a couple of years ago logging companies had been trying to get their hands on it to cut down the majestic trees. Because the land belonged to hundreds of owners, many living out of the state with the land being passed down through a few generations, the purchase became too complicated and costly even for large companies.

"You know, Gladdy, when the state forestry people first approached Mother and me last year, we were reluctant to part with the old land. Part of us wanted to give it to you and Dale for a wedding present or to Don when he graduates from school. Now, after seeing what they want to do to create a new state park here for everybody to enjoy, we've decided to sell it to the state as an investment in the future. Don, I don't think you'll even remember the place; it's been quite awhile since you were down here. All that's really left is the family cemetery and that's not actually on the old farm site. Let's see; when my dad died back in '31 Dale was about eight and Don, you were four years old. Mother and I try to come down every year but the last couple, with the war and all, well, it's not been possible. Anyway, since today is Decoration Day, we thought getting out of the cities and stretching the legs a bit would be a welcome relief. "

Dautin stopped the car on the side of the gravel road. As soon as the doors opened, Gladdy heard the beautiful sound of meadowlarks, that lilting melody that she missed from her own early years on the farm in southwestern Minnesota, near Worthington. The grass was not high yet and it was still too early for mosquitoes; all in all, it was a perfectly gorgeous day with blue sky and a gentle warm breeze. As they walked, Dautin pointed out where his great-grandfather, James Weldon, had first laid the foundation for a home.

"Back in 1859, the year after statehood, James moved the family from Indiana to here, near a few houses daring to call themselves Oakview. He decided to build the house on this little knoll, looking out over his farm that would gently slope down to the creek; see, right where that tree line is. Of course, this whole place was thick with huge oak and hard maple and whatnot. My father once showed me where James was killed by a tree he was felling, right about here." Dautin pointed to the ground where they now stood. Moving on, he continued, "James was buried in a coffin made from that tree. A neighbor arranged for the boards to be cut from the trunk up in Red Wing. I cannot imagine how much work went into that very kind gesture. People were real neighbors back then; thank goodness there are still a few like that around today. After James died, his son Isaiah, my grandfather, and his brother had to clear the rest of the trees to get crops planted. Don... Isaiah was about your age, I suppose, when all this happened. He had an older brother, like you do, named Mark. He eventually took over this farm, he and his wife... oh, what was her name now?"

"Her name was Rose", put in Esther. "Rose had been orphaned in the Sioux Uprising in 1862 and came to stay with the Weldons here. She taught school in Oakview and they fell in love and married. They never had any children, but I've heard she spread her mother's love over all her students."

Gladdy was enthralled with the story. Don was a bit more interested in the garter snake he was chasing through the grass. "Please, do go on. Dale's never told me much of the family history."

"Well, let's see. Isaiah fought in the Civil War, enlisted when he was sixteen or so. Was with General Sherman in his march through Georgia and all. He met a young woman down there and she became my grandmother, Beth. Her father was killed by some 'rebel scoundrels', as Grandpa Isaiah put it. They farmed on land a bit north and east of here; close to where the creameries were by the railroad as it heads up the grade over there. That land was sold by my father during the First War when I was in France. We used to visit Grandpa and Grandma Beth down here when I was a little boy. Lots of fond memories of those times, taking the train down to the creameries and always the smell of that rich, fat cream. Ummmm, I'd better stop that or I'll have to eat!"

"Father, let's walk to the cemetery now. I'd like to spend awhile there before we have to head for home." Esther was always the clock watcher of the pair.

"Yes, dear. Gladdy, I wanted to give you a sense of our family and what it means to all of us, with Dale in England. Our family, you see, well.... we've had someone protecting us in every generation since before America was even the United States. I just wanted to show you a little of that so you might feel encouraged, you understand?"

"Oh, yes, Dad. I understand completely, I think." Taking the hand Esther wasn't holding, Gladdy joined the other two in step as they walked into the woods along the creek. The sunlight filtering down through the new, young leaves just sprouting overhead, with the soft, moist soil under their feet made for an amazing walk. Each step brought up a wonderful earthy fragrance, so unlike the smell of asphalt or concrete. Don was following a bit behind, looking for squirrels in the trees. Birds were flitting here and there, a symphony of different calls sounding out alarm as the family walked up to a rise where Gladdy saw a half dozen or so headstones surrounded by an iron fence.

"Oh, my. It's perfect; the ideal place to rest while the world goes hustling by."

"Great-grandma Ruth, Isaiah's mother, chose this spot for James to be buried. His stone is over here", Dautin pointed to a natural outcrop of granite with 'James Weldon, 1824-1862' carved on it. "The same neighbor that had the coffin made chiseled out that inscription. No one has even thought to change it; it's so perfect. Ruth is buried next to him, Grandpa Isaiah and Grandma Beth are over here. There's his brother Mark and Rose; my father, Jack, and mother, Mary, are the newest here. You see, Gladdy, James fought in the Mexican War, Isaiah in the Civil War, Jack in the War

103

with Spain and against the Indians before that. Mother and I will be buried right over there; it's part of the agreement with the state park people. We have no right to insist on where anyone else ends up. I just wanted to introduce you to my heritage. Perhaps you'll have a chance some day to visit Mother's as well; it's a bit further to Iowa though."

"Thank you, Dad." Gladdy gave Dautin a strong hug and kissed Esther on the cheek. "You, too, Mom. When Dale comes home, I want this to be the first place we visit, the first chance we get! It's so peaceful here, I know he'll need some peace in his life when the war's over."

Don called out, softly, "Would you look at that?"

They turned to see two does and three fawns staring at them from only twenty or so yards away. It was enough to make all of them take in a long breath and let out an audible "Oooohhhhh".

Chapter 23
June 1944

England

Strange how things didn't seem different here in Deenethorpe; because it was far enough north and west of the other airfields the sounds of the invasion couldn't be heard. Dale imagined the flurry of activity that must be happening all over the south and eastern parts of England at the moment. But here nothing stirred, no unusual sounds, just the normal footsteps of the corporal making his rounds and waking the crews that would be flying today. He lay in the dark, absorbing the quiet of the early morning, knowing his turn was nearly here, when the cold brightness of the man's flashlight would be in his eyes and the quiet voice saying, "Lieutenant Weldon, wake up sir, briefing in twenty minutes, sir." Then the light and the voice would be at the next bed before it retreated out the door and down the hall to the other rooms. He heard the faint click of the door latch and a soft tread, respectful and full of duty.

Breakfast, briefing, pick up the Norden bombsight which they wouldn't use today but had to bring along just in case. Out to the plane where the gunners were already inspecting and loading the guns and ammunition cases into the ""Lucky Lady"". Dale climbed through the hatch beneath the nose of the plane, reached down and brought up the bombsight when the crew chief handed it to him. The routine included pre-flight checks on the Norden to make sure it was working; then the right cheek .50-caliber machine gun that he and the navigator used. Dale always took his favorite picture of Shorty out of his pocket, kissed it and put it back; in the pocket right above his heart. He took a few moments to pray for God's protection on this day as on all days. It was then he fully realized this day was different; this was 'The Day'.

When Dale joined the Army Air Corps eighteen months earlier, Nazi Germany had ruled over all Europe, northern Africa and a good sized piece of Russia. Now, after all the hundreds of ships, thousands of airplanes, tanks and trucks, millions of bullets and shells; now that several hundred thousand men had been trained, 'The Day' had come. He wondered what it all would look like from his seat in the nose of this B-17; what, if anything, would he see of the invasion of Europe? Today began the liberation of millions of people who were living under the heel of Hitler's boot. Today freedom was coming, delivered from the guns of thousands of young men from a dozen countries that called themselves 'The Allies'.

When the plane touched down, back from their third mission that day, Dale felt a surge of pride he'd never known before. He had not been able to see anything through the cloud cover over the beaches of France; had not seen the death and destruction on those sands of Normandy. He was not sure how he could have done what 'they' had done; those men in the landing craft when the front ramps went down and the enemy guns began firing at them. He could not imagine what that would be like. He did know there had been plenty of flak coming up at them today, though not a single German fighter challenged them on any of the short flights they made. Because the target was completely covered by the clouds, it wasn't possible to drop their bombload on this last mission. They were bringing back all twenty 500 pounders. If they had been flying over Germany dropping them anywhere wouldn't be a problem; but not in France. There was no point in that; dropping them on French civilians or farms or towns just to get rid of the bombs. The French were Allies, on our team; but the Germans were the enemy.

Dale rubbed his eyes, realizing for the first time just how tired he was. He had been up since before wake-up and had not been able to sleep the night before. It was a long day alright, but he knew it was longer for those guys down on the ground, over there in France now.

Minnesota

"Well, Commodore, the past few days have been quite exciting, to say the least." Dautin set down his glass, reached over to the pitcher and asked, "More lemonade?"

"You know, Weldon, this is perhaps the most delightful drink on a warm day. Can't say as I've ever tasted anything as refreshing; I'd like another glass, just one, then I really must be going. Visits to your home are most enjoyable, they really help me get my mind off the work."

Esther came into the backyard carrying a tray of sandwiches; as she set it on the table, Air Commodore Wallace smiled at her and began, "Did you know those are named after an English lord, the Earl of Sandwich? I'm not really sure just why, but I do know his great-great-something grand-nephew, probably another seven or so greats in there somewhere." His manner of joking told it all; even with the hard fighting going on in France and Italy, there was a lifting of the solemn, sober British demeanor.

"Commodore, have you heard anything besides what we're told on the radio here in the States?" Esther asked the question carefully, not sure exactly how to say it. "I'm not looking for secrets; I'd simply like to know the perspective of what's going on. It all seems so large and confusing to me."

"Well, madam; I'll see if I can summarize the situation as I know it. The landings in Normandy earlier this month were a triumph, though not of a scale we had hoped. The Jerries are putting up quite a fight; but with our air superiority, they cannot move around during the day without getting blown to pieces. We're expanding the amount of territory we control in France daily and putting ashore more men and equipment every day. I'm sure Hitler will not be defeated without much more fighting; we will have to smash his army all the way to Berlin this time. They didn't seem to learn their lesson back in 1918, right Weldon?"

Dautin had a smirk on his face and replied, "Maybe we didn't whup 'em good enough last time."

Commodore Wallace laughed hard at that; it took him a moment to continue. "Now, just in the past weeks, they've started hitting London with a new type of weapon; it's a sort of unmanned guided rocket bomb. We're trying to figure out a defense against them; actually that's why I'm back here in Minnesota now. At the same time, Rome was surrendered by the Germans just two days before the landings in France took place; so we're making progress there as well, though Italy is a hard place to fight with all of the mountains, valleys, rivers and the like. This you haven't heard yet, but should by the end of this very day; your Navy has won a tremendous aerial victory over the Japanese in the Pacific. The dispatch was read to me as I was driven over here. Apparently your carrier planes have shot down nearly 400 enemy aircraft with almost no loss to you. It's incredible to think of, really. We thought the RAF was doing a good job over London during The Blitz, but really, 400.... it staggers the imagination."

"That's wonderful, Commodore; thank you for telling us. Sometimes I feel like the war will never come to an end. But it seems like we're winning after all. I just want my son to come home, along with all the boys that are away fighting."

"I fully understand, Mrs Weldon. I miss my own wife Edith terribly; she's cooped up in the old country house, rattling around the 'big stone castle' as she calls it. We used to entertain quite frequently, though now it seems everyone has other business to attend to, like myself. I so would like to see the two of you, along with the rest of your family, sitting under the trees along the stream on our estate back in England one day. Do you enjoy trout fishing, Weldon?" Dautin nodded his agreement. Air Commodore Wallace went on, "We've stocked plenty of the nice, fat ones

108

there. Just the thing to help one forget what the rest of the world is up to at times."

"Commodore, I just want to say that you are always welcome here. Make yourself as comfortable as if it were your own home, really." Esther smiled and turned to go back into the house. Dautin and Wallace sat for a while longer, soaking in the beautiful day, listening to the gentle buzzing of the bees in the raspberry patch near them. They continued a conversation about the easy relations between their people, the English and Americans. Dautin recounted a story his father had told about an encounter during his time in Cuba while in the army. He had met a young British Lieutenant, fresh out of their military academy, Sandhurst; assigned as an observer from the 4th Hussars. Jack Weldon, Dautin's father, was an infantry officer escorting the foreign officers around parts of the country. He claimed to have introduced the Lieutenant to the particularly smooth tobacco used by the Cubans in their cigars. The young man later became a leader in Great Britain's military and government, rising to become their current Prime Minister, Winston Churchill; known for his love of Cuban cigars.

"Extraordinary, Weldon! You're father is to be commended for creating an image recognized around the world; Winston cannot be thought of without one! The next time I see the Prime Minister I shall have to tell him I've met the son and grandson of his first tobacconist. Marvelous, simply marvelous."

England

"Alright, men, you all know what's expected. Do it well and we're one day closer to the end of this war."

"Room. Attention!"

The pilots, navigators and bombardiers all stood and snapped to attention. The Group Commanding Officer strode purposefully down the aisle between the rows of chairs, past his men all standing tall. The primary target today was Berlin, 'Big B' as it was known. No milk run today for these crews; it seemed like a long while since they flew over Germany. The past month or more had been missions to France and Belgium in support of the invasion; now it was back to the dirty work of pounding the Nazi homeland into rubble. They were to hit a series of factories around the enemy capital city; a synthetic oil facility, an aircraft parts manufacturing plant and a railroad marshaling yard, where supplies and troops flowed by train through the area on their way to the front in France. Flak and Luftwaffe fighters were expected to be heavy; no surprise there. The weeks spent softening up France for D-Day had allowed the Germans time to build more fighters, train more pilots and lay in supplies of aviation fuel. Now the Mighty Eighth Air Force would pay the price.

"Weldon, Hoyle; have you two seen Wooster?" Their pilot, Bob Gracy approached them just outside the briefing hut. "The engine replacement on '"Lucky Lady"' won't be finished in time for today's mission. I've got to let him know he'll be flying in another plane. It seems there was an accident off the base early this morning and some officers were badly injured. In fact, you'll be flying in the same plane, Weldon. It's out on the hardstands, three past ours. Same position in the formation as we were supposed to be; good luck, Dale. See you when you get back."

It wasn't the first time he had to fly with another crew, but it was the first time the change had happened right before taking off. Dale wasn't sure about this; the crew had all eaten breakfast together, just like always. This change of routine was never a welcome event; flyers became used to their pre-flight routines and changes often resulted in disaster; all in all, they were pretty superstitious. He tried to put the 'bad omen' thought out of his mind while he walked to the bomb sight storage area.

They formed up without mishap and made good time to the target. Flak had been light over the coast of Belgium but was increasing with each mile they flew toward Berlin. The mission called for another Group to fly ahead of the main attack force to divert the enemy fighters away. It seemed to work as there were practically none opposing their flight over the capital. The pilot was able to fly the plane nice and steady for the final bomb run. When the bombs were gone, Dale let out a deep breath as he reported, "Bombs away, Captain."

"Well done, Weldon", was the reply from the cockpit. A few minutes later, as they were making their turn toward England, Dale's world turned nearly upside down. He heard the explosion as he felt the plane dip violently to one side. The spin caused him to be pinned to the side of the fuselage; his parachute pack was just out of reach. He knew he would black out soon because of the spin and struggled hard to get to the escape hatch.

"Must....get...parachute." The voice in his head was screaming it; no, it was really him screaming as he fought to maintain consciousness and get out of the plane. That was when he heard her voice; Shorty was telling him she loved him and everything would be fine. Everything went swirling into a deep, black pool....

Dale regained consciousness falling, plummeting to earth. He had no idea how long he'd been out or what altitude he was at. The "Lucky Lady" was below him, spiraling down toward the ground; it was surprising how long the sound of it crashing took to get to him. The air was thin at this height, but he could breathe; at 15,000 feet up it was bone chilling cold. He noticed two other parachutes open up and knew he had not been unconscious long. Pulling the ripcord, Dale felt an encouraging soft 'pop' as the restraining pin released the tightly packed parachute, saw the silk canopy rush upward out of the chest pack and felt the hard snap as it opened above him. It suddenly seemed as though he was going back up into the sky, like the feeling you get when an elevator slows at the bottom of a tall building.

He was coming down over farmland and could not see any city or town around. As he drifted down his thoughts focused on where he might land for the best chance of escape. He was sure the plane had been hit while they were still deep inside Germany, more than a hundred miles from France; even further from friendly front lines. He noticed a wooded area to the west and tried to guide his chute that way by pulling on one riser. That's when he saw the men on the ground; they looked like a bunch of farmers. Dale saw them pointing and running in his direction.

The earth seemed to be rushing up at him. He hit the ground hard, like jumping from a car going 20 miles an hour and rolled to a stop, looking up at an old man and young boy, both carrying pitchforks. "Hande hoch, hande hoch", the younger one said while motioning with the handle for Dale to raise his hands. When he tried to release his parachute harness, the older guy jabbed him in the butt with his pitchfork. Dale winced and the pain nearly made him pass out again. He was a prisoner of the Fatherland.

Minnesota

"Dale!!" Gladdy screamed it as she woke up. The room was dark with just a hint of shadows from the streetlight out on the corner. She was scared nearly to death; the dream had seemed so real. She could hear Dale calling her as the airplane he was in blew up and fell to earth.

"Oh, God, please, please don't let it be real. I love him so, I don't think I could live without him. Please, God; if he can hear me, let him know I love him. Tell him it will be alright. Oh, please...."

Esther came in after a soft knock on the door. The hallway light spilled into the bedroom. She could see Shorty sitting up, sobbing and mumbling; she couldn't quite make out the words.

"Honey, Gladdy. What's wrong dear? It sounded like you had a nightmare; are you alright?"

"Oh, mom.... I, I've just had the most dreadful dream. Dale's plane blew up and, and... it was so real. I heard him shout my name and oh...." She hugged Esther and buried her face in her bathrobe.

"There, there, dear. I'm sure it was all the talk you heard at dinner between Father and the Commodore. You know how those two carry on; honestly, it's almost like they don't realize there are others in the room. Sometimes it brings back all the horror of that time in my life as well. I don't think they remember that I was there, too. All the glory they speak of, the honor; well, what I remember are the broken bodies, the horrible wounds, the rasping sound of men trying to breathe after they had been gassed. Goodness sakes, now there I go; I'm terribly sorry, dear. I'm sure it was all just a dream. Why don't you try to get back to sleep; you'll feel much better in the morning."

"No, mom; this was too real to be a dream. Dale's in trouble, how much I don't know. I know, I feel it really happened; I don't know how. I'm going to keep praying that God will watch over him." With that she got on her knees next to the bed and began to pray. Esther knelt down next to her daughter-in-law and joined her in prayer.

Germany

The old man was right behind Dale, leading him down the road. The young boy had gone at a faster pace to alert the town folks and authorities up ahead. Dale was struggling; his behind hurt like hell and it was not easy carrying his rolled up parachute. It didn't help that he was in his full flight gear with sheepskin coat, pants and boots over the electrically heated coveralls and clothes underneath that. On the ground the temperature was nearly 80 degrees, not the -40 up where he had been 30 minutes earlier.

They were joined by another small group of men surrounding John Wooster. The co-pilot did not speak to Dale, only gave him the slightest nod of his head as a sign of recognition. Now there were nearly a dozen or so men guiding the two downed airmen into the village. As they passed a local pub, several more men came out; these guys were loud and looked mad as they could be. Dale couldn't understand anything they were saying; he didn't have to, their actions said it all. One approached Dale and punched him in the face; the salty, warm taste of blood filled his mouth. The same guy hit Wooster too; it looked like he broke his nose. Two more men came up carrying ropes, which they threw over the arm of a street lamp post. Both Americans knew their time was up.

At that moment a scuffle started at the outer edge of the growing crowd of old men and boys. A shot rang out and one voice bellowed over all the others. A man in a uniform could be seen shoving his way toward Dale. The man was a Luftwaffe sergeant, home on leave, and had been visiting his uncle, the local Gauleiter; the town mayor. The sergeant bullied his way to the front and, in disgust, tore down the two ropes and shoved his pistol right up to the face of the man who had hit the two. He commanded the group to break up and go home; he was taking these two as prisoners of war. He didn't give a damn what Goebbels and his propaganda ministry had ordered; these men were enemy soldiers and would be treated as such, not as criminals!

The sergeant sent one of the older boys, perhaps 13 years old or so, to get a wagon and horse from the Gauleiter. While he was gone, the town doctor was sent for to tend to Wooster's nose and Dale's wounds as well. Both of the Americans were relieved and John Wooster spoke that word that was understood by armies around the world; "Cigaretten?".

The sergeant smiled and reached into Wooster's front pocket. His smile grew as he pulled out the pack and said, as if in Hollywood, "Yah, Lucky Strrrrikes, mean vine tobacco." Dale took one also, lit it and said to Wooster, "No time like the present to start smoking."

The rest of the men in the mob slowly moved on their way back to their own business; the excitement of hanging two American airmen having evaporated, like a morning mist disappears after a sunrise. The Luftwaffe sergeant led Dale and John to the horse drawn cart where they deposited their parachutes and climbed aboard. With the sergeant watching them closely, the young driver shook the reins and the cart started on its way north and

114

east, leaving the small village behind. The two Americans were glad to be away from that place, yet neither was enthusiastically awaiting what the immediate future held.

Minnesota

The next few days were hard on Gladdy; though she imagined they were not as hard as those her husband was going through. It was difficult to focus on her job and Frank Rarig had offered her a few days off to "stay home and..."

"And what, spend all my time crying? No, Frank, I've got to DO something or I'll lose my mind. I don't know if what I dreamt was real or not; though I certainly FEEL like it was...is. I even phoned an officer I know here in Minneapolis; he said it could be weeks before I hear anything. I wrote Dale a letter right away, but that could take just as long to get an answer. I don't know.....I'm sure my mind will stop running wild with the thoughts I'm having. I want to keep working; I really think it will be best. All I ask is for your patience with an employee who suddenly starts crying for no outward reason."

"You do whatever you need, Gladdy. Everyone in the office knows the situation and understands. I can't think of anyone I know as friends or anything that hasn't felt the hurt this war brings. You heard my sister's youngest boy was killed last month in the South Pacific; his brother made the landing at Normandy, we think. You can count on the help of everybody that works here, OK?"

"Thanks, Frank. And to think when you first hired me, I was scared to death of you!" Gladdy smiled as she turned to go.

"Well, you just make sure everybody else around here still thinks that way! I want them to know this old dog still has teeth in his bite, even if his bark is getting quieter!"

Gladdy felt a bit better already; knowing she had the support of her boss and coworkers meant a lot to her. She sat at her own desk and began calling the various plants and factories to schedule visits over the next weeks. Air Commodore Wallace was not due for another tour until August or so; she wanted to make use of the time until then to catch up on her audits, especially the reports that were already piling up. She thought about times when people just made things; if there ever was a time when the government didn't need to know every little detail about who hired who or how many of what nationality or race. She wondered how things will change when the war comes to an end and a few million men return, all wanting jobs. Will there even be the jobs when the plants no longer have to make guns and ammunition, or any of the other items the war demanded.

That evening she got home a little later than usual; paperwork had, again, delayed her. She put the package on the kitchen table when she came in the back door. It was one the Air Commodore had mentioned he was sending to her for Dautin. She read the note on the table. Esther was already at the USO, Don was at a wrestling match in St Paul and Dautin had gone to watch him. She was fixing herself a cup of tea when the front doorbell rang. When she answered the door, the Western Union boy was there, his bicycle leaning against the step railing.

"Mrs Weldon? I have a telegram for you; sign here please."

He wasn't more than fifteen, Gladdy thought, as she signed the receipt ledger he offered. She thanked him and tipped him a quarter, which he thanked her for with a smile and an 'Alright!' Gladdy closed the door and looked at the yellow envelope with the telegram inside. She slowly walked to the table, pulled out a chair and sat down. She assumed it was for her, though it might have been for Esther. She carefully opened it and began to read.

"The Secretary of War regrets to inform you......"

116

"Weldon, Dale A... Lieutenant... 760056"

"Yes, yes Lieutenant Weldon. Come, sit down. I know exactly what you will tell us; you're not the first to be in this office. In fact you are about the thousandth or something to sit here. My name is Hauptmann, er... Captain Weimar. We have to complete some paperwork so the Red Cross can officially notify your wife.... let me see, yes.... Gladys, you call her Gladdy? Funny how Americans have nicknames for nearly everyone; it must be somewhat confusing. You graduated from Saint Louis Park schools; that would be in Minnesota, in 1941, ah... you and your wife were in school together! How quaint."

Dale tried hard to hide his absolute astonishment that this German Luftwaffe officer would know these things about him! How in the world could they know this, let alone get the information and tell him these things so quickly; it had been less than a week since he'd been shot down.

Dale was seated in an office in Dulag Luft; it was a main interrogation center, just where he was he didn't know exactly. John Wooster and he had been brought in together and then separated; he had not seen John for three days now. In the office with him was an American airman, a Captain. The flight gear he was wearing told Dale he was a fighter pilot..... or he could be a German agent posing as one. The pilot nodded at Dale when he came in.

"I have just finished questioning Captain Hoover, here." Hauptmann Weimar continued. "You see, we don't need you to answer any questions at all. We already know things like what squadron you flew in, how many planes there are assigned to it; that sort of thing. It's really no secret, you know. Your American newspapers are a wonderful source of information for our intelligence bureau. We have thousands of folks working every day gathering and organizing information on all of you officers in

117

the United States Army Air Force. Would you like a cigarette, Lieutenant Weldon? How about you, Captain Hoover?" Weimar pulled out a pack of Lucky Strikes and offered them each one.

"You know, I wonder if the New York Yankees will win the World Series again this year? I was quite disappointed when they beat the St Louis Cardinals last fall. Personally I hope it will come down to the two St Louis teams, the Cardinals and the Browns. I spent two years in St Louis myself, before the war. I enjoyed the Mississippi River nearly as much as the Rhine River here. Excuse me a moment..."

Another Luftwaffe officer appeared in the doorway. Hauptmann Weimar strode to the door and spoke quietly with the man for a moment before he returned to the desk.

"If you will pardon me, gentleman; I'm requested to assist in the questioning of a couple of English fliers. I won't be long; please help yourself to the cigarettes on my desk."

Dale and Captain Hoover watched as Weimar entered an adjoining office and left the door opened a bit. The two Americans were witness to something neither would ever forget. The two English pilots were tied down on a table, faces up. The Germans each put on a pair of coveralls, picked up what looked sort of like baseball bats, and proceeded to beat the two prisoners to death! The sound of the bats striking the men was fearsome; neither of the Englishmen could possibly resist, though their cries and screams filled the rooms. Dale looked at Hoover, who was looking at him; both had tears in their eyes, convinced that their turn may well be next.

It was over in minutes. Hauptmann Weimar returned to his desk after taking off the coveralls. He was wiping his hands on a towel as he picked up the Lucky Strike pack and withdrew a smoke. Lighting it up, he turned to the two Americans. "Where were we, ah yes, I do so want the St Louis Cardinals to win the championship this year. You two look frightened..... no need to

118

be. It's simple, really. We like you Americans very much; we don't like the British at all."

Their interrogation was over; neither man had been asked a single question. It was all completely unnerving to Dale; he could not understand any of what he had just witnessed. The complete disregard for life that Hauptmann Weimar had shown was beyond anything he imagined a human could do. He began to realize that his time as a guest of the Third Reich would be unlike anything he had ever known.

The next day a group of Allied prisoners, all officers, were herded into a railroad boxcar and shipped north to Stalag Luft One, near the North Sea town of Barth. Twice during their journey north the train was bombed or attacked by Allied aircraft. Once the engine had to be replaced as it was destroyed by a strafing British fighter. They arrived to the view of an extensive compound, covering hundreds of acres and surrounded by double rows of barbed wire, fences, watch towers with searchlights and soldiers carrying machine guns. Stalag Luft One had recently been expanded to accommodate the increasing numbers of American officers shot down over Germany and the occupied countries of Europe. Several thousand officers were currently prisoners in the camp; Dale was added to that number. He was assigned to a room in Block 4 of the North Compound; his home for the foreseeable future.

Chapter 24
July 1944

<u>Minnesota</u>

The past several weeks had gone by quickly, something Gladdy was happy about. The telegram had explained that Dale was 'missing in action'. That meant no one knew yet if he was alive or not. Esther had taken it very hard; believed that Dale was probably dead. Gladdy would not hear of it; she maintained that Dale was alive and probably a prisoner of war. Only time could prove which was true. Despite their difference of opinion the two women were a source of strength in the household. Don had seemed to lose interest in attending his final year of high school; he wanted to join the military right away and, in some way, avenge what had possibly happened to his brother. Even Dautin slipped into a time of depression, not wanting to do anything more than sit in the back yard in the shade of the tree.

On his birthday in mid-July, the family had a barbeque; Gladdy had saved ration points to buy a large beef steak to cook. It was a warm, sunny day with those huge, puffy white clouds gliding across the bright blue sky.

"Now you be careful with that chunk of cow, sir. That's every bit as precious as anything I can think of right now. Don't burn it!" Esther was feeling much better today, enough so to poke fun at Dautin's ability to cook.

"Yes, ma'am. You know, Mother, you said that just like the orders you used to give out to us doughboys in France. I've been thinking about those days a lot recently, maybe too much."

"Well, today is your day, dear. You do whatever you want, as long as you don't want to incinerate that steak!"

Gladdy came over with a birthday gift; it was the package she had brought home the day the telegram arrived about Dale. "Here, dad; why don't you open this before you start cooking. It arrived awhile ago from Commodore Wallace; he asked me to give it to you."

As he opened it up, he made sure no one else could see what would be inside. He put it on his head and turned around.

"What on earth is that?" exclaimed Gladdy. Esther took one look and started laughing until she had to sit down. Don had a one word expression, as usual... "Cool".

"I've wanted one of these for twenty or more years; and it's even the right size. Fits this old, bald head perfectly."

Esther managed to speak, between laughs, "It's as ridiculous on you as the one's they wore back then, Dautin. Why on earth would the Commodore send you a World War 1 German officer's helmet..... I can't remember what they were called. What was it, dear?"

"It, my all-knowing dearest wife, is a Pickelhaube. As you are aware, these were all the rage, a real fashionable item in Germany during the Great War. This is incredible; I've got to go in and write a thank you letter to Wallace right away. This is great, I don't think I'll take it off the rest of the day."

"I will never begin to understand the male mind, Gladdy. They fight each other to the death and, years later, relish in wearing parts of an enemy uniform." Esther was shaking her head. "Well, I might as well start with the steak. That man will not be much use for the rest of the day. Maybe we could use the spike on that thing he's wearing to get the olives out of the jar."

It was at that moment that the mailman walked around from the front of the house. "Excuse me, ladies. I have a parcel for the family of Dale Weldon here and brought a letter from England as well."

The parcel had been sent from Bob Gracy, Dale's pilot and friend. It contained everything of his from the air base in Deenethorpe, all neatly packed with a letter from Gracy on top. Gladdy didn't want to read the letter until after the birthday celebration; but she did want to share the letter from Air Commodore Wallace with the family. Esther went in to the house to get Dautin while Don carried the package in. When they had all returned outside, Dautin still in his gaudy headgear, Gladdy began to read the letter.

8 July, 1944

To my friends the Weldons,

Greetings to my Yankee "mate" and his family. Sometimes news is hard to put on paper but I will endeavor to do my best. As you know my daughter, Kim, was married to an RAF officer last month. It was a joyous affair, full of fun and laughter in the middle of this awful war. Ted, her husband, is now in France at a forward airfield flying missions against the Boche; he's turned into a rather good pilot and has a nose for finding the enemy wherever they hide. Kim has taken a posting in Scotland, far from the fighting where she is already preparing to make me a grandfather! Young people don't seem to want to wait to start families anymore.

Now the hard part comes; my heart is, again, fairly breaking as I write this. My wife, Edith, who I have adored and cherished all these years is no more. Two days after the wedding a German guided rocket hit our beloved home, killing my darling along with three others that were there. I was inspecting an airfield in the north of England at the time. It's only in the past week or so that I've been able to return to the war effort; one that must go on for the sake of Edith and all the others that have died thus far! This brings me to some business at hand.

Gladdy, I'm wondering if you would consider becoming a housekeeper for a doddering old Englishman at his new 'digs', as I'm told Americans call their homes, in the state of Florida? I've decided to accept an assignment as part of the air staff to the Joint Chiefs in Washington. I'll be working primarily in your southern states so thought it best to acquire a home down there. I've heard from Frank Rarig that you've experience in this area; but I must add that the title 'housekeeper' may not be exactly correct. I'd like for you to manage the household, not wash the windows or empty the dustbins. There will be other duties, all proper and above board; you know we English are a stuffy lot.... I would appreciate your answer soon. I hope to move in and commence my duties the beginning of August.

In closing, I must not neglect wishing a very Happy Birthday to my war time chum, Dautin. Your mate against the *Boche* forever....

William Wallace

Germany

"Weldon, I'd like to explain a few ground rules we have here. First, there is still a chain of command, nothing much different than you're already used to. Your flight is this barracks, squadron is the block; for you that will be Block 4. Ahh, Group is the North Compound. Our senior allied commander here is Colonel Zemke. Keep track of those nine bed boards the Krauts issued you; they'll be checking for those nearly every day. Don't let them get away; make sure any request for one comes down through the chain of command. Since those boards can be used for many things, including tunneling, the Krauts keep a pretty close eye on them. So do we; the penalty for losing some is pretty stiff, usually a week or more in solitary confinement." The officer giving him this briefing was a Captain Elliott, his squadron commander. The briefing lasted nearly an hour and covered everything from chow to using water to rules on curfew and such. Dale knew there would be much more to learn about. There seemed to be so many rules for a place where you did very little. The one thing

Elliott said that impressed Dale the most was, "Around here, we try hard to keep everyone busy. Your body may suffer some from the food, but we don't want your mind to go away."

Daily routine, as Dale was already beginning to learn, revolved around two subjects; chow and roll call. Chow was normally twice a day, morning and evening. It was important that Red Cross food parcels continued to be distributed to the prisoners; a body could not last long on what the Germans provided alone. Not only was food becoming scarce in the Third Reich, the transportation network, trains and roads were being bombed daily throughout the country. What food was issued by the Luftwaffe often consisted of nearly rotten potatoes, coarse black bread that was hard to digest and sometimes had pieces of glass or stones in it, and some barley to make soup with. When meat showed up, and rarely did, it smelled horrible and no one asked what kind of animal it had been. The Red Cross parcels contained canned milk, tinned meat, coffee and other foods prized by the prisoners. Parcels might also arrive from families back home; sometimes baked things like cookies or breads. Also welcome were packages containing tobacco and cigarettes. All things considered, it was an enormous advantage to be in an officers' camp run by the Luftwaffe. Other POW camps were much worse off.

Dale was in his third week as a prisoner when he heard an unmistakable voice, loud and at a pitch that kind of grated on your nerves; above all it was very loud. Dale said to no one in particular, "That has GOT to be Jack Hale."

"Well, I'll be go to hell, if it ain't Dale Weldon! You must have done something right after washing out of pilot training after all. When did you land in here, Weldon?" Jack Hale was still about the loudest person Dale had ever met. They had been together in training back in Texas during the summer of 1942. That seemed like a lifetime ago. The two spent an afternoon catching up on what they had been doing the past two years. It turned out Hale had never progressed beyond two engine aircraft and had become a C-47 pilot. He had been shot down after dropping weapon containers full of machine guns and ammunition to the Maquis, the French resistance fighters, two months before the landings at Normandy. The Germans had not been nice to him during his interrogations; the beating they had given him had ruptured one of his eardrums. Now that he couldn't hear on one side, he compensated by talking even louder. There was no such thing as a whisper to Jack Hale.

"Hey, Dale, did you know that there are more of us here? I mean more of the guys we went through training with. Phil Harris, remember him? He's in the South Compound; Phil was shot down early on, I think he's been here a year or so. We should look him up tomorrow."

"Thanks, Jack. I'm really glad there are some guys I may know here. I think I'll ask around and try to find some more. What do you say we get together every day about this time? I'm sure we can find something to do." Dale heard the whistle for afternoon roll call. He hurried to fall in line with the rest of his flight and squadron. No one was missing or unaccounted for, but the Krauts hauled one man away from the ranks and put him in solitary. He was short two boards.

Dale spent the next week trying to find other men he had known from training. He discovered that all three of his own roommates from flight school had been killed; one had died when his plane collided with another bomber over England. Several guys he knew from gunnery school and bombardier training were either dead or missing. Two men he had graduated from high school with were also dead, although another was in the South Compound, right here at Stalag Luft One. He couldn't help but wonder if he had been asked about that by his interrogator, like Hauptmann Weimar.

Every day he wrote to Shorty. He had been given a journal in one of his Red Cross parcels. Although letters were rarely sent out of camp, he found that writing to his sweetheart became a way of keeping a record, a diary of sorts, of his time in the camp. In it he also made lists of what his first meal would be when he returned home, detailing precise things like 'cream in coffee at breakfast, but heavy cream on the corn flakes'. He soon discovered he was not alone in writing about food; nearly everyone did. Many prisoners would have contests over who could come up with the perfect menu for that first day of freedom. Winners might get extra cigarettes or some other prize.

Dale also joined a group that wanted to put on a special show for Christmas; provided the war was not over by then. Most felt it would be; that Germany could not last long under the terrific pounding the American and British air forces were giving them. News of the war was passed around daily both by word of mouth and by an official newsletter. It was hand written and read in the barracks each evening; someone in camp had made a radio and was able to tune in to the BBC radio broadcasts from London. There were even times when the German guards would ask the prisoners how the war was going; apparently they didn't completely believe their Propaganda Minister, Herr Goebbels who continued to forecast 'a glorious victory and a thousand year reign of the German people'.

Chapter 25
August 1944

<u>Florida</u>

The train pulled into the station under a bright Florida sun. Gladdy had thought it would be oppressively humid on the station platform, but the breeze off the ocean a few blocks away made the day pleasant. Don was busy getting their bags with the help of a porter. An RAF officer in his crisp gray blue uniform approached her.

"Mrs Weldon? Flying Officer Hutchins; Air Commodore Wallace sends his respects, ma'am. I'm to bring you and your travel companion to the villa and see that you get settled in. I'm afraid the Commodore will not be here for several days, perhaps a couple of weeks; he's been delayed in Washington. He did say you are to make yourself quite at home and to enjoy the sunshine until his return."

"Thank you, sir. We'll be ready to go in just a few minutes I'm sure."

"Hey, Gladdy. Can you believe it? I mean, look over there; that's a real palm tree! They're all over the place; man, this is the place to live. Feel that sun; mmmmmmmm, boy I'm I going to enjoy the next two weeks."

Don had come along with Gladdy to provide company and to give him a chance to see some of the United States before he started his senior year back in The Park. Dautin and Esther had arranged his tickets through Commodore Wallace's office; travel for civilians

127

was still restricted and without the military clearance it would not have been possible.

As Flying Officer Hutchins drove to the villa, Gladdy and Don were able to enjoy the view; the ocean waves calmly lapping the white beach, a few people playing a game of volleyball on the sand. It looked so peaceful and fun; it was hard to image that just a few miles offshore there was still the very real threat of German submarines and the dreadful torpedoes they used to send Allied ships, and sailors, to a watery grave.

"Nearly there, ma'am. When we arrive, Mrs Winsted, the cook, will likely show you your rooms while I get Master Weldon settled in the guest cottage."

"Guest cottage? I'm liking this more and more; it makes me feel like I'm in some kind of Hollywood movie or something." Don was wearing a grin three sizes too big for his face. He imagined what his classmates would say when he walked into school the first day, all tanned and full of stories of sunny, warm Florida.

The car turned off the main road, through a large gate and headed up a gravel drive. Through the overhanging canopy of cypress trees, the front of the villa could be seen. It looked almost like a plantation from "Gone with the Wind". Tall white columns flanked the front doors and the house was wrapped around by a large veranda. There were three or four other buildings nearby. Hutchins explained that from the second floor windows there was a fine view of the ocean. When they stepped out of the car, a most delightful aroma filled the air; sweet and fresh.

"What is that wonderful smell?" Gladdy asked.

"Oh, ma'am. There is a large orange grove behind the house. Plenty of fresh citrus including lemons, limes and even grapefruit anytime you'd like. This place makes me forget there's a war on. Ah, Mrs Winsted; this is Mrs Weldon. Would you be so kind as to show her to her rooms? I'll take young Weldon here to the guest cottage out back and get him settled in."

"Certainly, sir. Glad to make your acquaintance, ma'am. We'll have your bags brought up directly. Would you follow me, please?"

Gladdy's head was almost spinning. She had not expected that even the cook would speak with that clipped, British accent. She learned that everyone working here, with the exception of the gardening crew, were from England. Commodore Wallace had brought his entire staff over; those who had survived the bombing of his estate back home. Here, in the deep South, was a little piece of his home. She began to wonder just how well she would fit in and whether the staff would follow her instructions, being the newcomer to the Commodore's world. How different her own had become; how different Dale's must be right now.

For weeks Gladdy had been unable to make a decision on whether to come here. Not knowing where Dale was made it impossible to leave Dautin and Esther; she also needed to stay put so she could be contacted with any update from the Army Air Corps. Ten days ago another telegram had arrived with the information that Dale was, indeed, a Prisoner of War. It gave her instructions on how to contact him and what she should, and should not, write to ensure he got the letter. Gladdy, Dautin, Esther and Don had sat down and immediately written short notes to him which they mailed in a single envelope, entrusting the Red Cross to get it delivered to a place called Stalag Luft One, the prison where he was being held.

Germany

"Sorry, mate. It's the best we can do here. I hardly feel like the dentist that I am with this contraption being all I've got to work with. You do have the option of me just yanking that tooth out with pliers. Just so you understand."

129

The medical officer was Australian; he'd been captured in North Africa fully two years earlier. He was also the only trained dentist in the North Camp. Dale sat, looking at the system of pulleys and gears and whatnot, powered by another prisoner peddling as fast as he could on the old bicycle frame.

"Really, before the Jerries let me have this thing, the only option was the pliers. Now at least there is a choice. Some of the blokes here fancy getting a little exercise, pretend they're on the Tour de' France or something. Try to relax, that tooth looks pretty bad; must hurt like hell. Sorry I don't have anything to numb it. It will feel better when I'm done."

Dale watched as the dentist came closer to his face with the drill. He could actually see the bit turning. He closed his mouth, shook his head; then he told the Aussie he'd rather have him yank it out. The dentist smiled, nodded and put the drill back. The cyclist looked rather disappointed that his turn on the peddles was over.

"You know, most all of you Americans say the same thing. I guess you're just too soft for this type of dentistry. That's alright; we'll have a go at that blighter with the pliers. This won't take long; we'll do what we can to ward off infection afterwards. Let's have a look see, shall we?"

A few minutes later, Dale was outside; the side of his face still throbbed, but it actually felt a little better than before the tooth was pulled. He sighed and thought it was just one more reminder of how far from home he was. He could hear another prisoner quietly whistling 'Somewhere Over the Rainbow'. Dale had to chuckle; he certainly wasn't in Kansas right now.

"Hey, Weldon. There was a letter for you at mail call while you were at the dentist. I put it in on your rack." It was Jack Hale; even without looking around, Dale knew by the way other guys in the yard jumped at the volume of the announcement. Listening to Jack was nearly like sitting directly under the speakers at Memorial Stadium during a Gophers game; they could make you hard of hearing for a week. Dale smiled, turned around and thanked Jack; then he hurried back to his barracks. It was the first piece of mail he'd received since his arrival. His hands shook a bit as he opened the envelope.

My darling,
I write this, just minutes after receiving a telegram that you are safe and a prisoner of the Germans. How relieved I was to know you're alive and well. Then I cried, knowing you are in prison. It's been scary here, not knowing anything. I'm sure it's been much worse for you. We all miss you so much. I hope and pray you are treated well and I look forward to the day we will be together again with nothing to separate us. This note is mailed with others from Dad, Mom and Don. Hopefully you'll get them all. I'll write often and send as many food parcels as I'm allowed to through the Red Cross. I'm going to their office in Minneapolis tomorrow to learn exactly how to make sure you get everything we send. At this moment, my love, know that I'm sending you all my love. I will always love you, no matter how long it is until we can hold each other again.

Shorty

Dale read the notes from the others, then read Shorty's again.... and again. He kissed the note where her lipstick was and carefully folded it up. He noticed the number '1' written under the return address, and wondered how many more he would receive before he saw her beautiful face again.

Chapter 26
September 1944

<u>Florida</u>

Today was the day Air Commodore Wallace was due to arrive in the afternoon; the house had been gone over top to bottom by the staff and everything was in its proper place. The groundskeepers had the outside looking beautiful, with every blade of grass looking perfect. Gladdy was a bit surprised by all the fuss; she had regarded the Commodore as being less than the fastidious master the others around here made him out to be. She had made arrangements for the other guests as well; her instructions were that a few gentlemen would be accompanying the Commodore and the guest cottage and extra bedrooms needed to be prepared. She had even obtained two staff cars from an Air Corps base nearby to be leant for the use of the RAF for the week.

With everything as ready as possible, she took the time to go and freshen up before their arrival. The Commodore had sent instructions for her to purchase additional 'clothes and such as she deemed appropriate' for her position as his housekeeper and American liaison. After she had seen Don off on the train back to Minnesota, Gladdy had spent an entire day shopping for what she needed. Today she would wear a dress that spoke 'business'. Her dress was a lovely shade of brown, just the right length and cut with a hint of military to it. Flying Officer Hutchins had said anyone in the RAF would know whose air force she was cheering on. She made a point of wearing a miniature U S bombardier's pin on it; just in case they didn't.

She sat on a veranda out back overlooking the gardens and, beyond, the citrus groves. A wonderful breeze was softly filling the air with the delightful scent of orange blossoms. She reflected on the past weeks since her arrival here; Don and she had spent a couple of wonderful days enjoying the beaches and sun. The only reminder that a war was on came two nights ago. As they were getting ready for bed Gladdy had noticed a dim glow out over the waters of the Gulf. Flying Officer Hutchins had explained it was from a freighter that was burning after being torpedoed by a German submarine. Such attacks were not nearly as frequent now but it served to warn everyone that the fight was not over. It had cast a bit of gloom over the two Americans as she and Don spent time talking about Dale and the rest of the family before heading to their rooms for the night. Along with Dale in the German POW camp there was her own brother fighting somewhere in France as well as several of Dale's cousins scattered around the world from Africa to the Pacific islands and Australia. Gladdy and Don spent time thanking God that none of them had been killed or wounded as far as they knew. They also reminded one another of the need to be careful in what they wrote in letters to Dale; they had been cautioned not to mention Gladdy's work with the RAF in particular.

Mrs Winsted came out on the veranda and spoke softly, saying a call had just come in; the Commodore and the other men had arrived and were on their way. They should arrive in a quarter hour or so. Gladdy thanked her and busied herself making sure there were no last minute surprises that had been overlooked. She was in the front entryway when she heard the sound of tires on the gravel approaching the manor. She glanced at the large mirror one last time and quickly adjusted her blouse and jacket, smoothing it for the hundredth time.

"Ahh, Mrs Weldon... splendid. I'm so glad you decided to come and join our little corner of Britain down here. I say, you've not gone and actually joined your husband in service to the United States, have you? With uniforms like that, you should beat the

133

hun much faster than our own rather frumpy RAF jumpsuits, what?"

"Thank you, Commodore. I wasn't exactly sure what you felt would be appropriate to my position here; Flying Officer Hutchins has been most helpful and has quite an eye for fashion, I must say. Your entire staff has made me feel most welcome and I'm ready to get down to business whenever you direct, sir."

"Yes, yes... all that in a short time. Hutchins shall be made a Flight Lieutenant for this. Right now I'd like to introduce you to some chaps you'll be getting to know. They'll be working here and, I'm sure, bumbling their own way about learning American customs. Perhaps you could also instruct them, as needed, in addition to your other duties? This is Group Captain Smythe, Wing Commanders Brandon and Wilson, Squadron Leaders Hall and Lincoln. A few others you'll meet tomorrow when they get here. Things are going to get a bit busy around here, I'm afraid."

"Not to worry, Commodore. Your rooms are ready, gentlemen; the staff will show you to them and arrange for your bags to be brought up. Please pardon me if I stumble over your ranks; I'm not even comfortable with our own yet. I've taken the liberty, a curious habit here in the states, of arranging for some refreshments before dinner. If you'd all care to freshen up, we'll meet on the large veranda out back in thirty minutes."

"Splendid, splendid, Mrs Weldon. I say, that Mrs Baston deserves a commendation or medal for recommending you when I made my inquiries about needing assistance." Commodore Wallace was genuinely pleased; Gladdy caught a wink from Mrs Winsted and, from the corner of the room, Hutchins gave her a quaint American "thumbs up".

As they were climbing the stairs to their rooms, Gladdy overheard the Commodore speaking to the Group Captain, telling him about how Dautin and he had "practically fought together" back in France during The Great War. She made a mental note to be sure and include that tidbit in her next letter to the folks. First, however, best check on those refreshments...

Germany

Dale awoke from the dream, again. The past week had been the same each night; a few hours of sleep and then the dream. Each time it was identical; the awful beating he'd witnessed of those English pilots. He would wake with the sounds and the smell of the Lucky Strikes he and the other American were smoking. Only now the Englishmen would raise themselves off the tables and point their bloody fingers at him, as if to say "What are you doing about this, mate?".

As hard as he tried, Dale couldn't shake the dream. It came back, night after night. When he told others about it, many would shrug and say that they had their own to deal with. Not that it wasn't terrible, but that there was nothing to do about it while they were here. Maybe someday there would be help; or maybe the dreams would stop. Dale wasn't so sure. He feared he would never be able to forget the things he'd experienced and especially what may lay ahead for him.

His first two months in the camp had taught him much; in fact, he'd learned about all there was here as a *Kriegie*. He knew not to venture out of the barracks at night; once "Lights Out" sounded, guard dogs were let loose in this particular compound. It was kind of an experiment the Germans were trying... see if the dogs alone could guard the prisoners at night. The first night one man was killed by the dogs and another was torn up badly and still might not survive. After hours communication between barracks had suffered until the prisoners set up a system of Morse Code tapping faint enough for the guards to not hear. The dogs didn't seem to pay it any attention either; it was slower but it was working, for now.

Escape from the camp was difficult, nearly impossible. The Germans had learned to build camps more securely as the war

135

went on. Most prisoners felt the war was winding to a close now and the risks of getting caught and suffering the penalties were too great. The clandestine radios in camp had picked up the BBC broadcasts about the capture of Paris by the Allies and the great gains made on the ground across France by American General Patton's Third Army. Many felt their liberation and the end of the war was, at most, a couple of months away; certainly no later than Christmas.

Even the guards' attitudes were changing; they didn't seem to lord it over the prisoners quite as much. Some were even seen to smile or show an act of kindness once in awhile, seeming to know that some day, perhaps soon, they might be the prisoners instead of the guards. To Dale, time now had become a daily routine of getting up, standing for roll calls throughout the day, trying to keep busy; most of all, trying to not think about food. He knew he'd already lost ten, maybe fifteen pounds and he'd only been here two months. Others would reassure him that the weight would stop coming off soon, when he reached whatever weight his body could adjust to. Some men had lost as much as 50% of what they weighed when they were captured. Others had only seemed to lose a few pounds; mostly they had been the skinny ones to begin with. The highlight of every day was mail call; that time when a letter would drive the boredom into the background for awhile. Even if he didn't get a letter himself, one friend or another would read about things back home. Dale did the same when he got a letter; of course, there was always those parts he wouldn't share. The men developed a sort of honor code; don't ask about the personal stuff.

<u>Florida</u>

"Confound it, man! I've needed to speak with Admiral Harrison for two days and you're telling me he's still not available? Have I got to hang over you every minute to make sure you're trying to do your job? That's all the better you can do.... to tell me he's not available? Why... where is he... Oh, keep trying to get him on the phone. What nonsense and stop your blithering about things."

136

Obviously the day was not beginning well. Gladdy could hear the Commodore's voice through the door, down the hall, up the stairs and through the doors to the study she knew were closed. Stopping by the door of the Commodore's office, she poked her head in and asked his adjutant, "Everything OK"? The look she got in return was one of bewilderment and resign. "Sorry, ma'am, I'm not having any luck with your Pentagon people and the Commodore needs to speak to someone there."

"Here, let me try. Who does he need to get through to? Could you write it down, please? Thanks." Gladdy sat at the empty desk and picked up the phone. In two minutes she asked the adjutant to see if the Commodore was available to speak with Admiral Harrison. He practically tripped over himself getting to the Commodore's door. A half hour later the Commodore came through the door.

"That, my dear, was truly fantastic! How is it my staff cannot accomplish a simple task in two days that you performed in two minutes? Utterly fantastic!"

"Well, Commodore, there are secrets outside the military, you know. If you want to get through to a General or the Director of a large company, or a Governor or whomever, you never ask for the person directly. Here in the States, you ask for their assistant and explain things, that's all."

"Mrs Weldon, I cannot thank you enough, again. I would ask of you two things, please? First, would you agree to take on the running of my office and staff; not the household staff. You've already got them running like a Swiss timepiece. I mean the affairs of this office. I am not able to find, apparently in the half of the Royal Air Force stationed here in your country, one individual that is up to the task. I'm sure I can get it cleared through our people, what with salary and all that; your security clearance has already been checked and approved."

"Commodore, am I to understand you're asking me to become your secretary? Your daughter warned me about this some time ago, you know." Gladdy smiled, the smile of a friend.

"Yes, yes, I remember. I've even tried getting her back, with my son-in-law, mind you. He's not interested in staff work, prefers to fly against the Hun and all that; she just won't cross the Atlantic again, she says. Of course, you'd have to learn to read my writing, what?"

"Commodore, I'll let you in on another American secret. Over here we use what's called shorthand. You dictate and I'll get it down right the first time."

"Hmmph; Mrs Weldon, we English may appear somewhat stuffy, if that's the proper term. I'll have you know modern shorthand was first developed by an Englishman! I simply cannot find someone in our color of uniform that knows it!"

"Sir, I'll not trade my olive drab for RAF gray, but I'd be honored to help you with the war effort; one ally alongside another. Anything to get my husband home faster, I'd say."

"Splendid, splendid. Adjutant! In here at once... show Mrs Weldon where all of the files and whatnot are and cut yourself orders back to an airbase in England. That's a good lad; no wait. I've a better idea; cut orders for another like yourself to report here. Mrs Weldon shall have two assistants; an Air Commodore rates a staff at least this large. Get me Flying Officer, I mean, Flight Lieutenant Hutchins will you?"

Chapter 27
Fall 1944

<u>The World</u>

Paris had fallen to the Allies. Germany's once vaunted Wehrmacht was being beaten, badly, on all sides. Russia was driving toward the homeland of the Third Reich from the east; in Italy, the Allies were making headway toward the border with Austria. The empire that was to last a thousand years appeared to be on the brink of destruction after only half that many weeks.

In the Pacific the Allies were also making headway against the Japanese. The anchorage of Ulithi in the Caroline Islands had been taken and the U S Navy would soon build it into the largest base in history to plan for the future invasion of Japan. The bombing campaign against the German homeland continued, disrupting transportation and cutting fuel supplies for the German army and air forces. Food distribution networks were also affected and shortages and starvation began throughout areas of occupied Europe. The lack of food only worsened the plight of hundreds of thousands of prisoners held by the Axis, including those of the Allied military.

In Germany and Italy, POW's were still receiving Red Cross parcels and mail from home. Those held in camps run by the Luftwaffe were, perhaps, more fortunate in the treatment they received. Americans held by the Japanese were systematically beaten and starved; worse things happened to those from other nations.

When it seemed the war would end in a matter of weeks, Hitler unleashed a surprise attack on British and American army forces in an area of the Ardennes, in Luxembourg. About the same time, Japanese Kamikaze's, suicide pilots, began flying their planes into American ships in an attempt to stop the U S Navy. The war took a frightful, awful turn; rocking the Allies back and threatened to undo a year's worth of victories.

Chapter 28
December 1944

<u>Minnesota</u>

"Gladdy, it sure is swell having you home again. I know Mom and Dad have enjoyed telling others about all you've been doing and the places you've seen these past months. What's it really like working for the British?"

Don had grown another inch and filled out a bit since the summer when he and Gladdy had last seen each other in Florida. He was in his senior year now at Park High and was looking forward to his chance to "get into this fight". He planned on joining the Marines or the Navy when he graduated, if the war was still going on. A month ago he would have bet it was going to be over by now. The fighting in Europe had increased, not in a good way, with the Nazi's attack. A cousin, Dick, and Gladdy's own brother, Bob, were both in the Army involved in that battle. Another cousin, Bobby, was a Naval Aviator in the Pacific now, flying off a carrier battling the suicide pilots Japan was sending in waves to try and destroy the American ships.

"You know, Don, they keep me so busy there are days I'm not sure even what city I'm in. I find myself thinking about how to get to a particular office or war plant and then remember I'm no longer even in that same state. The only thing I know to do every day is to write a letter before bed. I send one to Mom and Dad every week; my sisters get one, too. Of course I write Dale every other day. I've not gotten one back from him at all yet, but I still look forward to the first one. Every two weeks I send him a special

141

package; none have come back and I hope and pray he's getting them. The hardest thing is not knowing how, or really even where, he is. When I read of our Air Force, and the RAF, bombing Germany at night and by day, I'm scared that they may bomb the prison he's in by mistake. I really just wish the war would end. I like to think the work I'm doing may help bring that about. By the way, thanks for picking me up at the air field. I wasn't sure you'd get the telegram I sent from Washington."

"So, sis, what's that new Pentagon like? I've seen pictures of it; is it really as big as it looks? You'd think they could fit the whole army in there."

"Don, you would not believe it; it's absolutely huge. I've been in some of the factories where they're building new bombers and they seemed gigantic until I went into the Pentagon. You almost need a road map to find your way around; each office and hallway looks like another one. It would probably be worse if I wasn't 'one of those Brits' as they call us. Sometimes I love the looks I get when I open my mouth and good old Minnesotan comes out." Gladdy smiled at the humor of it. "They expect that clipped, English accent and get American with a touch of Scandinavian twang, as I call it. It really is funny sometimes."

"Well, plenty of opportunity to speak it this week. Mom has outdone herself for tomorrow's Christmas meal. Grandpa Rundquist even got his hands on a turkey, and Uncle Roy shot a goose this season. Plenty to eat, that's for sure. All the same, I wonder what Dale will be having?"

Tears welled up in Gladdy's eyes as she, too, thought of her darling. She pictured him sitting, possibly alone, in a dark cell somewhere with little or nothing to eat.

Germany

"I tell you, Jack, this is undoubtedly the best day I've had since getting here. I haven't laughed this hard in at least a year. That was the best musical ever and those dames were actually kind of cute." Dale was a bit tired from the laughing and the muscles in his gut hurt. It was a welcome hurt.

"I know, I know. Who'd have thought costumes like that could be made from Klim cans and paper mache? Those wigs we helped with looked pretty good too, huh? Good to laugh like this, especially now. It's tougher being in here when we thought it'd be over by tomorrow; I mean Christmas and all. How do you suppose Hitler scraped together enough men to attack us? That new guy, the one who got here day before yesterday; what did he say? The Germans had tanks twice the size as ours? Where did they come from? Even the damn weather is on the Nazi's side; if the skies would clear up we could bomb the crap out of them. Right now we can't even see 'em."

"You're right, Jack. But you wait, the clouds will go away. When they do, I wouldn't want to be on the receiving end of guys like Patton and Bradley! Can you imagine how mad our guys are right about now? Give them a chance and they'll be in Berlin in three weeks, you watch. I'm more worried about those Japs; we were told they've started flying their planes right into our ships on purpose. Suicide pilots they call them. How can a man do that? They really are devils or something, I guess. No regard for their own lives at all. I mean, I'd die to save a buddy, we all would I think. But to just go and blow yourself up like that?"

"Well, Dale, as a weapon of war it's pretty smart I suppose. One plane, one aircraft carrier or battleship; pretty cheap. It makes the war a lot more expensive for our side; can you imagine how many men we'll lose if we have to attack Japan itself? I'm hoping you and I, and all of us here, get to watch the end of the Pacific War from home, that's all I'm thinking about. Oh, and what we're going to have for Christmas dinner, that too."

"Jack, Jack; don't remind me of that. It makes me hungry thinking about what I'd be eating at home. My mom makes the best turkey and Shorty's mashed potatoes......" Dale's sentence was cut short by the chorus of "Shut ups" that surrounded the two of them.

Later that evening, the revelry turned to quiet reflection as the men in their compound held a Christmas Eve service. As they sang carols and listened to a message from their Chaplain, each man was gripped by his own thoughts of home, the war, their situation and the chances of freedom in the future. The Chaplain, towards the end of his talk, suddenly stopped and, gesturing for everyone to listen, opened a window behind him. All could hear the sounds of the guards, in their own service and language, singing "Stille Nacht". The Americans gently joined in until their own voices, and those of their enemies, together proclaimed a desire for peace on earth and good will to all men.

The next day's meal, barley soup and a potato, was made special by the memory of the previous evening. Word went around that some POW's and guards even shared and traded bits of Red Cross parcel "treats" and cigarettes for Dutch chocolate and real bread.

Chapter 29
January 1945

Washington D C

The Colonel in the adjoining office came out with a quizzical expression on his face. He had overheard his adjutant discussing, with a woman, a problem about granting the RAF access to a B-29 manufacturing plant in Wichita. When he heard the young lady's name was Weldon, something clicked in his mind.

"Pardon me. Ma'am, did you say your last name was Weldon? You're not, by chance, related to a Dale Weldon? I know you're not from England by your speech. My name is Walther, Colonel Walther."

"Yes, Colonel, Dale is actually my husband, a Bombardier in the Eighth Air Force. At present he's a Prisoner of War in Germany. I work for Air Commodore Wallace as part of his staff. We're trying to obtain permission to visit a war plant in Wichita while we're touring the central United States. Commodore Wallace is the RAF liaison..."

"No need to explain who Commodore Wallace is. As part of Operations here, I'm aware of the RAF's mission and plan on cooperating with it. I'm relieved to hear that your husband is alright, as it goes. Sorry about his being captured; we'll do all we can to see his return is a safe one. I knew your husband when he was in pilot training. In fact, I had to wash him out of the program because of an oversight he made. He struck me as a very bright young man; even though he wasn't able to continue in pilot training, I feel confident he will do well as a bombardier and an

145

officer. Captain, issue the passes... and allow the Commodore and his staff access to any other plant they desire. Mrs Weldon, it has been a pleasure; best of luck to you and your husband."

Gladdy left the office with the passes and a letter granting access to practically anywhere. She carried with her something infinitely more precious; the knowledge that her husband was held in esteem by others. The thought that this Colonel would remember Dale out of the hundreds, perhaps thousands, of other cadets he had been in charge of was all she could think of in the taxi back to the hotel.

"Good heavens, Gladdy. The Commodore will believe you can conjure up nearly anything when he sees this. How on earth did you manage to get this out of Operations when we've been unable to get access to some plants making paint, of all things?" Flight Lieutenant Hutchins was truly impressed by this one; he had come to see Gladdy as someone who could cut through red tape like a very sharp knife indeed.

"Oh, it's actually easy when you're married to the man I am, I suppose." She smiled at Hutchins and the twinkle in her eye said there was a story here. Hutchins poured tea and ordered a cup of coffee for Gladdy and waited for her to tell it. When she was done, Hutchins admitted the Weldon family was, indeed, a bit special. He counted on his fingers events like the Commodore and Dautin's friendship, the meeting of Wallace and Dale at the hospital in England, Gladdy being able to "work miracles" as part of their staff.

"I suppose, when this is all over, you'll have met Churchill himself, along with your husband. Perhaps even the King."

"Now, really Hutchins. Don't go overboard and make this bigger than it is. Then again; you never can tell." Gladdy replied.

The Commodore was very pleased by the letter Gladdy had obtained at Operations. They would all, the entire staff, go to dinner this very evening to mark the event. He asked her to draft a letter of personal thanks to Colonel Walther from himself; Gladdy responded it was on his desk awaiting his signature. Wallace looked up and with a nod, said simply, "I say, good show Mrs Weldon, very good indeed."

Germany

It wasn't the cold that woke Dale; he'd been awake since shortly after midnight. In the distance he could hear the dull thump of explosions from the RAF's bombing of Rostock, about 30 miles to the southwest of Stalag Luft One. In his mind, Dale reflected on a time when the idea of dropping bombs on an enemy was patriotic; it had gone from that to almost pity after he had seen some of the destruction up close with his own eyes and had witnessed a bombing while on the train as a new POW. Now his only reaction was a mixture of anger that the Germans didn't just surrender to stop this wasting of civilian lives and their cities and the jealousy he felt; at least Rostock was warm at this moment because of the fires. He shook his head at the idiotic thought and focused instead on remembering home; what it looked and smelled like. He felt a small cold wind chiseling a hole in his blanket. He found a small crack between two boards next to his bunk and stuffed a piece of cloth, torn from a wash rag, in it to stop the arctic intrusion.

The Germans allowed one chunk of coal per prisoner every night; in this barracks that meant sixteen pieces, each of which burned for a whopping three or four minutes. The prisoners took turns placing a piece in the stove in the middle of the room; tonight Dale's was the first. The game became one of how long each man could wait until he placed his piece, in turn, into the fire. Too soon and the stove seemed to eat it faster; too late and the piece may not start to burn from the embers of the previous offering, causing the room to get even colder. Last night one man slept past his turn and the fire went completely out; restarting the fire cost nearly a whole piece. Dale was sure that man would not sleep through his turn again after the chewing out he received from the others. "Funny", Dale thought, "what becomes important in a place like this".

His thoughts turned toward what he would buy first when he got home. He was sure the Air Corps would feed him well, really fatten him up, before anyone in the States would see him. So it wouldn't be food; maybe some new clothes? No, a newly issued uniform would do fine; besides, he had plenty of his old clothes in his dresser and closet at home. He smiled, knowing they wouldn't be too tight. How about a new dress for Shorty? No, he'd prefer her to wear... don't think on that! Let's see; got it. A new fishing rod and reel; this war has got to end before summer and by the time I get home there'll still be plenty of time to fish through the fall. Yeah, that's it... a new reel. Maybe one ... the thoughts and images of rocking in a boat on a warm, sunny, summer day put him to sleep before he'd even landed that first walleye.

The next morning the news spread through camp that the American and British armies had finished "mopping up" the mess left over from the Battle of the Bulge; Germany's attack through the Ardennes Forest in December had failed. It had started as the largest defeat the American Army had ever suffered. Now the drive on Berlin could continue; and the Soviets had captured Warsaw! So the squeeze was on the Nazis from both sides. Then a follow up was announced that the Americans had landed in the Philippines; the Japanese were being driven back as well. The men's emotions soared; this day would be remembered by all of them. Dale and Jack agreed that the men who had built their little clandestine radio should get a medal, maybe two.... and a good, thick steak as a bonus.

Chapter 30
March 1945

<u>Florida</u>

It was wonderful, being back in the relative warmth and sunshine of the South. Though the two week swing through the central United States had provided much needed information and contacts for the Air Commodore's mission, the weather had been less than perfect. Storms had caused them to cancel only one manufacturing plant visit, but it had also delayed several others that cut short the time planned for tours. All things considered, Wallace was pleased with the results and appreciative of the effort that went into making sure they got to see as much as possible. All of the RAF personnel were overwhelmed at the scale of manufacturing potential they had seen.

In particular the B-29 Superfortress, being used to bomb Japan, had impressed the team. To realize the thousands of individual parts that went into each one and the scale of the plant rolling one finished plane out every few hours was amazing. In a fully pressurized bomber, the crew did not need bulky clothing or oxygen masks while flying at high altitude. The Air Commodore was able to secure a ride in one and was thrilled at the size and abilities of the craft. He went on and on for days about "the weapon that will end this war". To try to picture hundreds of these giants in the air, dropping bombs and incendiaries over the large, wood and paper cities of Japan was difficult and somewhat horrific to Gladdy. It was the first time she came close to realizing what Dale had been doing before he was shot down over Germany.

She stretched out a bit in the sunshine and penned a letter to her husband:

My Darling,

I hope and pray this letter finds you in good health and spirit. I have read that the winters in northern Germany are much like at home; maybe you can share tips with the other men on how to keep warm. Did you receive the package I sent with the wool scarf, mittens and socks? I've heard from others that packages often don't arrive at the camps and are opened and stolen by the Germans. Everyone at home is fine and looking forward to spring's return. I'm looking forward to the return of something much more precious... you.

Gladdy glanced up and saw the Air Commodore's car swing into the lane leading to the estate. She folded up the letter; she would finish it later. Standing up and smoothing her skirt, she went in the house to make sure all was ready for the arrival of Wallace, and the guests for tonight's dinner and meeting. She was aware that all of the high ranking British officers in the United States would be in attendance. The feeling of the staff was that important decisions about their status, with the war obviously coming to an end in Europe, would be determined this evening. The Yalta Conference, a meeting of Roosevelt, Churchill and Stalin, had been held a month earlier and showed the world the determination of the Allies in defeating Germany and Japan. It put a bit of hesitant expectation in the air. Flight Lieutenant Hutchins had admitted to Gladdy that as much as he missed England, he knew life there would be much less colorful and fun as his country recovered from this terrible war. Here in the United States, the economy was booming, everyone was at work making more money than ever before and even rationing of most things was coming to an end.

Germany

Dale had just finished one of the classes on electronics, studying how devices like radios and the new invention of television worked. Now that the prisoners felt certain the Allies would win this war, senior officers had emphasized the need for the men to keep busy. Many of those captured had college degrees in technical majors; some had even been college professors before the war. Now classes in subjects like drafting, chemistry, mathematics, art and music were attended by greater numbers of those looking forward to a better future when they returned to the States. Though they didn't have textbooks or laboratory equipment, everyone sensed the knowledge gained here would put them ahead when they enrolled at real schools after their release.

Daily reports of the Allied army advances, across Germany, up Italy, into Austria and even in the Pacific against the Japanese, were culled from the hidden radios and written in the camp newspaper, the POW-WOW. As hard as the guards tried to find out about the radios, they were never successful in locating even one. Lately, they themselves began to listen to the BBC broadcasts instead of their own Nazi propaganda. The closer the Soviet Army came to this part of Germany, the more nervous the guards became; some began to show overt signs of friendliness. Dale had recently spoken with one nicknamed "Old Bananas" who was so frightened by the idea of being captured by the Russians that he would visibly shake when they were mentioned. Everyone began to speak, quietly, of the tables being turned.

Yesterday while the men were enjoying the warm spring sunshine outdoors, a couple of Luftwaffe training planes had flown over the stalag from an airfield nearby. As the prisoners watched, a British Mosquito came diving out of the clouds at them; the Mosquito was a twin engine fighter built of plywood that was incredibly fast and maneuverable. The two trainers went down in smoking wreckage in moments as the prisoners cheered and waved. That evening an order came from the camp commandant that no prisoners would be allowed outside when aircraft were around; any found doing so would be shot on sight.

Chapter 31
April 1945

Germany

"Roosevelt's dead."

The word had been passed around the camp within a few minutes of being heard over the radio. No one waited for it to be written in the day's paper; no one was concerned about the Germans asking how everyone knew this so quickly. Prisoners stopped what they were doing when they heard; around the world, people did the same. The man who had led the United States nearly as long as the airmen had been alive was gone. Heads bowed and most shed unashamed tears; men who would not cry over their best friends' deaths or their own imprisonment, wept for their country. Many had no idea who Harry Truman of Missouri even was; now he was their Commander in Chief, the new President.

Florida

Flight Lieutenant Hutchins came through the door quickly, giving Gladdy one brief, incredibly sad glance as he walked to the Air Commodore. He whispered something to Wallace, turned and walked back out of the room. Gladdy's heart went cold at what could have caused the look on Hutchin's face. Thinking of Dale, and the worst, she put down the pad of paper and her pen. "Sir, Commodore, what is it? What news, if I may ask?"

"Mrs Weldon, it grieves me deeply. The Lieutenant has just been told that President Roosevelt passed today in Arkansas. I'm deeply moved and sorry for you and your country."

Gladdy was stunned. It seemed he had always been President, would always be; what would this do, now, with the war so close to its end? She felt the need to cry and a hatred for the enemy at the same time.

"This letter can wait; no one will be reading it for several days anyway. Please take today and as long as you need to reflect on this; we'll get back to your work when you can, Mrs Weldon."

Minnesota

As the word spread across the country, schools closed and work stopped. The sadness spread like a dark cloud over the land. Dautin felt alone as he worked at typesetting the evening's special edition newspaper before he left to go home. Esther was sitting at the kitchen table crying as the radio repeated the story; Don walked in from school and joined her there.

Elsewhere, in Germany and in the Pacific, the pause was brief. Soldiers, sailors, airmen and marines steeled themselves with greater determination than ever. This war will be over, will be won.... for him.

Chapter 32
May 1945

Germany

The sound had been getting louder for several days. At first Dale thought it was a distant thunderstorm since it had rained yesterday. Now the realization hit home to the prisoners; this was the approach of the Russian army. Because the camp was located almost directly north of Berlin, no one had been sure whether they would be liberated by their own troops or those of their "red" allies. It seemed now there was no doubt that the Soviets would get here first. Calls of "Come on, Uncle Joe" could be heard at all hours now; a reference to Joseph Stalin.

Captain Elliott came in the door. "Hey, Dale, I just got briefed by Colonel Zemke himself. The Commandant told him to get all the prisoners ready to leave; that we'd be marching from camp to avoid the Russians. Guess what the Colonel told him? He said that there are 9,000 prisoners who will not be going anywhere; that even if the 200 guards start shooting, we'll win and stay put. It was up to the Luftwaffe to choose whether to fight or just leave us here! The Colonel also said we need to be ready; he thinks the krauts will pull up stakes and be gone any morning now."

"No kidding? They must really be scared of the Russkies; though, by the sound of that artillery, I wouldn't want to face 'em either." Dale could hardly wait to spread the word around the barracks. The men had been talking about how close it was coming to the end, though many feared the Germans would either force them to move or just start killing them. They had all heard of the reports of the concentration camps and work camps that had been liberated in the past couple of weeks. The night before last it was reported on the BBC that nearly 500 French POW's had been literally marched to death to keep them from being liberated. It had steeled the nerves of most of the prisoners; they knew they would rather fight and die than just give up and let themselves be starved or killed.

That night the guards seemed to be holding some sort of party in their area just outside the compound. Music was being played over loudspeakers and all the lights were on; strange because the lights made it a perfect target in the blackness of the Baltic night. The next morning the answer was discovered; there were still guards in every tower but all the Luftwaffe trucks and other vehicles were gone! At first light the guards could be seen to be Allied prisoners acting as part of a "Field Force" that Colonel Zemke had organized. He had actually been told by the German Commandant the day before of the guards' planned departure. With fighting still going on in the area, Zemke thought it best to keep the gates closed to prevent POW's from wandering around and risk being shot. The kriegies still celebrated, spilling out of the barracks into the compound. Dale expressed his joy by joining in the jumps and hugs and shouting. Most of the men were hoarse and worn out in short time.

It was now the 1st of May and, late in the morning, several Russian staff cars pulled into the camp! Part of the Second White Russian Front army had driven the Germans out of Barth and arrived to liberate the camp. When a quick inspection showed that the enemy had taken all the remaining food supplies with them, General Borisov, the Russian commander, ordered that more than 200 cows be herded into the camp compound. The prisoners lost no time in butchering them and soon the smell of fresh beef cooking filled the air. A few hours later, dozens of American built trucks marked with the red Russian star began unloading crates filled with foodstuffs for the hungry POW's, including good old Minnesota SPAM from Austin. That evening all the prisoners were entertained by the Russian equivalent of a USO show complete with dancing and singing female soldiers.

The fences surrounding the camp were soon torn down and hundreds of prisoners began to wander away; some into the city of Barth to hunt for souvenirs, many more started walking west, on their own, to try to find the British and American lines. Dale and most of his comrades decided to stay put. Colonel Zemke, along with other senior allied officers, began working with their Russian counterparts to organize transport for the thousands of men. It was even arranged for letters home to be sent out, the first in many months.

It took nearly two weeks for the Allies to negotiate the evacuation of the prisoners of Stalag Luft One back into American and British controlled areas. At the end of the war, both Western and Eastern Allies had captured and secured the release of each others' soldiers and airmen. Many former Ukrainians had fought for Germany and now did not want to be returned to the Soviet Union; nearly 10,000 were forced to go back where the faced certain slow death in the work camps of Siberia. They were the price paid for the return of American and British ex-POW's.

On May 12th and 13th, dozens of American B-17's landed at the Luftwaffe base next to the prison and began ferrying former prisoners out; the RAF to England and the Air Corps officers to Camp Lucky Strike in Le Harve, France. There they would be given needed medical care and made ready for their return to the US. Virtually all of the POWs were undernourished and, like Dale, severely underweight. It would take weeks of good meals and careful exercise to bring them back to better health. There were other, logistical matters to attend to as well; many of the men had been prisoners so long they were due promotions and changes in pay. Their time at Camp Lucky Strike served several necessary purposes.

<u>Florida</u>

"Mrs Weldon, I've some news for you. We've received a report from the Combined Chiefs in Washington that the prison camp at Barth has been liberated by Russian troops. It means your husband will soon be on his way home. I've been placed in charge of the return of our RAF officers from Germany and will have to return to the European Theater until the end of summer. I'm sure you'll want to take advantage of some of that time to return to Minnesota to prepare for your husband's homecoming. I also want to offer the use of the villa here, and the housekeeping staff, to you and Lieutenant Weldon in my absence, once he arrives in the States. I honestly hope you'll accept the offer and allow this place to become a quiet spot for you both to enjoy and get reacquainted. You know the war, at least that part against the Nazis, will be over in a matter of a few days. Be assured, if the opportunity presents itself that I may see your husband, I'll be sure to. You have been the most wonderful person I've had the privilege to work with, I mean that. Best of everything to you and your family in the future; I do so hope we'll meet again one day." Air Commodore Wallace extended his hand and heartily received a hug, complete with a kiss on the cheek.

"Thank you, Commodore, it's really too kind. Working for you has been the best thing to happen to me. Sincerely; next to getting married, I mean." Both shared a laugh before Wallace strode out of the room. The next hours were spent finishing the final few details on closing out their mission and making arrangements for the military staff's transportation back to England. Gladdy also booked her own, by train, back home. She told Mrs Winsted she would be in contact soon about coming back with Dale. That evening the final goodbyes began with dinner and ended well past midnight with toasts and singing; both English and American favorites. Just when most of the revelers were thinking of getting some sleep, the radio announced the unconditional surrender of all Axis forces in Europe. The "good nights" were postponed for several emotional rounds; toasts to the King of England, the President of the United States and to each and every branch of the military from both countries. The celebrating finally ended as the sky in the east began to brighten.

Chapter 33
June 1945

<u>Camp Lucky Strike</u>

"Lieutenant Weldon? I'm Flight Lieutenant Hutchins; if you'd be so kind as to follow me, sir."

Dale was thoroughly perplexed, having no idea who this RAF officer was or why he had been on this errand. All he was doing was enjoying a chocolate milkshake, actually his second of the day; he had to be careful not to put on too much weight! Now he was being ushered down a hall in the main administration building of the camp by an Englishman, of all people.

"I'm sure you're wondering why you're here, sir. Rest assured there is no hint of you having done something wrong. Air Commodore Wallace is inspecting the camps, I believe you'll remember meeting him. He's learning how you Yanks are handling the return of POW's; the Commodore is in charge of our efforts and has come to appreciate American ingenuity through the example of someone you know quite well. I, too, have gleaned much from the way Gladdy cuts through red tape and all, as she calls it."

"Gladdy? You mean my wife? What the dickens has she got to do with this whole deal anyway? I know she met Wallace once a year or so ago, but..."

"Yes, well, she couldn't really write you that she worked for the RAF, with you in the Stalag and all, now could she? She's actually been a vital asset to the cooperation between the Air

Corps and ourselves in manufacturing and development. I should let the Commodore explain it himself. Ah, here we are; please step in here, sir."

Dale stepped in the office, right into the outstretched hand of an Air Commodore; one with a large smile on his face at that. "Bloody good, bloody good. Welcome home, lad, or nearly anyway. It's so good to see you again. I can only imagine the welcome you'll get when you finally arrive back in Minnesota, Lieutenant Weldon. I've come to appreciate your family quite a lot; particularly your father, another old war horse much like myself."

"Commodore, if you'll excuse me, sir. I'm completely in the dark on this; you've met my father along with my wife?"

"Oh, yes, had some of your mother's delightful lemonade and even took in a wrestling match, or part of it, that your brother Don was in. This war has not been entirely unpleasant for a few of us, I suppose. There is someone else here I'd like to introduce you to. He's had rather a tougher go at kicking the Nazis than I, you know. He's never met your father but does, however, seem to recall spending a few weeks with your grandfather in Cuba. Lieutenant Weldon, may I introduce Prime Minister Churchill..."

Dale almost fell down; out of the shadow stepped the leader of England in the flesh! He shook the offered hand and, swallowing hard, managed to say, "It truly is an honor to meet you, sir. You've been an inspiration to all Americans in this war."

"Most kind of you, sir; but I will admit, your family is also quite inspiring. I hear we owe a great deal of thanks to your wife. I know I personally owe my fondness for a certain habit to your grandfather; another of, I gather, a long line of Weldons who have nobly served their country. A token of remembrance, if you please." With that the Prime Minister handed Dale a very long cigar. "Made of the finest Cuban tobacco, I assure you."

Boston

It had been three days since Gladdy left Minneapolis on a train to the east coast. She had spent one night in a sleeping car and last night in a hotel after arriving in the city. The troopship carrying Dale and several thousand other returning POWs was due to arrive in the harbor shortly. Gladdy had put on the dress she wore the day he left, hoping that if Dale didn't recognize her, at least he might remember it. She thought back to the briefing the Army doctors at Fort Snelling had provided her, along with the wives of other returning POWs. Their advice was to expect little emotion from their husbands, and to make plans to adopt if children were desired. After all, former prisoners of war had difficulty fathering. Gladdy certainly planned to test that theory!

When she told the cabbie why she was going to the harbor area, he turned, smiled and said, "Well ma'am; you just sit back and enjoy the ride. This one's on me. My baby brother is due back next week; he's been a prisoner since North Africa. I sure am looking forward to seeing him." They had a nice chat through the traffic. He managed to let her off closer than she thought would be possible. "Give him a welcome home he'll never forget", he said as he waved and drove off.

Gladdy joined the throng of people; older couples waiting for sons, wives, some with children. It seemed everyone had a small American flag to wave, too. Just as she noticed, one was handed her by a smiling young girl, maybe ten or so years old. "We even got out of school to come and cheer them home" she said to Gladdy; who at that moment knew she had not brought a large enough hankie for the tears she would shed today.

"There she is!", someone shouted and everyone strained up on their toes to try to get a glimpse of the arriving liner. A band struck up "America the Beautiful" and thousands of voices began to cheer. The minutes did not diminish the sounds at all as the ship slowly made its way to the pier. Gladdy searched through the thousands of faces lining the rails and peering through portholes on the sides of the great vessel. She felt lightheaded and her heart was racing like a Kentucky thoroughbred. The gangplank was lowered and a rush of people nearly swept her off the ground. Ahead, as men began to walk, then run, down the sloping ramps leading to the pier, shouts of joy, peals of laughter and squeals of delight sounded out. Together, it made for the happiest time anyone could ever imagine. She looked and looked, up and down the rails, everywhere returning men in uniform mingled with women and children; but she couldn't see Dale. Just as she had the slightest tinge of doubt, she was caught up and spun around. The face she saw, inches from her own, had tears flowing down the cheeks. The lips that met hers were wet with them, mixing with her own. She could not even hear the words; could only read the lips as they said, "Shorty, oh Shorty, I'm home."

Minnesota

Naturally, everyone wanted 'only a minute' with Dale when he arrived. Family and friends stopped by Dautin and Esther's house by the score; a seemingly endless procession. After a few days of this Dale, along with his dad and brother, managed to steal away for awhile to go fishing. They came home smelling of gasoline, beer and fish. Even Esther admitted it smelled like "old times". The next day Dale and Shorty drove off by themselves for the afternoon; Dautin had given her the directions and Esther had packed the lunch. When they arrived at their picnic spot, the grasshoppers were everywhere and the blue sky competed with and complimented the puffy, white clouds. The grass was so green it almost hurt the eyes.

Crossing the bubbling creek, Shorty recounted her own feelings of the first time she had been here, a year earlier. Dale remembered the place from his childhood, but through the now grown up eyes, it had a particular beauty. As they entered the quiet place, with the headstones surrounding them and the trees creating a cathedral ceiling above, they both stopped and soaked in the atmosphere. The two of them went from one marker to another, running their hands over the cool stone and reading the

161

inscriptions. When they reached his grandfather's, Dale turned to Shorty and spoke. "I haven't told you who I met in France before shipping home. We will have to take some time, a lot of time in fact, for you to tell me all about your job with the RAF. Commodore Wallace showed up and introduced me to Prime Minister Churchill himself. I was completely thunderstruck by it; and then he told me about meeting my grandpa in Cuba. There is just too much whirling in my head for me to make much sense of anything right now."

"I know, darling. It's why I've waited to tell you the next, the best, news. Commodore Wallace will be in England until September, maybe even October. You and I get to live in his villa in Florida until then, to get you all fat and rested up. Just the two of us along with the housekeeper, cook and gardener; do you think you could stand a few months of spoiling? We'll have all the time we need to tell each other all about everything that's happened since we got married."

Epilog

Dale and Gladdy proved that ex-POWs certainly are able to quickly adjust back to a free civilian life; their first daughter was born less than a year after his return. The family settled in The Park and stayed there for several decades. A total of four children filled the house they bought. Dale returned to school and continued to study electronics before working for, and retiring from, a large telephone company. Gladdy (Shorty to family) went back to work at the school district once the kids all started going there. Dale seemed more inclined to share his experiences in the war than many other former soldiers and POWs; though there were incidents he didn't tell anyone until many years later.

Air Commodore Wallace retired from the Royal Air Force at the close of his assignment with the returning Prisoners of War. He repaired his family home in England and lived there with his daughter and son-in-law and a growing nest of grandchildren. He remained a friend of the Weldons and hosted Dale and Shorty on a visit they made to England years after the war. He passed away a few months after that visit.

Don joined the Merchant Marine service after graduating in June of 1941 and made two convoy runs up to Alaska before the war ended. He returned to The Park and lived there several years before moving to California.

Dautin and Esther enjoyed many years with family, especially the grandchildren. Dautin retired from the newspaper and the two of them traveled frequently. Both are now at rest along with the earlier generations of Weldons in that quiet, wooded spot.

GLOSSARY

Airborne	American paratroops.
AP	Aiming Point; when the bombs are dropped.
Auguring	When a plane spins and falls to earth.
Birds	English women.
Bogie	Enemy aircraft.
Boche	Slang term for German soldiers.
Brass	High ranking American officers.
Clay Pigeons or Clays	Clay targets for shooting; like small saucers.
Echelons	Formations, assemblies, of troops.
Fubar	Fouled Up Beyond All Recognition.
Heinie	Slang term for German soldiers.
Hun (Huns)	Slang term for German soldiers.
IP	Initial Point; when the bomb run begins. The plane is flown by the bombsight computer until the bombs are dropped.
Jerry (Jerries)	Slang term for German soldiers.

Kriegie	Nickname for an American POW in Germany.
Luftwaffe	German Air Force
Mae West	An inflatable life preserver named for the Hollywood starlet.
Minority Group	Term used to describe a non-white person.
RAF	Royal Air Force (English)
Stood Down	Past tense of stand down; to not fly a mission.
Wehrmacht	German Army

Made in the USA
Charleston, SC
18 February 2016